ALSO BY VERONICA CHAMBERS

The Joy of Doing Things Badly:
A Girl's Guide to Love, Life and Foolish Bravery

Miss Black America, a novel

Having It All? Black Women and Success

Mama's Girl

KICKBOXING
GEISHAS

HOW MODERN JAPANESE
WOMEN ARE CHANGING
THEIR NATION

Veronica Chambers

FREE PRESS

New York   London   Toronto   Sydney

*f*P

FREE PRESS

A Division of Simon & Schuster, Inc.

1230 Avenue of the Americas

New York, NY 10020

Copyright © 2007 by Veronica Chambers

FREE PRESS and colophon are registered trademarks of
Simon & Schuster, Inc.

For information about special discounts for bulk purchases,
please contact Simon & Schuster Special Sales at
1-800-456-6798 or business@simonandschuster.com

Designed by Kyoko Watanabe

Manufactured in the United States of America

1   3   5   7   9   10   8   6   4   2

ISBN-13: 978-0-7432-7157-8

For the Kim women:

Sharon Kim-Gibbons, Dr. Jin Young Kim, and

the indomitable Caroline Kim.

And for Louise Masako Mitsuda Hillman.

CONTENTS

1

KICKBOXING GEISHAS

The funny thing about my love affair with Japan is that it was never the country of my dreams. The country I loved, the bad boy I could never get to walk me down the aisle, was France. Two days into my first trip to Paris, I called my mother from a pay phone on the Boulevard Saint-Germain. "Sell everything I own," I said dramatically, "I'm staying." Even as the words came out of my mouth I knew they were untrue. I was twenty-four years old. I worked for the *New York Times* at a job that journalists twice my age would kill for. All that, and I didn't own much worth selling. I had just enough money to cover the cost of my trip and I was too pragmatic to play the starving artist. But the sentiment, the desire to stay, said everything I could not about how deeply I had fallen in love with the city, how I longed to follow in the footsteps of all the writers who had made Paris their home before me.

I spent the next five years trying to get to Paris, watching French movies, reading French *Elle*, studying French, visiting whenever I could. I was twenty-nine and working at *Newsweek* magazine when a colleague named Greg Beals suggested I apply for a fellowship to go to Japan. "But I'm not trying to go to Japan," I told him. "I want to go to Paris." He rolled his eyes. Anyone who had spent any amount of time with me knew that I was gunning for *Newsweek*'s Paris bureau. "Yeah, well, they're not giving out fellowships to go to Paris," he says. "You should apply for this fellowship, check out Tokyo."

I had visited my friend Mina in Shanghai just a few months before. I remember overhearing a lengthy discussion among foreign correspondents at a bar in New York about the difference between those who go to China and those who go to Japan. China folks were serious. People who went to Japan, said the journalists I was with, only filed superficial stories about music and fashion. They said this as if it were a bad thing, but it piqued my interest nonetheless. I *liked* music and fashion. I adored the writer Banana Yoshimoto, author of *Kitchen*, and her warm, frothy tales of young women coming of age in Tokyo. I took the application from Greg and promptly forgot it.

God bless Greg Beals. Two months later, he came by my office. "Did you apply for that fellowship?" I shook my head no, dug it out from the "Don't Forget" pile on my desk and was sad to see that I'd missed the deadline. "Maybe next year?" I said weakly. An hour later, Greg was back. "You're in luck," he said. "I called over there and they've extended the deadline."

In Tokyo I stayed at International House, or I-House, a kind of Harvard Club for Western writers and academics in the Roppongi section of the city. Roppongi is known for its high-density population of foreigners, nightclubs, and restaurants. Later, I would look down on Roppongi as a *gaijin* ghetto, *gaijin* being the Japanese word for foreigners. But for me, it was a good starting place: filled with clubs and restaurants and a lively street life that kept me from feeling completely isolated.

I grew up in New York City, so I knew a thing or two about crowds. But in Tokyo, density is the thing. Tokyo is the most heavily populated city in the world: more than a quarter of the nation's population live crammed into an area that represents less than 2 percent of the country. It's got a good ten million people on Mexico City, Sao Paolo, or New York. So the second most important phrase I learned was *"sumimasen,"* a hybrid of "excuse me" and "I'm sorry." It is the oil that keeps the wheels of social grace turning. You say *sumimasen* when you bump into someone on the train or when you want them to know that if they don't move, you will bump into them. *Sumimasen* is used when you want to catch the attention of a friend, colleague, or stranger, or when you want to ask a question, the time, directions, anything.

But it is also a kind of thank you. A way to say, "I'm sorry that I've taken up some of your precious time. I so appreciate it." The first time I took a rush hour train and watched a white gloved official literally shove us into the subway car, I realized that *sumimasen* was the vocabulary equivalent of those white gloves. In a city of twelve million people, you are bound to step on some toes. But *sumimasen* smoothes it out.

In one of my favorite poems, Yusef Komunyakaa writes about a black man's sense of isolation and humiliation in the American South. The poem is called *I Apologize For the Eyes in My Head*. In Japan, I apologized constantly, but it did not make me feel ashamed or isolated. *Sumimasen* was the thread that wove me closer to the fabric of Tokyo.

It was five years before Sofia Coppola's soporific tale of a young woman in Japan, but I soon began to live out my own *Lost in Translation* scenario. I had studied Japanese for six months before my trip. I did not yet dream in Japanese, but occasionally, I daydreamed in the language: a kind of Romper Room fantasy where various brightly colored objects would be pointed out to me and I would, correctly, call them by their Japanese name. When I arrived in Tokyo, I was immediately set up with a series of translators. I asked if the translators could take a back seat, filling in where necessary. "Well . . ." my fellowship adviser said, "we'll see." As any visitor to Japan and I suspect many other Asian countries soon learns, you are rarely told a straight-out "No." Instead, your host oh so politely sidesteps a yes.

During meetings when I greeted the interviewee with a simple *"Ohayo gozaimasu,"* there would be much exclamation about how wonderful my Japanese was. If I introduced myself and said where I was from, there would be more amusement and praise. Once I started to ask a question in Japanese, however, my interpreters firmly stepped in. Later, they would tell me that I could speak a little Japanese, but they were there to make the interviewee feel at ease. It was important to a Japanese artist or executive that he or she not be misquoted or misunderstood.

There were more dangers in my trying to express myself in Japanese. If I spoke more Japanese than my counterpart spoke English, this would cause them to lose face. Losing face being of course, the utmost dishonor. Finally, my translator explained, I was a representative of the United States and the Japan Society, who had been kind enough to give me this fellowship. Did I want to risk repercussions to fall down upon my country and future fellows should I make some sort of careless mistake? This confirmed the comical *Lost in Translation* scenes that anyone who has worked with an interpreter has experienced. You ask a question to a dignitary, say, the mayor of Yokohama. Your interpreter asks the question in Japanese. The mayor gives a long, elaborate answer in Japanese. There is much gesturing and emotion and nuance. You don't need to understand the words to know this: you can see it, you can feel it. Then your interpreter turns to you and says "He says yes." The interpreters are always filtering and yet it is so easy to put yourself in their hands.

There were two main interpreters I worked with. One I secretly called "Mama-san." She was a fifty-something woman whose only child had gone off to college and who had recently reentered the work force. I called her "Mama-san" because she was a Japanese Doris Day: prim and proper, always in skirts and sensible shoes, a frilly pink umbrella by her side, in case it should rain. She showed up early for every appointment and dragged me, like a child, down the streets of Tokyo at lightning bolt speed. She told me what I should or shouldn't do and what I should or shouldn't say.

It was March when I arrived, and colder than I had expected. *Sex and the City* was the hit show back at home and following Carrie Bradshaw's stylistic lead, I had stopped wearing stockings. This did not escape Mama-san's notice.

"You aren't wearing stockings," she pointed out.

I muttered something in a twelve-year-old's voice about this being the style.

She sighed, "Maybe no one will notice."

I was stockingless again the next time she saw me. "Your legs must be very cold," she said.

I was, in fact, freezing and I had tried to remedy the situation. "I went to the store, but they didn't have any stockings in my size."

She could hardly argue with this. Japanese women are universally tiny. I am universally not. She clucked, "Maybe no one will notice."

* * *

I-House was located on a side street of Roppongi, at the high point of a small hill. If you went down the hill, you found the streets and clubs along the wide street Roppongi-dori. It was great for people watching: men in shiny suits pressing strip club flyers into the reluctant hands of passersby; young club girls teetering around in high heels while looking for foreign boyfriends; salarymen—the Japanese equivalent of the man in the grey flannel suit—working women, students, and lots of foreigners from all over the world. At that time, spring 2000, schoolgirls, the *joshi kosei*, were all the rage. It was not uncommon on a Sunday afternoon to pass one group of girls dressed up like the court of Marie Antoinette, walk one block down and see another group of girls dressed like Hello Kitty and then turn the corner and bump into a bunch of leather-clad biker chicks. It wasn't so much that these girls pioneered one particular style, as it was that they were fearless and relentless in their ability to cycle through every period in fashion history. These Japanese had long been the master of a certain kind of copycat culture. But the teenage girls, who took care of every detail—from the right period shoe, to a three-hour makeup job to get the punk rock look just right—took the copycatting to another level. This was a case of "Anything you can do, I can do better."

The obsession with teenage girls was not relegated to street culture. For a retrospective of his work at the Tokyo Contemporary Museum of Art, seminal designer Issey Miyake invited over one hundred cheerleaders from local high schools and colleges to perform in the museum's courtyard. It was the very antithesis of the fashion scene, a hundred girls in brightly colored sweaters and miniskirts, shaking their pom-poms around, but Miyake declared that the girls captured the joy he felt when "making things." At the Venice Biennale, the following year, the Japanese pavilion was called "City of Girls" and visitors traversed through a stark white structure, white pebbles underfoot, white trees to the left and right, in and out of hundreds of portraits of Japanese girls. The fact that the girls were both super trendy and trendsetters had morphed into something more. Back home in Brooklyn, my minister always said at every christening, that life was our most powerful answer to death. He would hold the new baby up to the congregation and remind us that whatever and whomever we had lost in the past year, here was new life, here was new hope. I saw Japan as doing the same thing. After the economic depression of the nineties, when big business had been this country's religion, Japanese teenage girls were a symbol that all was not lost. Japan held the girls up, in art and in the media, and eventually in business, as a symbol to the world that new life coursed through its veins.

Any weekday afternoon, you can still spot the *joshi kosei* in front of Shibuya 109, a legendary department store in one of Tokyo's most popular shopping areas. *"Moshi-moshi!"* one will screech into her cell phone. It's one of her friends, and if you ask, she'll pull out a fat album of *purikura*—tiny sticker photos that she and her friends have taken in photo booths at game centers all around town. The phone rings again. *"Moshi-moshi!"* she calls out again. It's another friend, asking if she knows the plan for tonight's late night karaoke session. With mock exasperation, she rolls her eyes. It's tough being popular.

The cliques of girls who roam Tokyo's streets like to identify themselves by wearing something that matches: they sport the same Coach handbag or hang the same Hello Kitty charm on their cell phone. They believe that the sameness strengthens the bond of their friendship.

The schoolgirl craze, while concentrated in Tokyo, commanded national, even global attention. On my first visit, every weekend in Shibuya, in Ueno Park, in Harajuku, you could find foreign photographers and foreign news crews, shooting pictures of schoolgirls in their blue and white sailor-style uniforms and other more outrageously dressed Japanese teenage girls. In all the Western fascination with these girls, it shouldn't be lost just how sexualized the images of Japanese teenage girls were and continue to be. Google "Japanese teenage girls" and you get a glut of porn sites. Google "American teenage girls" and you get hits ranging from fashion to music to health issues. The teen girls who were being pursued by the foreign press in Tokyo's most stylish quarters, are part of a long tradition of Westerners traveling great distances to see exotic Japanese women. From the seventeenth century to the mid-nineteenth century, Japan's borders were closed to foreigners. When Japan was open to the West in 1868 at the beginning of the Meiji era, Japanese women were quickly stereotyped as beautiful, docile, sexual, and selfless. Shuttered from the rest of the world for nearly two hundred years, the Japanese woman was perceived as both exotic and innocent, pure and highly desirable. Such stereotypes continue to this day. In *Contemporary Portraits of Japanese Women,* Yukiko Tanaka discusses about how powerful and perennial the image of the Japanese female is: small, pale, delicate, childlike, sexually sophisticated, and submissive. This most recent foreign obsession with schoolgirls is in fact part of a much longer tradition.

It is hard to overestimate how the worldwide fascination with Japanese girls plays into the stereotype of the Japanese as a nation of cartoonish, eccentric people—"Oh those crazy Japanese"—who are too polite or too stupid, to know that they are the butt of the joke. In the newspaper I read an outrageous tale—complete with photographs—about girls who were having their lips sewn together to create a Hello Kitty smile. Whether or not this was actually true, I'm not sure—it was a proper newspaper, not the Japanese equivalent of the *National Enquirer.* But I thought it was telling that the boyfriend of one of the girls pictured said that what he liked best about his girl-friend's new look wasn't how *kawaii* she looked—*kawaii* meaning supercute, and the Japanese catchall equivalent to cool. What the boyfriend liked about his girlfriend's Hello Kitty lip job was that now she talked less. (Cue the cameras, "Oh those crazy Japanese!")

I had to admit, I found them fascinating too: laughing elementary age girls, traveling in packs like wolves, their school uniforms immaculate, Hello Kitty key chains and other brightly colored decorations hanging off of their backpacks, with the full confidence that only comes from knowing you are in charge. Before long, I began to realize that as dominant as the schoolgirls were in the popular culture, they're weren't the only Japanese women making bold statements, and not all of those women were playing the part of the shopping-crazed child.

During my Roppongi strolls I developed a fascination with a lurid group of young women who stood out on a street it was hard to stand out on. These were the *yamamba* girls, slang for old mountain hag, but they were more like Palm Beach divas than spinsters. They had deep George Hamilton-like tans, dyed platinum blonde hair, and wore high platform shoes and white lipstick.

Their behavior and dress was shocking to a nation of conformers and each day, some new tale recounting a *yamamba* girl's exploits appeared in the paper. One woman in her early twenties said that before she adopted the *yamamba* look, she was constantly being hit upon—on the subway, at school, at her part-time job. "Now," she said, triumphantly, "nobody touches me." Lascivious salarymen on the train are legendary for their wandering hands and typically, the younger the victim, the better. All around the subways, official government posters portraying a pretty young working girl scolding a red-faced businessman. The poster says, in both English and Japanese, "NO TOUCHING!" By adopting a look that was so extreme as to be referred to as "old mountain girl" this *yamamba* girl felt like she was protecting herself from being groped in public.

Yamamba girls were rumored to smell. It was said that to make their tans last longer they showered rarely. They were rumored to be promiscuous and in a shocking F-you to the powers that be, they were choosing to have their babies as single mothers. Baby's Mamas! I thought, thinking of the term that we used in Brooklyn for someone who is more than a girlfriend and less than a wife. As in "That's my baby's Mama" or "She's my brother's baby Mama." In Japan, where even today, fewer than 1 percent of children—in any class strata—are born out of wedlock, feminists applauded the *yamamba* girls for breaking the rules.

Their fashion wasn't only garish, it could be lethal. One girl was brought up on charges of manslaughter after her ten-inch-high platform heels made her lose control of the car she was driving. Even after they had children, you could still see them on Roppongi-dori pushing their strollers in these same sky-high heels, cigarettes dangling from their exaggerated white lips. They reminded me of a story I once read about Gore Vidal, in which he recounted how his mother covered his head with a burping cloth to catch the ashes, since she smoked as she nursed.

Yamamba fashion has now evolved. You can still find sleeker versions of the blonde-haired tan Japanese girl in Harajuku, emulating—one imagines—Paris Hilton, who is a familiar face in Japanese fashion advertisements. In time, I realized that an even more revealing window into the changes going on in Japanese women's lives was the phenomenon of the parasite single. She is decidedly more upmarket than the *yamambas*. A parasite is—or at least aspires to be—the Japanese equivalent

of the Park Avenue princesses described in Plum Sykes'
Bergdorf Blondes.

While *Sex and the City* remained more an aspirational fantasy than a reality for American women, in Japan women
across the country lead a life right out of the HBO sitcom. As
Peggy Orenstein reported in her *New York Times Magazine* article, "Parasites in Prêt-à-Porter," nearly half of all Japanese
women thirty and under are single and nearly all of them live
at home. They may earn on average the equivalent of $27,000
a year, but they're not expected to pay rent or contribute to
the household in any way—hence the term parasite singles.
Their money is earmarked for luxury goods, which is why you
will see them out in force when you stroll Ometesando,
Tokyo's leafy boulevard equivalent to the Champs-Élysées,
lined with flagship stores of Prada, Chanel, and the mother
ship of luxury goods for Japanese women, Louis Vuitton.

Yet one of the things I was to learn while reporting this book
is that the stereotype of the shop-happy Japanese woman masks
more complex realities at play in the women's lives. After all,
what do all those handbags mean? Opinions differ. To feminist
writer Yoko Tajima, the handbags are little handcuffs, keeping
Japanese women tied to the purse strings of corporate Japan.
"Japan is considered number two in the world in GNP," she
says. "Even though the economic position is stagnating, women
have the money to spend on brand-name handbags, so they are
somewhat satisfied. They have their handbags, so they don't
speak up." Case in point: Japan, despite being a relatively small
country, accounts for more than 55 percent of Louis Vuitton's
global sales. Akira Miura, editor in chief of *Women's Wear Daily
Japan* has said, "Almost every grown-up Japanese woman
already owns at least one Louis Vuitton item." The question, as
raised by Yoko Tajima, is how much independence do you swap
for that Louis Vuitton bag?

The tradition of Japanese women and their obsession with luxury goods goes back much further than the mid-nineties when the parasites made their debut. It started in the years after World War II, when Japan was becoming an economic behemoth and the modern salaryman came into being. He commuted then, as he does now, upward of two hours a day. He left before dawn and worked till after dark. But at the end of the day, he could not go straight home. In Japan, the real wheeling and dealing does not take place between the hours of nine and five. There are company dinners and drinking parties, entertaining clients and the courting of senior staff. The salaryman does not get home until after 11 P.M. At 5 or 6 P.M., in Shinagawa station—in the neighborhood where I now rent an apartment whenever I'm in Japan—it is crowded, but not abnormally so. The real stampede begins at 10 P.M. when thousands of employees try to make the last train home.

If you are a salaryman and you leave the house every morning before your wife wakes up and come home every evening after she falls asleep, how do you make it up to her? If you are the Cary Grant-esque actor Koji Yakusho in the international hit film *Shall We Dance?*, you seek the answer to the missing passion and dulling bureaucracy in your life by secretly signing up for ballroom dance lessons. If you are the average Joe, or Yoishi as the case may be, you buy your wife a Louis Vuitton bag. In the U.S. we don't really go for the old buying your wife an expensive gift to beg forgiveness anymore (even in the 1969 film, *Cactus Flower*, when Walter Matthau tried to make up with Goldie Hawn by buying her a mink coat, she thought he was a square). But in Japan, neither public displays of affection nor private displays of affection are common, even among married couples. A Louis Vuitton bag is just so much easier.

The parasite singles, though, have the disposable income

to buy the bags for themselves. I wondered, are they really being handcuffed? Retail therapy is a term I've never actually heard used in Japan, but I can't help but believe that it's more than mere materialism that keeps the masses of Japanese women swathed in Louis Vuitton, Chanel, and Prada. They want these high-end items because they make them feel loved, adored even. In interviewing so many Japanese women, I quickly learned that the number one complaint was that men, even the young ones, were too reserved and unemotional. There is a phrase in Japanese, *ishin denshin*, which means that people share a "vibration" and that there is no need for words. In the U.S., love means never having to say you're sorry; In Japan, love means never having to say "I love you."

Japanese women are so widely thought of as materialistic, that it's easy to misundertand all the forces at work in their lives. Take for example, the phenomenon of *enjo kosai* or compensated dating: wherein schoolgirls and young women agree to have sex with middle-aged salarymen in exchange for luxury goods. Although recent surveys suggest that the initial media outcry against *enjo kosai* were overhyped, even conservative numbers suggest that an average of 5 percent of teenage girls have participated in *enjo kosai*.

These are not the poverty driven, teenage sex workers of southern Asia. *Enjo kosai* is middle-class prostitution at a level never before seen. No pimps. No street corners. The girls merely exchange cell phone numbers with men who approached them in department stores, subways, or increasingly, online. The men then make arrangements to meet the girls at Japan's infamous "love hotels" by calling them on their cell phones, often when the girls are eating dinner or doing their homework under their parents' watchful eye. How the girls are paid is the telling thing: with cash, yes, often $400 or $500 a pop, but they are just as often paid with "tributes"—such as a Louis Vuitton or

Chanel bag. One teenage girl in an interview with *Time* Asia, explained her experience this way:

> "I started doing *enjo kosai* my second year of high school. On most of my dates, I had sex. That's the weirdest thing I've ever done—meeting someone for the first time and screwing him the same day . . . I was going to school like usual, but I was bored and had no money. My boyfriend, the guy I lost my virginity to, had just broken up with me. I wouldn't do *enjo kosai* if I had a boyfriend. Losing him was really rough. So I just left a message about myself on a cyber message board and chose a sex partner from the guys who wrote back. It wasn't hard. Guys who want sex and dinner, guys who just want sex, guys who just want dinner—they're all out there . . . Most guys pay some sort of tribute to me. Guys always pay homage. But all the guys who wanted to screw me were old! Like, in their thirties. And none of them were attractive. One guy gave me a Gucci ring but I didn't keep it. Using it was gross! I sold it and spent the money on snowboarding. I bought lots of cute accessories and went on snowboarding trips . . . I stopped doing *enjo kosai* after a while. When I did it, all I was thinking was that it's only for today so it doesn't matter. Stuff like, "No problem, don't worry that it's not someone you like." At the time I didn't think that I was doing anything bad, but now I think it was bad. So I don't go shopping as much as I used to, even though I love Gucci's new stuff. I used to wear *kosai* fashion too, but not anymore. Now I have a part-time job in a Japanese inn serving breakfast and stuff but I also know some store managers here in town that give me day jobs, so I make about 30,000–40,000 yen a month. My dad gave me this Louis Vuitton purse . . . Yeah, it's small, but it's a brand name."

Stories like this about *enjo kosai* are disturbing, but all of the media coverage may have deflected attention from more important issues affecting young Japanese women's lives. Yasuka Nakamara is president of Boom, Inc., a marketing firm that specializes in informing companies about the latest styles popular with teenage girls. To Yasuka, the media reports about *enjo kosai* and other scandalous teenage behaviors get tiresome. "Teenage girls have such negative portrayals in the global media and the result is that our girls have a bad reputation in other countries," Nakamura says. "All the journalists care about are the high school girls who sell their underwear, wear the short skirts, or the long, loose socks. They look like sexual objects even if they are good students. They may wear short skirts, but they still study hard. Some members of my research team are high school girls who have the potential to go to Tokyo University because they are just so good, so smart. But everything picked up by the mass media is always about their short skirts or long, loose socks—they always pick up the negative side and I just hate it so much."

There's so much hype about how trendy and shop-happy Japanese girls are, it can be hard to get at the complexity beyond the pop culture portrayals. In 2005, Tokyo's fashionable females not only inspired much of Gwen Stefani's multiplatinum solo album, but both her tour and multiple videos featured a quartet of Japanese girls, Stefani's twenty-first century take on doo-wop girls. As she sings in her song, "Harajuku Girls,": You got the wicked style/I am your biggest fan." There's a perception that Tokyo is, as it was portrayed at the Venice Bienale in 2001, a "City of Girls." But all you have to do to learn how much more complex the reality is for Japanese women today, is talk to a woman who is trying to break the rice paper ceiling in corporate Japan.

When I first visited Japan, I thought I was going to find the most forward-thinking society in the world. (If I had been a teenage boy, raised on Japanese animation featuring sexpot girls with big eyes and barely any clothes on, I might have known different.) With all their sleek style and high-tech prowess, I expected to walk into Japanese companies and find a modern day version of the *Jetsons*. What I found instead was that for the most part, men still played all the key roles. If there was a smart young woman—or even a smart, older woman— she may attend meetings, write reports, develop new products, and contribute intellectually, but she was still expected to make and pour the tea that is served in every kind of Japanese meeting. It was like a *Mary Tyler Moore* episode: There was Mary, an associate producer, but basically a glorified secretary, in the midst of Lou, Murray, Ted, and Gordy. Even in 2000, in most Japanese companies it was still 1974.

It's hard to imagine when bombarded by images of Japan's crackerjack technology—The cars! The microchips! The itsy-bitsy phones/computers/video players!—just how traditional male-female relationships still are in Japan. I once visited a *juku* school in Kobe, a cram school where kids go to get the leg up on the competition, and asked a classroom full of eight-year-old girls, "What do you want to do when you grow up?" The answer from each and every girl was, "I want to be a house-wife." Similarly, I spent an afternoon interviewing girls at a hip-hop record shop in Tokyo. These girls were tanned, made up, impossibly cool in their miniskirts and thigh-high boots. When I asked them what they wanted to be, they too answered . . . a housewife.

Japan has the lowest representation of women in govern-ment among all developed nations. Forty-three women recently won seats in the Japanese lower house of Parlia-ment—the highest number since 1946, the year that Japanese women were granted the vote. Women represent less than 10

16

percent of the 480-seat lower house. According to the Geneva-based Inter-Parliamentary Union, with women occupying only 7.7 percent of Parliamentary seats, Japan still ranks below the Arab states where women occupy 8.8 percent of the seats in the lower house.

Yet, what is also increasingly clear is that major change is underway in Japanese women's lives and roles. In 2005, when Prime Minister Junichiro Koizumi wanted to privatize the post office and lost the support of his Liberal Democratic Party, he decided to harness the energy of ambitious women in Japan and invited an unprecedented amount of them—many with no political experience—to run on his ticket in the September elections. Even before the votes came streaming in on election day, the women were already a threat. In particular, three of Koizumi's picks for the lower house captivated the media's attention: Satsuki Katayama, a high-flying finance ministry bureaucrat and a former Miss Tokyo University; Yuriko Koike, a former news anchor and current environment minister, and Makiko Fujino, a TV chef who is often referred to as the Martha Stewart of Japan. These three women were the Charlie's Angels of Koizumi's ticket: beautiful, powerful, and effective. The fifty-three-year-old Koike, for example, was reported as steamrolling through her working-class district, shaking hands and kissing babies, an army of girl power supporters in hot pink T-shirts following close behind her. "This is a ground battle for reform," Koike shouted through her bullhorn, "let's change Japan." No wonder the old boys club began to refer to the women as Koizumi's "assassins."

What I didn't quite catch on my first visit was that just as in the U.S. of 1974, the times they were a-changin'. Though Japanese women may be angry that their country's corporate structure has little room for bright, educated women, women my age are forging their own ways: starting their own businesses, learning languages, traveling. As two Japanese guy friends I made on that first trip, Kazu and Haruki, were to reveal to me later, many Japanese men are absolutely intimidated by Japanese women today—and I think a little jealous. Kazu and Haruki are salarymen now. Kazu works from 8 A.M. to 10 P.M. on most days, with a two-hour commute on each end. In order to meet me and my husband for dinner, he makes arrangements to stay in a capsule hotel, a men's only establishment where the rooms are literal capsules with a single bed and a small TV suspended inside. At about $30 a night it's a cheap and common refuge for salarymen who miss the last train or are too drunk to make it home. In comparison to Kazu's life, many of the women I've gotten to know in Japan have it made: one has her own cosmetics company, another runs her own comedy troupe, and a third one works a desk job and studies salsa for performance (a la *Strictly Ballroom*) at night. My Japanese girlfriends are breaking the mold and it is anything but easy. Blazing trails is hard work. And maybe, just maybe, the fires burn brighter when viewed from a distance.

With Koizumi's assassins, *enjo kosai* and parasite singles so much in the Western news, and such hot debate topics in Japan, it can be hard to get a handle on what real women's lives are like in Japan today. The easiest thing to do when one is studying Japanese women is to see them in extreme contradiction and as victims: of men, in the broadest sense, but also of economics, politics, materialism and a cult of femininity and sexuality that has captured the Western imagination for literally hundreds of years. The hard thing is to marry the very real facts about compensated dating, parasite singles, and other popular darlings of the Japanese and Western media with real women doing interesting work.

It took several trips to Japan after that first one for me to start discovering the more interesting story of the dramatic changes going on in Japanese women's lives. On one trip, I met a hip-hop DJ. On another trip, I was introduced to a comedienne. But it wasn't really until I started writing this book, and made studying Japanese women the sole focus of my work, that I began to break through the *shoji* screen that separated real women from the public eye. In the U.S., you can pick up a magazine like *Glamour* or *O, The Oprah Magazine* and read about an interesting woman playwright, or physician, or comic book illustrator. In Japan, the media is dominated by personalities: especially by insipid teenage "talent-os," young people chosen from giant casting calls to play a role or sing in a band. Like the eighties Latin phenomenon Menudo, talent-os have an expiration date. By the time they leave puberty, for the most part, their time in the spotlight is done. Finding real women who would talk to me was hard. I spent hours scouring through newspapers, looking for mention of smart women with interesting work. If I saw a profile of an interesting looking "real" woman in a Japanese publication, I had the text translated. Once I read it, I would contact the woman for an interview. My contacts at the Foreign Press Center (FDC) were amazed by the scope of women I was able to find. I found award-winning industrial designer Fumie Shibata, on the cover of a design publication I saw at the Hara Contemporary Museum of Art. I figured if she was on the cover of a magazine, she would be worth knowing, or at least worth having the interview translated to get a sense of what she was about.

For a number of months, I sent a series of requests to the FPC in Tokyo. Could I interview women executives, engineers, physicians, and researchers? Some of these requests were denied simply because I'd asked for someone who didn't exist: a female president at a Japanese car company, for example. Eventually, through my FPC connections, referrals from friends in Japan and the U.S., and my own plowing through magazines and newspapers for mentions and profiles of women who looked engaging, I started to meet an amazing array of women of many different ages. One day it would be a high-ranking executive at Canon, the next day a jewelry designer, a prominent industrial engineer, a graphic artist, or a ballet dancer.

Once I'd found the women, getting them to open up to me was the second hurdle. In the U.S., an hour-long interview with even a very famous person, can easily spill into two or three hours if the person feels comfortable. In Japan, settling in for a nice long chat with a total stranger is simply not done. If my interview began at one o'clock in the afternoon, it was expected that I start wrapping things up at a quarter to two. When I interviewed someone in a corporate position, they were always joined by a company minder. For most high-ranking interviewees, a list of questions was requested beforehand. On one occasion, I was handed back a list of typed responses and was expected to leave after the polite handshake and "Nice to meet you." While everyone else stood up, I sat down and tried to figure out how not to be rude and still get what I needed. I had follow-up questions, I sputtered. For the next forty-five minutes I asked my follow-up questions as the entire room wore tight smiles that made it clear how rude they considered me.

My being a foreigner was its own icebreaker. The more I interviewed women, the more people in Japan told me that it was easier to open up to a foreigner. When my time in Japan was over I would go home to my own country. They could tell their thoughts to someone outside of their society because there would be no need to maintain polite relations for years on end. One night, I invited eight women in their twenties and thirties, all of whom who knew one another to varying degrees, for a girlfriends' dinner at T.Y. Harbor restaurant in my Shinagawa neighborhood. The restaurant, one of my favorites, sits on the river and is one of those treasured wide-open places in a very cramped city. The women ordered, ate, and drank for two hours while I asked the most personal questions. At the end of the evening, Mie, who was the common link among the women, admitted that she'd learned more about her friends in a single evening—what their parents did for a living as well as their opinions on marriage and childbirth—than she had in years of acquaintance.

Again and again, when I told people that I was writing a book about the changing roles of Japanese women, they asked me why. Why would a *gaijin* be interested in Japanese women? *Gaijin* men, obviously, love the Japanese ladies. Even today, a *gaijin* woman who lives and works in Japan stands out. The bullet trains, noodle shops, and nightclubs are filled with American and British men whose affection (obsession?) with Japanese women is hard to parse out from their passion and respect for Japanese language and culture. It is all part of the package.

Long before Vegas coined the term, there has been a tradition among men who traveled to and worked in the land of the rising sun: what happens in Japan, stays in Japan. One only has to look at the classic James Bond film *You Only Live Twice* in which 007 teams up with his counterpart in the Japanese secret service, a raffish fellow (no emasculated images of Asian men here) named Tiger Tanaka. After a long day of fighting the forces of evil, Tiger suggests they take a bath and with a snap of his fingers, a small harem of Japanese beauties appear. Tiger explains that these women will bathe James Bond. When James suggests he is entirely capable of bathing himself, Tiger lets him know that there are only two rules for getting along in Japan:

Tiger Tanaka: Rule number one: Never do anything yourself when someone else can do it for you.

21

James Bond: And rule two?
Tiger Tanaka: Rule number two: In Japan, men come first.
Women come second.
James Bond: I just might retire here.

While James Bond movies went on to become dated tales of cads gone by, in Japan, Tanaka's truism remains. Below the surface, what Japanese women really knew was that the depth of their intelligence, their capabilities, and their creativity was far greater than Bond, Tanaka, or their fellow travelers could ever understand or acknowledge.

The more women I talked to, the more obvious it became that women are breaking the traditional mold in many ways, and that a revolution is underway not only in their lives, but in the whole culture. Not a day goes by in Japan that women don't make the front pages of the newspaper *and* make some waves across the business pages. I chose the subtitle of my book, How Women Are Changing Their Nation, because I can see all the ways that as Aretha Franklin and Annie Lennox sang, "Sisters are doing it for themselves."

I was even to find that today, Japanese men are looking to the women for leadership and change. "I think women have always had the opportunity to be educated, but they haven't been given the light to shine," says Takeo Kami, a twenty-six-year-old man who works in finance. There's a perception, especially among men that things have never been better for Japanese women. But this obscures the fact that for working women, especially those who aspire to the Japanese corporate track, there are still many obstacles—and a great deal of back-lash. "You look at major Japanese companies and you're not gonna see women CEOs or women on the board—it's very rare—I can only think of one," says Takeo Kami.

In fact, because in Japan, it is still considered true that "the nail that stands out gets hammered down," women are reluctant to proclaim a revolution, or position themselves to be at the front of it. They often demurred when I asked to interview them on the subject. Sometimes it helped to drop the names of some of the more famous women I'd interviewed: Diet member Makiko Fujino (the Diet is like the U.S. Congress) or outspoken feminist and TV personality Yoko Tajima. Other times, mentioning those names provoked a lengthy correspondence wherein the woman I wanted to interview declared herself "not worthy" to stand among this illustrious set, and I paced my apartment, kicking myself, for making her feel uncomfortable.

If successful women were reluctant to speak to me, that's for sure in part because of the backlash in the traditional portrayal of women executives. Women in the workplace, those who are most publicly breaking the traditional molds, have been subjected to the greatest amount of insult. One recent article in *Japan Today* newspaper proclaimed that "women who become obnoxious while in their cups are on the increase." The article then went onto describe three high ranking Japanese female supervisors and their outrageous behavior. Ms. A was thirty-eight years old and the guest of a salesman for a manufacturing company. Ms. A asked her salesperson to bring along some of his younger colleagues, then proceeded to hit on the men as if they were on the menu. "Fawning over her like that, we felt more like employees of a host club than business associates," the salesman complained. Contestant number two fares no better in this journalistic equivalent of Dunk the Alpha Chick. Ms. B is the supervisor in a small company with fewer than fifty employees. She is also, according to her thirty-three-year-old male subordinate, having an affair with the president of the company. When Ms. B has too much to drink, the employee complains, "She'll start lecturing, for instance, complaining to older employees that their bows are not deep enough . . . It makes me want to throw up."

The article offers no testimony from the women executives, nor does it offer any concrete advice. Admitting that she is right, the article warns, will only earn you her contempt. The only way to deal with a drunk female, we are told, is to "flatter them for their capabilities at work. Then the next day at the office you can call on them for favors." That some women in power behave as poorly as men in power is no surprise. That such a one-sided article could be presented as journalism is the real shock.

The hundred million yen question is of course: Given how traditional Japanese society still is, why this change in Japanese women now? There are as many answers as there are bullet trains coming in and out of Tokyo Station. One answer was expressed well by finance worker Takeo Kami: "I think one of the major reasons that Japanese women are beginning to stand out so much now is because we have been in a major recession for so long. During that time it gave the general population the time to think: 'Hey this man-driven culture hasn't put us where we're supposed to be,' and it gave women the opportunity to say: 'Hey, we can do this now.'"

In the course of ten years, Japanese women have gone through a massive social, cultural, and economic shift. During the go-go eighties, the nation rode high on the wave of economic groundswell. It was widely believed that this tiny island would swallow the global economy whole. Then the economic bubble burst. While Japan is still reeling from the burst's effects, a new economic paradigm has given way to a generation of women who don't play by the same rules. Until their economy collapsed, the typical Japanese woman in her twenties was married, a housewife with no plans—or need—to work outside the home. It was the eighties, but for all intents and purposes, Japan was caught in a time warp circa-1962, some-where between June Cleaver and Betty Friedan's problem that had no name.

Post-burst, the men were no longer the financial titans everyone had made them to be, and women began to see opportunities in places that didn't exist before. The birthrate plummeted, the average age of marriage went up by five years and this was when Japanese teenage girls began to drive the national economy with their joyful, trendsetting consumerism. Everything the girls touched turned to gold: from platform shoes to pastel-colored cell phones, from Hello Kitty to Louis Vuitton handbags. Today, it is Japanese women of all ages who drive what *Foreign Policy* reporter Douglas McGray so memorably called Japan's new GNC, "gross national cool."

The women, in particular teenage girls, now determine the course of the country's cultural economy. It's entirely possible to imagine that Japan is on its way to becoming the Italy of Asia: not a power player in manufacturing or politics, but a timeless travel destination, renowned for its art, its heritage, and its food. You can already see this happening in depopulated rural villages where there is no industry, but where a group of housewives open a soba shop and a gift shop and tour buses soon arrive to show city dwellers an older way of life.

Although no other country in the world speaks Japanese, its fans are growing. According to the Japan Foundation, in 1997, 127,000 people around the world were studying Japanese. In 2004, that number had exploded to three million. Sushi is becoming as easy to find globally as a Big Mac. In Sao Paolo, there are now more sushi restaurants than Brazilian barbecues, and residents consume an estimated 278 sushi rolls per minute. Hello Kitty has become to the twenty-first century what Mickey Mouse was to the century before: a global symbol of wonder and culture, instantly recognizable to children and adults alike.

In this internationalized Japanese culture, women are the ones who are truly international. While a typical salaryman may request his vacation, it's a good sign of loyalty and ambition to not actually take it. You come in on a Monday morning and your boss says, "Sato-san, I thought you were going on vacation." You reply, "I couldn't possibly take vacation when there's so much work." Women, on the other hand, who have less invested in corporate Japan, travel extensively. For many of the women I spoke to, this was not just the difference between themselves and their mother's generations, the global perspective was the difference between feeling liberated and feeling limited.

"When I was seventeen or eighteen, if you traveled outside of Japan, you still needed a visa," says Miyuki Hentona, thirty-six. "You had to show how much you had in your bank accounts. Then all of a sudden there were these cheap tickets and you could see the world without a visa. That happened and the old values started collapsing."

Kazuko Koizumi-Legendre remembers thinking as a student that "Japan is an island country. We can be very happy, just living among ourselves." But she wanted to know more. At the university, she studied American Literature and English. "I wanted to go abroad. English is a communication tool. If I learn it, then I can speak to other people outside Japan." She eventually fulfilled her dream, earning a post at the Japanese embassy in London. Now that she's a manager at the FPC, she notes that it's still the women who learn English, it's the women who reach for the world beyond the borders of Japan. "Ninety percent of the interpreters we hire to work with foreign journalists and diplomats are women," she says. "Very few are men."

Another woman, Ai Fukasawa, twenty-six, says, "My mother lives in a frozen world. She doesn't have any foreign friends. She doesn't speak English or any other foreign language. She can't get information outside of Japan. She can't understand if it isn't written in Japanese." Ai is sympathetic. In her own way her mother made big leaps. When her mother was a young girl, she moved from Kobe to Tokyo, a radical move for a young woman in the 1950s. For Ai, the leaps were bigger. At the same age her mother moved from Kobe to Tokyo, Ai moved from Tokyo to New York.

Award-winning industrial designer Fumie Shibata sees the bubble bursting and the effect of international travel as having a tandem effect on women in the past ten years. "After the economy collapsed, people—especially women—people learned that they need to be responsible for their own life by doing their own thing, not only by continuing to work for companies, because those companies went bankrupt," she says. "And marriage is not necessarily the perfect tool to make them happy. The job isn't either, unless it is their own special something." Fumie, who's forty, says, "In my generation there are many women who made trips abroad to find who they are. If you live in this country you need to get out for a while to find out who you are and to see things for yourself."

The first time I read Banana Yoshimoto's *Kitchen,* I was twenty-two years old and just a few years out of college. I knew nothing about Japan, I did not know that the year I turned twenty-eight, the age Banana Yoshimoto was when she wrote *Kitchen,* I would move to Tokyo for one magical spring just before the cherry blossoms bloomed. What I knew was that I was completely and totally hooked by the first paragraph:

27

"The place I like best in this world is the kitchen. No matter where it is, no matter what kind, if it's a kitchen, if it's a place where they make food, it's fine with me. Ideally, it should be well broken in. Lots of tea towels, dry and immaculate. White tile catching the light (Ting! Ting!)."

I've read *Kitchen* over and over again. I even used the rhythm of its short, simple sentences, the stunningly swift passage from grief to love in one hundred and five pages, as a model for my novel *Miss Black America*. I don't think anyone noticed. Who would think to compare a writer from Brooklyn to a writer from Tokyo? But to me, *Miss Black America* was a book forged in the soul kitchen of Banana Yoshimoto's words and memories of my seventies childhood—and the combination has made me happy.

In *Twenty-One Love Poems*, Adrienne Rich writes about the thing outside of ourselves that brings us back to ourselves, that was here before us, and knew we would come. For me, in Japan, this is Banana Yoshimoto's novel. It is a touchstone, the hidden panel that reveals a secret passageway between the girl I was in my early twenties and the woman I am becoming in Japan.

I'm not unique in what critics call "Bananamania." Banana's novel *Kitchen* has sold over six million copies worldwide; at the 1993 G-7 summit, the Foreign Ministry proudly gave a copy of the book to each delegate. Since then, Banana has kept her fans happy with an array of novels, short story collections, and a book of essays called *Song from Banana*. The forty-year-old author herself remains intensely private, although she does make sporadic postings to her fans on her Web site. Her site, besides giving out her birthday, also reveals her blood type. In Japan, blood types are considered markers of personality and are studied with the same passion with which horoscopes are read in the West. Not surprisingly, Type A's—Banana's blood type—are considered the most artistic of all the blood groups. She has a partner, and recently had a child, but she has been quoted as saying that marriage is "unnecessary"—perhaps because her own mother fell in love with her father, while married to another man. Her father, Takaaki Yoshimoto, is one of the most well-known philosophers in Japan. Her sister, Haruno Yoiko, is a famous cartoonist. Born Mahoko, she took the name "Banana" while a university student so her readers wouldn't know if she was a girl or a boy. The young woman writer whose early influences ranged from Stephen King to Truman Capote, knew that to launch a writing career in Japan in the days before teenage girls ruled, it might help to if not hide your femaleness, then to obscure it. These days, a writer's female identity is a pure positive.

In many ways, this book is a continuation of a dialogue between Japanese women and I that began the first time I picked up a book by Banana Yoshimoto. It was Banana's books that first got me wondering, to paraphrase Madonna, what does it feel like to be a girl in Japan? As I graduated college, searched for my first job, moved in with my first roommate, fell in love for the first time, I read Banana's books and saw a mirror version of myself, living the same young life in Tokyo. Once I began to visit Japan, I longed to know more about how my Japanese counterparts dealt with issues of career, marriage, and motherhood in a country that seemed amazingly modern and sleek to me and at the same time, a generation behind my own.

It used to be that Westerners, mostly men, came to Japan as students to sit at the feet of Zen masters and learn what they could from what they perceived to be a rich, ancient culture. Like the naive Luke Skywalker learning from his wise sensei in *Star Wars,* they sought guidance in every part of life, not just work or love. I was after something more narrow, less ephemeral, and, at its core, less hokey: I wanted to learn from Japanese women how they married the traditional with the feminist, how they balanced work with marriage and motherhood. A sensei may have helped in this search, but in twenty-first-century Japan, I already knew that the force was with the women.

2

A MILE IN HER KIMONO

Japan's Costume Culture

Sometimes it seems like all of Tokyo is one big fashion runway. You see girls dressed up like Little Bo Peep complete with staff and stuffed animal sheeps. You see the punks and the Goth kids and the dandies in bowlers and English-style hats. Donald Richie, the film critic and Japan expert, points to the fact that in Japanese restaurants, the chefs still wear white coats and toques and that when Japanese families go hiking they still wear boots and alpine horns. "Oscar Wilde once said, 'It's only shallow people who do not judge by appearances,'" Richie said in a conversation with *Interview* magazine's Ingrid Sischy. "And of course that's true—the surface truth is always the real truth. This is something that all Japanese people believe. You proclaim it, you put it on your name card and that's who you are." It's not that you are locked into one costume, one identity—it's just that you dress for every occasion, in the accepted costume of the environment. It's the reason why there's no such thing as casual Fridays at Japanese companies and why, if you are hiking in the countryside, you will see whole Japanese families

31

dressed up like the Swiss Family Robinson. It's not just a costume; those are their "hiking clothes."

The title of Ian Buruma's landmark book on Japanese popular culture goes a long way toward explaining all the different roles bubbling beneath Japan's quiet exterior. The book is called *Behind the Mask: On Sexual Demons, Sacred Mothers, Transvestites, Gangsters and Other Japanese Cultural Heroes.* As Buruma writes, "Life in Japan [seems] highly theatrical to the outsider. Even the way people dress often appears a little stagey. Japanese, on the whole, like to be identified and categorized according to their group or occupation, rather than simply as individuals. No Japanese cook worth his salt would want to be seen without his tall white hat; 'interis' (intellectuals) sport berets and sunglasses, like 1920s exiles on the Left Bank of Paris. And gangsters wear loud pinstriped suits over their tattoed bodies. In brief, everybody is dressed for his or her part."

Gwen Stefani sings about the Harajuku girls and their "wicked style." But Harajuku is also an anthropological petri dish of young women and how they are choosing to react to all the changes in their lives. From the thirty-plus-year distance of our own American women's movement, it's difficult to remember how many women were terrified of equal rights. In Japan, you can see that same kind of "fear of flying" at work, in strangely theatrical, uniquely Japanese ways. The latest and most popular style of street fashion is the Lolita. Named, but not styled, after Nabokov's enduring heroine, the Lolita actually dresses in Victorian fashion: replete with ribbons, lace, and bonnets. Her counterpart, the Gothic Lolita, dresses in the same Victorian dress, dyed completely in black. The Lolita's accessories are steeped in her infantilism: frilly underwear, lacy parasols, and teddy bears are common. It's not uncommon to see them, flopped on the floor like babies, legs splayed wide as if the streets of Harajuku were their own personal Romper Room. You can't help but feel that there is a sex-ualized element to all of this—Japan is, after all, the country where until very recently there were vending machines that sold used schoolgirls' panties, playing on the popular business-man fetish of the young virgin in her sailor-girl school uni-form. If geishas are off limits—look, but don't touch—and the modern woman is baffling independent—touch, only with her permission—then the Lolita is an adult version of Hello Kitty, one tug on her bonnet and she's good to go. Lolitas insist, however, that they are acting out a costume drama that is more Merchant Ivory than Benny Hill. "I'd like to go back in time, like the era of Marie Antoinette. I wish the whole world was like this," one twenty-four-year-old nurse told a reporter from the *Wall Street Journal.* The young woman was, at the time, wear-ing "a red pinafore, a gigantic white bow in her hair and white, high heeled Mary Janes."

Rika Kayama, a Japanese psychiatrist as well known as Dr. Phil, believes that what ails the Lolitas, along with many young women in Japan, is a sense of insecurity about the future: eco-nomically, but also emotionally and professionally. Dressing up like a Victorian doll baby, she asserts, is a way to get back to childhood when life was simpler.

Tokyo is the ideal place to witness the extremes of Japan's contemporary costume culture at work. Every weekend, young people from all over the region come to parade the latest and most outrageous in Tokyo street style. Although there are broad groupings among these trends—*kawaii,* or the culture of cuteness; gothic; Lolita, etc.—the young women (and some men) who embody these street styles thrive on their individu-ality. Hence, you might see a girl in a French maid's uniform with bright orange knee-high socks and *I Love Lucy* red hair. If it is true that the nail that stands out gets hammered down, then the most blatant exception is the "Fruits" as photographer

Shoichi Aoki calls them in his well-known book—those young people who are in between high school and corporate life and are free to "deuniformize" and express themselves as creatively as they wish. As Brian J. McVeigh writes in *Wearing Ideology: State, Schooling and Self-Presentation in Japan,* "The de-uniformizing period is 'betwixt and between' childhood and adulthood, socialization and employment, training and production and studying and working . . . These students are not yet considered adults, or *shakajin* (members of society; literally, 'social person')."

Kawaii, on the other hand, is about creating a fantasy of never-ending girlhood. In Harajuku, I've seen twentysomething women dressed in full Little Bo Peep gear, complete with a staff in one arm and a stuffed baby sheep in the other. According to McVeigh, there are three elements of the *kawaii* culture: 1) having features of an infant, 2) arousing a protective instinct in others, and 3) having the desire to be liked.

I believe the costuming of today's Japanese young women reveals, in a powerful way, how for many young Japanese females, Japan is a hard place to become a grown-up woman.

The Harajuku Little Bo Peeps and Lolitas may be the most visually striking young women in Japan these days, but not all Japanese young women are drawn to these styles; many reject the babying of their gender at every opportunity.

What does it mean to be a real woman in Japan? In a costume culture where on any given day, you can see women in kimonos and girls dressed up like Hello Kitty and everything in between, what makes you, in the words of Carole King, feel like a *natural* woman? I asked Miss Monday, the hip-hop superstar who is as popular in Japan as Queen Latifah and Lauryn Hill are in the United States. She is twenty-nine years old and every one of her albums has gone platinum. "I don't know what *real* means to other people," Miss Monday says, "but for me, I think it means to accept everything about oneself. Your strength, your weakness, cool parts, and not so cool parts."

It's hard, even for a modern Japanese woman, to wear her strength on her sleeve. If there's a Japanese equivalent to Rosie the Riveter, I don't know about her. I do know that for some Japanese young women, hip-hop culture is one way not to become a Lolita: a grown-size doll baby, swathed in Victorian lace. All over Japan, you can see these hip-hop girls: dressed in Timberland boots, baggy jeans, and tops from hip-hop inspired designers like Phat Farm and A Bathing Ape. It may be true that this is just fashion—these boots are made for walking, not taking a stand—but it is hard not to compare how much more grown-up the hip-hop girls seem compared with the Lolitas.

An island off the northern coast of Japan, Sapporo is a thriving center of this hip-hop craze. An American urban planner designed Sapporo, which means it's one of the few cities in Japan that was built on a grid system of numbered streets. Agricultural experts from the U.S. were brought in to develop the farming industry in Hokkaido. Most famously, William S. Clark, a former professor at Amherst College taught at the university in the late 1800s. Upon his departure, he famously intoned, "Boys, be ambitious!" It's a trademark phrase in Sapporo where there are several monuments built to Clark, and his image graces many of the local souvenirs and products. Sapporo brewery even markets a "Dr. William Clark" brand of coffee. Its slogan "Boys, drink coffee!" is a natural follow-up to "Boys, be ambitious!" When I ask my DJ friends Naomi and Trish what they think of this slogan, they just laugh. Boys may be ambitious, but at FM North Wave, the female DJs are getting the job done.

* * *

It's 10 P.M. and way too early to start clubbing in Sapporo. But I'm hanging with Naomi and Trish, so in effect, wherever we go is where the party's at. Naomi Chida and Trish Nakano are the top DJs on Sapporo's FM North Wave station, the biggest hip-hop station on the island of Hokkaido. Naomi is like a Japanese version of Sarah Jessica Parker—she's got a Modigliani-shaped face, perfectly tousled hair, and a wardrobe that manages to combine vintage style and Gucci without looking pretentious. Trish is a little more tomboyish: she favors boot cut pants, Ferragamo shoes, and funky hats. In Sapporo, Hokkaido's capital city, these women are as popular as any MTV VJ in the States. Even the American consul, hardly the person one would expect to listen to rap music, is a fan of Naomi's "Chat and Beat" show.

Our first stop is a new club called Blondie. Like many of Sapporo nightclubs it's housed in a typical two-digit-story office building. The club is basically a suite with strobe lights and an IKEA style bar and stools. But the crowd at Blondie doesn't come for the interior design, it comes to dance. And even though it's early, the dance floor is full of young men and women getting their groove on. The men are dressed in standard homeboy gear: baggy pants, designer boxers with labels that peek above their beltless pants, and because this is Japan, they have dyed hair, mostly shades of blonde. The women are dressed in variations of African-American ethnic styles: they sport braids and dreadlocks, head wraps, and African prints.

Sometimes, it makes Naomi mad that it's so easy to get dressed up as a *b-kei*, fan of black culture. "It's a costume mentality," she says. "You want to be something else, so you put on certain clothes or change your hair." She is especially contemptuous of Japanese girls who are obsessed with black men, but haven't really studied black culture. "Some of these girls are really hoochies," she says, using the hip-hop slang. "They don't even know Run-D.M.C. They've never read *Vibe* magazine." On her show, Naomi tries to put some context to the music. "If you go to a movie like *Four Brothers*," she explains, "it helps if you understand who Tyrese is, who Andre 3000 is, and who John Singleton is. Then you can enjoy it even more. On my show, I try to be an open door for black music and black culture."

On the dance floor, it's the men who dominate. They bust moves that are so flawless, any one of them could be on tour with Janet Jackson. They've got it all down: from Busta Rhyme's trademark shoulder jiggle to Will Smith's clown prince spins and turns. Naomi explains that many Japanese hip-hop fans are shy about dancing, so many of them take classes with professional dancers from the U.S. It's something she tries to dissuade her listeners from—the Japanese need to be perfect, to analyze and study practically everything they partake in. "It's just music," she says with a shrug. "Enjoy yourself." But the MTV-ready moves and artfully arranged head wraps and baggy pants were proof that the Blondie crowd had been doing its homework.

In many ways, Sapporo is the last place you'd expect to find hip-hop culture. If you ask folks in Tokyo, the northern island is a wasteland—the Alaska of Japan. But that's why I went. Sure, I've danced to hip-hop in clubs where Diddy and Mariah Carey hang out in velvet rope VIP areas. But what I love is searching out the beat in unexpected places: Indian bhangra music in London, reggae español in Barcelona, hip-hop in Sapporo.

I had first visited Sapporo in the spring, one year earlier when I was on the fellowship from the Japan Society and had been living in Tokyo for two months. As I've spent over a decade writing about African-American culture, the Sapporo

37

American Center had invited me to give a talk on hip-hop culture at Hokkaido University. I accepted immediately, but my Tokyo friends were disparaging, urging me to cut my trip as short as possible. "There's nothing up there but snow, fish, and Eskimos," they insisted, although none of them had actually visited Sapporo. By the time I boarded my flight, I was so filled with Tokyo myths and jokes about Sapporo ("You come right home if they don't speak Japanese!" is a popular one) that I half-expected to land on an Arctic tundra, to be picked up in a sleigh driven by huskies and to spend the night in an igloo.

It was quite a shock to discover that Sapporo is the fastest growing city in Japan—and that it had everything I loved about Tokyo, without the crowds. I've struggled to come up with the right American parallel for Sapporo. In some ways, it's the San Francisco to Tokyo's LA. It's growing music scene reminds me some of Seattle, some of Atlanta. The northern side of the city, bustling with students from Hokkaido University, makes me think of Boston or Denver. The American comparisons aren't entirely inappropriate: the island of Hokkaido was colonized by the Japanese in the late 1800s, with significant help from American advisers. The central meeting point in town, the Tokeidai Clock Tower, is hardly a tower at all. It's a white clapboard house that looks like it was beamed straight off the set of *Little House on the Prairie.*

André Breton once wrote that the "eyes exist in an untamed state." The same could be said about Hokkaido. The island encompasses one fifth of the landmass in Japan, yet only 5 percent of the nation's population lives there. It's the only place in Japan where nature outnumbers people. There are dozens of national parks and from the western most tip of Hokkaido, you can see Russia. On the island, Tokyo and the other industrial cities in Japan, feel a million miles away. Hokkaido was originally inhabited by the Ainu eskimos who called the island

Ainu Moshiri, which translates roughly as "human world." Even now, the name seems to fit. Each summer the island is besieged by outdoorsy types seeking to escape Tokyo's brutal heat. And each winter, the tourists come to snowboard and ski. It's as if Hokkaido were the place where urban Japanese go to reconnect with nature and their humanity. To quote the old Club Med slogan, it's the antidote to civilization.

I am following Dr. Clark's advice to be ambitious on this club crawl. After visiting Blondie, I follow DJs Naomi and Trish to Pulse. The street soldiers at Blondie had the fashion and they had the moves. I especially appreciated DJ Saitchi's heavy rotation of old-school hits: playing everything from Notorious B.I.G. to Leaders of the New School. But Blondie couldn't compete with the authentic flavor of the Jamaican hip-hop club, Pulse.

I grew up in the Flatbush section of Brooklyn—a Caribbean-flavored neighborhood where I spent many summers eating beef patties, sucking on sugar cane, and grooving to the dance-hall beats of artists such as Beenie Man and Shaggy. The Japanese promoters of Pulse knew the roots of the American reggae scene and had incorporated as "Flatbush Presents." The minute I walked in the door, I knew it was more than just hype. The crowd was, as they say in Jamaica, straight from the yard. The selectors, as Jamaican hip-hop DJs are called, were trophy winners and kept the crowd jumping by rapidly mixing and scratching a large stack of LPs. Their taste was impeccable as they moved from Dawn Penn to Chaka Demus & Pliers to Junior Murvin and back again. The beats were relentless. It was the sort of DJ set where every time you think you'll take a break and hit the bathroom or the bar, they play another favorite and you find yourself back on the dance floor again.

At times, I would close my eyes and believe that I was back home in Brooklyn. Then I'd open my eyes and see that I was surrounded by beautiful Japanese dreadlocked girls and Japanese men with long, black wooly hair and rasta caps. I'd look around, take in the scent of incense, the music, and the clothes and marvel at the power of Japanese imitation, their unique ability to not only mimic a cultural phenomenon, but make it their own.

Although I've hung out with Naomi on her home turf in Sapporo, it's not until we meet for lunch in Tokyo that I learn her story. Naomi grew up in Toyokoro, a small town in eastern Hokkaido. It is the one part of the country where the land—the wild, uninhabited space—outnumbers the people. Hokkaido people, Naomi tells me are "frontier people." So breaking down barriers comes naturally to her. She tells me about a famous frontiersman called Benzo Yoda who was a proponent of the famous "one pig, one pan" theory. If you can make it with one pig and one pan, you can do anything. "Hokkaido is like Australia," Naomi says. "It was a place where frontiers people and prisoners were sent to build roads. We have that kind of history."

Her great-grandfather came to Hokkaido more than two hundred years before. Her grandfather owned a store and she lived in a traditional intergenerational household with both grandparents, her parents, a younger sister, and her father's younger, unmarried sister. Naomi knew, from an early age, that her mother felt stifled. "She was always happy to take a break, if something needed delivering from the family store to a neighbor's house, she would be the one to go," Naomi says. With a note of sadness, Naomi remembers that sometimes, she was a useful accomplice to her mother's schemes. "When I was little, she used to say that I was sick and that she needed to take me to the hospital. Then she'd go to the department store and look around. She'll never admit it, but I remember."

Her mother took refuge in window shopping, but Naomi's escape was music. She took piano lessons, though she says modestly, the only reason she enjoyed the tutorials was that the teacher always had doughnuts and Naomi loved the Western treats. One elementary school friend had an older sister. Naomi was six years old, but this older girl introduced her to Abba and other seventies music. They were incredibly isolated; there are parts of Hokkaido that are closer to Russia than to Tokyo. "We didn't have an FM station, but there was a national NHK station that I could catch." Around the same time, Naomi's next-door neighbor became interested in jazz. "He was a high school student. I was just a little kid, but I could look into his bedroom. He had posters of black artists like Miles Davis. This is how I got interested in foreign countries."

While both her parents worked hard at the family store, Naomi and her younger sister had to amuse themselves. From an early age, Naomi's ambitions were clear: "I wanted to go abroad, speak English, and play the piano." When she was a teenager, Naomi delivered newspapers. It was an unheard-of job for a girl, but she needed the money to buy records. She delivered newspapers for four years. "People kept telling me, 'Girls don't do this.' But I didn't care. My curiosity won."

When she was in high school, her parents took a vacation to Hawaii. She asked them to bring her back some records. One of them was an album by New Edition. Even in a small town, in the middle of the Japanese wilderness, Naomi managed to hit the right moment in the cultural zeitgeist. Many people trace the Japanese obsession with hip-hop back to New Edition band member, Bobby Brown. When his single, "My Prerogative" hit, both the singer and his flavorful blend of hip-hop bravado and old school R&B set the Japanese fans on a *miha* (fanatical, lifelong) obsession with black culture that has yet to wane. "Before that New Edition album," Naomi says, "I didn't know how much I loved black culture. I had listened to Stevie Wonder, but to me, it was just foreign music. After New Edition, I was more conscious of the genre."

After high school, Naomi wanted to study music, but her mother told her that she would never make any money that way. Her mother encouraged her to marry a public servant, even going so far as to suggest that Naomi take a romantic interest in one of her single high school teachers. Naomi went to junior college in Sapporo instead. It's hard to imagine her, the cool DJ with the national fan base, on the road to being a Mrs. But Naomi says, "I thought that if I listened to my mother for a while, I'd eventually be free." Her major at the junior college? Domestic science.

This was the late 1980s. It's hard to imagine even a small-town American girl majoring in domestic science at that time. Yet it remains a common major in Japan to this day. Like so many of the women I interviewed, Naomi felt that she'd be locked into a traditional housewife role unless she went abroad. She agreed to major in domestic science because the junior college had a program: you spent two weeks doing a homestay program in England, then you traveled around Europe for two weeks. London was a revelation. Every night, Naomi visited hip-hop clubs and after the uni-racial experience of growing up in Japan, she was elated to see "so many races, dancing to one kind of music." When Naomi got back to Japan, she visited hip-hop clubs whenever she could. But "just to make my Mom happy, I got a job."

The job was at a pharmaceutical company and her mother's dream was fulfilled. "I was a typical 'office lady'—navy skirt, white blouse," Naomi laughs. "It wasn't that ugly." But the restrictions were great. In the morning, you couldn't drink tea or coffee at your desk, the only drink that could be displayed—out of respect for the company—was the energy drink that the company produced. Men could smoke at their desks, women could not. Naomi knew there was no future—office ladies are strictly not on the career track and cannot be promoted. Feeling that her job was quickly "becoming a cemetery for her life"—she quit.

Around this time, she got married and divorced, though that marriage and divorce are not something she speaks of in her public life as a DJ. For a very long time, a young woman who had been divorced—even one who worked in a field as fluid as media—was considered "bad news." Seeking a new start, Naomi moved to England, continued to study English, and got a job at the Kyodo News Service. She was twenty-four, but already felt that she was too old for a second chance at marriage. She was, after all, in the traditional Japanese hierarchy, close to being stale Christmas cake.

The stale Christmas cake label, while no longer in much use, is huge. From the 1950s to the 1990s, it was assumed that a girl in Japan, if she were to marry at all, would get married by the age of twenty-five. If she did not, she was like stale Christmas cake that nobody wanted after December 25. This was a cultural designation that crossed classes and geography. It wasn't just an annoying thing you heard from family members around the holidays—when are you going to get married? Are you really happy being an old maid? It meant that your chances of getting married were slightly better than nil. Japanese men were simply not interested in marrying, or even seriously dating, a girl in her late twenties. After the age of twenty-five, you might as well hang it up, get a cat, and take up embroidery. It's hard to imagine, from an American perspective, that such an arbitray timeline could hold so much power and weight.

A divorcée at twenty-four, Naomi felt her life was over. Now, she just laughs about it. "In the last ten years, things have changed so much," she says. "When I was twenty, my friends who were twenty-five said, 'I'm too old for everything.' Now twenty-five is nothing." Anxious to put her divorce behind her, Naomi got a job in London working for a Japanese company, an easy thing to do, in those heady years before the bubble burst. She admits, "I was really spoiled. I had no problem getting money. For my Mom's generation, you needed money and you saved, for a refrigerator, for a color TV. After the eighties, we had everything from the very beginning. It wasn't until the Bubble burst, that you realized how materialistic you'd been." Naomi tells me about how now in Japan, the worse thing someone can call you is lower class. As in, "You may have Louis Vuitton, but you're still lower class. You have a Hermès bag, but you don't really care about how you eat or where you live." Naomi says, "During the Bubble, money was power. Now we know better."

After the bubble burst, Naomi's parents asked her to come home. "They wanted to see my face," she says, sheepishly. She got a job at an English school, in part because of her continued fascination with hip-hop, then at FM North Wave—the station she works for now. It helped that she was fluent in English, an important trait for a Japanese radio personality who must often interview American stars who come to Japan on press tour. She asks me if I remember Jeffrey Daniels from the group Shalamar. How could I not? When I was in sixth grade, Jody Watley—then lead singer of Shalamar was my idol. Naomi explains that back in the late eighties Jeffrey had a program on North Wave, "a cool, urban, night program." Naomi became his assistant DJ. When Daniels left to do production work on a Michael Jackson album, Naomi took over the show. She's been spinning beats ever since.

These days, Naomi is thinking about leaving her show and becoming Big Apple *issei*—moving to New York. She has a boyfriend there, a black guy from the Virgin Islands. When I ask her why for so many Japanese women a love of hip-hop culture translates into the desire for a black boyfriend, she gives me the flip answer first. "Well, you know what they say," she says, "once you go black, you never go back." Then she gives me a more serious answer. "After the age of thirty-five, it's really hard to find someone single in Japan," she says. Even if the stale Christmas cake label no longer applies, younger women are still prized. "Foreigners don't really care about your age," Naomi says. Moreover, she feels that the ties between black culture and Japanese culture aren't so tenuous. "We can feel sympathy for what's happened to African-Americans in the 1960s and 1970s because we've been through it too," Naomi says. "Our grandfathers' generation really suffered. After World War II, we lost everything. We can relate to black people in that sense." Clearly for Naomi, her hip-hop style is much more than a costume, and is in no way an expression of insecurity.

The way that Naomi is able to connect hip-hop culture with post–World War II Japan is emblematic of how for Japanese women, there is a strong effort not to throw out the baby with the bathwater. Even with all the wild costuming one can see in Harajuku, not all Japanese women—or not even *those* Japanese women—are repudiating all aspects of traditional Japanese women's culture. There's still a great deal of respect for many aspects of traditional Japanese femininity. A friend of mine tells a very funny story of being approached by a rowdy group of hip-hop girls in Tokyo. They wanted him to take their picture. While they posed, they called out all kinds of curses— things they had obviously learned from gangsta rap songs like "Fuck tha police!" and "Smack that bitch up!" He took several pictures of the girls and when he was done, they all smiled, bowed, and said *"Arrigato gozaimasu!"*—Thank you—in the most dulcent tones you could imagine.

There is still a great deal of respect for traditional Japanese femininity. Even the hippest Tokyoite might get dressed up in a kimono for a special occasion, and revel in it. While kimonos and geishas go hand in hand in the Western imagination, a kimono is a formal dress, the Japanese equivalent to our ball-gown. Geishas wore kimonos, but they are distinguished more by their wigs, white-painted faces, and cherry-red lips. Geishas occupy an interesting territory, emblematic of so much stereo-typing, but also symbolic of a certain kind of grace that even a modern Japanese woman aspires to. It's important to under-stand that as Japanese women are changing, they are building on a foundation of Japanese womanhood, of which they are justifiably proud.

On her weblog "Sushi and Sensibility," Tokyo-based culture critic Kay Itoi keeps a very clever "Geisha Watch," a running commentary of all the ways in which Japanese culture and Japanese women are perceived and misperceived. The most stereotyped image of Japanese women is, of course, that of the geisha, and the most common misperception is that a geisha is a prostitute. The word *geisha* means "arts person" and the geisha is trained in the art of intriguing men with her most effective tool—her mind. Although relationships have devel-oped between geishas and their customers, she is the consum-mate hostess: a brilliant conversationalist, trained to entertain Japanese men with both her mastery of traditional arts from calligraphy and flower arranging, to singing, dancing, and playing the *shamisen,* a three-stringed type of banjo.

You can get dressed up as a geisha in Japan, and its some-thing that I highly recommend, if only because it's not some-thing that only tourists do. At the photo studios where you are transformed, you can see Japanese mothers and daughters being made up, young brides being made up, husbands dressed as samurais, and wives dressed as geishas for family portraits. You hear and read stories about what dressing up as a geisha means to Japanese women. One eighty-five-year-old client told the proprietor of a studio, that she had adored the *maiko* [the geisha in training] since girlhood and wanted to try dressing up as one before she died. Another girl, age twenty-five, came to Kyoto for the usual makeover and discovered that "this was a world that was close to my dreams." She quit her office job, "spent three years studying dance, *shamisen,* Japanese flute, drum, and the tea ceremony; worked hard to pick up the Kyoto dialect; and then made a formal debut as the geisha Kikuryu." It was more than a pipe dream. She is booked solid and quotes a fee of $1,000 for a two-hour appearance.

If nothing else, dressing up as a geisha enables you to wear an authentic kimono, which would otherwise cost you a few grand. But I was to discover that the ritual of assuming the elaborate costume of the geisha means a good deal more than just that. There is no equivalent in American society; a way to dress that piles layer upon layer of history and culture on your very being. The closest equivalent would be the not-very-sexy practice of quilting, so richly and evocatively described in Whitney Otto's *How to Make an American Quilt.* Being invited into an American living room with women of different ages and races to help weave scraps of fabrics into a quilt would give any foreign woman an unprecedented insight into American culture. Similarly, getting dressed up as a geisha enables a Japanese woman, and even a non-Japanese woman, to wrap herself in the very fabric of Japanese history.

I've dressed up as a geisha twice; once in Kyoto when I was all alone and once in Tokyo with a friend who wanted to immerse herself in the experience. I've also watched my mother-in-law plunge into the makeup and dress. The first time I got dressed up as a geisha, it was exciting but also a little embarrassing. I was afraid that I was becoming one of those Americans who takes her Japanese fascination too far. But the second time around, in the company of my girlfriend Michelle, who was there to share the experience, I found that my fascination had more to do with my love of Japan; I express that I am a fan by presenting a kimono-clad self to the world, or at least to my friends.

I was interested to find that while I considered the traditional geisha kimonos as quaint, in Japan just the opposite was true. Young designers are constantly working and reworking kimono fabrics into new shapes, as well as taking traditional kimono elements, such as the dolman sleeves, in different directions. There's a historical basis to the kimono's modernity. Shoichi Aoki, a street fashion photographer who is also the author of the wonderful book on Tokyo style called *Fruits*, writes in his introduction: "The average Japanese person's perception of their own traditional kimono culture was of an avant-garde and unconventional medium—adventurous, bright and colorful. Therefore the introduction of Western fashion and modes of dressing (e.g., the suit) seemed by contrast, drab and limiting." Aoki's observation adds another layer to my geisha dress-up: when I am in a traditional kimono, I discover that I do feel like I am breaking the mold of fashion. Kimonos are so adventurous, bright, and colorful. In one of my favorite movies, *Mahogany*, Diana Ross plays Tracy, a fashion model and aspiring designer who takes the chance to move to Europe and pursue her dreams. There are the usual movie ups and downs (including one really off-the-wall performance by Anthony Perkins as Mahogany's mentor and Svengali), but when Tracy finally gets to design her own line, it is a kimono-inspired collection, complete with kabuki music and makeup. After dressing up in a kimono, I was able to appreciate in a new way why they make such a powerful fashion statement, and why they are still so precious to so many Japanese women.

In Kyoto, time stands still. The Gion district is as famous for its geishas as New York's Christopher Street is for its drag queens. The district conjures up old Edo, as Tokyo once was called and it is not by accident that Kyoto is a palindrome of Tokyo. In Kyoto, one feels as if the *shinkansen,* the bullet train, is hurtling into to a slower, more graceful and simpler time. There, the hierarchy of a geisha's life as described in *Memoirs of a Geisha* came alive for me. I slept in a two-hundred-year-old traditional Japanese inn, a *ryokan,* in a *tatami* room and on a futon mattress. The door to my room was a *shoji* screen and when I turned out my light, shadows danced across it like the finger puppet figures my brother and I made with a flashlight at night when we were children. I read every night about Sayuri, the *maiko-san,* who arrives at the Nitta Okiya to train as a geisha. I shuddered at her harsh treatment from the geisha impresarios "Granny" and "Mother," cheered for her falling in love, and was reminded how rare "happily ever after" endings are when you and your beloved are from different classes and you live in a time and place where status is not fluid. It reminded me of one of my favorite novels, Lorene Cary's *The Price of a Child* about the love between an escaped slave and a free black man in Philadelphia.

During the day, I followed Sayuri's footsteps along the Pontocho alley, Kyoto's infamous red-light district, now a collection of charming restaurants and *ochaya,* or teahouses. I watched the young people hanging out at the Kamogawa River and tried to imagine the scenes that I read at night, playing themselves out on streets that have remained miraculously unchanged. *Kabuki* was born in the Gion, and geishas, who still populate the area, have been here since the early sixteenth century. When the day finally came for me to undergo my transformation into a *maiko-san,* the traditional term for a geisha in waiting, I arrived to find three middle-aged women, none of whom spoke a word of English, waiting for me. We got through with simple phrases and hand gestures. They were not mean, but I felt a little like Sayuri as they laughed and joked, drank Coca-Cola, and snacked. They covered my face in white paint, changed the shape of my eyes with black liquid liner. It took more than an hour. When I reached for a bottle of water, they told me I could not drink since my lips had already been painted. When they wrapped me so tight in my kimono that I could hardly breathe, I was told, "*Maiko-san* suffers for beauty."

The point of the elaborate costuming was that at the end of getting dressed up, I would get to walk the streets of the Gion, a real geisha in the eyes of all who might cross my path. But there was one problem: the geisha wig did not fit over my dreadlocks. There was much clucking and fussing about this. I was so lost in the flurry of Japanese flying back and forth over my head, that I almost missed the woman with the scissors who thought she could solve the wig problem by cutting off all of my hair. It was a stand-off. "*Maiko-san* suffers for beauty," I was told once again. But I had been growing my dreadlocks for nearly *ten years,* and I was not going to cut them off so I could wear a geisha wig for one hour. Finally it was determined that they would pin the wig to the front of my hair and that my dreadlocks would be tied in a bun in the back.

This meant that I would not get to walk in the Gion because my dreadlocks would give me away as a fake geisha and that would not do at all. But we agreed that I could do my photo shoot in the studio, maneuvering my head so that my locks would not show. So I spent an hour, feeling a little like Mary Pickford, acting out simple dramas while my hosts took pictures. "*Maiko-san* go shopping!" they called out and I took my traditional purse and baby-stepped my way across the room in my wooden slippers and thick white socks. "*Maiko-san* go strolling!" they called out and I walked back and forth with a parasol to protect my pale white skin. (Let me tell you this: it takes a lot of white paint to make me look pale.) "*Maiko-san* pour tea!" they said and I sat, knees demurely to the side, my kimono fanning ever so delicately over my legs. By the end, we were collapsing in giggles as I tried to mix it up with some moves of my own. "*Maiko-san* do the Cabbage Patch," I said, referencing an old hip-hop dance they neither knew nor understood. "*Maiko-san* do Saturday Night Fever!" one woman called out so I obliged with some Travolta moves.

While I was getting cleaned up, I watched with interest the clients who were waiting in the reception area. A Japanese businessman and his much younger, much more blonde American girlfriend. A mother and her teenage daughter. I wondered what the women would look like in their photos and what the transformation to geisha might mean to them. Geishas were sometimes scorned because they were entertainers and a step below wives. But according to some women, geishas were also more free than any wife or single woman could ever hope to be: living alone, making their own money, seeing the world. I took the long way back to my *ryokan*, pausing to stop on Pontocho Alley, then rushing back to my room to finish reading Arthur Golden's book, feeling closer to Sayuri than ever before.

Reading that book at this point was strange, because when I was first awarded the fellowship to Japan, I was constantly being asked if I had read *Memoirs of a Geisha*. When I admitted that I had not, people would say, "Well, you must before you go." As it turned out, I never got around to it, but I packed it in my bag, confident that I would read it eventually. I am so glad that I was able to read it, fresh and new, in the city in which it takes place. Never before and never since have I had the experience of feeling so immersed in the world of a novel. I could look out my window, walk down a street, and imagine the characters before me. It was a tremendous gift that Arthur Golden gave me, his words made Kyoto come to life. If I had relied solely on guidebooks, I might have missed it, seeing instead a Japanese version of colonial Williamsburg.

That dive into geisha style opened my eyes about the tradition of costuming that young Japanese women are riffing on, and I began to see how, in an ironic way, they are having fun with what is in fact a tradition that runs so deep in their culture.

The second time I get dressed up, I dive into the world of geishas in quite a different locale. We are in Tokyo; the Harajuku district, to be more specific. It is a sprawling metropolis of teenagers, fashionistas, and other creative types, a wild blending of the old and the new costume culture. Not necessarily the spot for foreigners to experiment with ethnic stereotypes. Michelle and I take the subway to Meijijingmae, then follow a map through back alleys to the Katsura studio. It is 3 P.M. on a Tuesday afternoon and the streets are thick with people. All my *maiko-san* innocence fails me as I press past bodies and feel them press past me. I feel the hair on other people's arms, I smell their soap, and I inhale their cigarette smoke. After a few inevitable wrong turns, we arrive at the studio.

In Harajuku, Michelle and I are transformed into geishas by three twentysomethings who are everything but traditional ladies; they're kind enough, but their attitudes say they might as well be working at a local record store or tattoo parlor.

While there are many strains of street style that run through Harajuku, I'm most intrigued by *kawaii,* and how different it is from the geisha costume I'm about to don. The kimono, like a tuxedo for an American man, inspires respect—if not for the person itself, then for the social situation. At the geisha photo studio, everyone is young and hip—engaged in a costume culture of their own. Izumi-san is the Japanese doppelganger of all the hip-hop girls I grew up with in Brooklyn. Her hair is straightened to the point of being slightly nappy around the edges. She's wearing bamboo earrings and an asymmetrical ponytail a la the rappers Salt and Pepa. Oriel is petite, delicate, and strong, like a ballet dancer. She is wearing a kimono fabric halter, low-slung jeans, and a white and silver studded belt. Nijon the photographer is the only man; he wears a traditional indigo jumper, nubby cotton-dyed by hand, the kind that Edo was once famous for and, as I understand it, was also popular among the Geechee in the sea islands off of South Carolina. I am reminded of the MTV makeover program *Made* that I sometimes watch at the gym. And it strikes me as funny and interesting that I have come to the nexus of Japanese hipsterville to be "made" into a geisha.

We begin, like brides to be, with a look book of exquisite kimonos. Every aspect of a kimono tells a story: the fabric, the color, the sleeve length, as well as the *obi* (the wide sash that ties around the waist of the kimono) provide clues as to a woman's marital status, social class, and the season. A single woman, for example, wears her kimono with sleeves that flow almost to her ankles, a married woman wears a kimono with shorter, more modern length, sleeves.

Flipping through the pages, we begin to imagine the fantasy that we are stepping into. I choose a sky blue kimono, the kind of color that is so primary and bright that it reminds me of a nursery school classroom. Michelle, who is from New York, chooses a jet black kimono with red accents. Then we must choose our poses. For one hundred dollars (usually $120, but we have clipped a coupon from the paper), we will receive three five-by-seven-inch portraits that will display us in one of three poses. We choose to take one photo together. Then we each choose a standing pose and a sitting pose. The sitting pose is actually a kneeling pose; our knees can barely take it, much less with the heavy weight of the kimono. We are sitting in a drawing room, on a leather sofa the color of sea foam, and we are wearing our street clothes and the house slippers that we were handed at the door. The day is young; we have only just arrived and we have every confidence that our MTV-like team of stylists will transform us into believable geishas.

Before we change, Michelle decides to take a bathroom break and returns from the restroom, delighted to report that there are "toilet slippers"—navy blue and vinyl with TOILET written across one foot and SLIPPERS written across another. Sanitation is everything in Japan. Earlier that day we had been turned away from the city recreation center in Minato-ku for not bringing along "indoor sneakers." It had never occurred to us that sneakers that had touched the sidewalk would be too dirty to wear on an elliptical trainer or treadmill.

In the dressing room, we are told to take off all of our clothes and our jewelry. I ask if I can leave my wedding ring on. I have just celebrated my third wedding anniversary and I have become newly paranoid about losing my ring. Once, at a day spa, I lost a coral bracelet that my mother gave me, one of only a few family treasures I own. I had flown to Japan with Michelle and without my husband, the day after our anniversary, how could I fly home without my ring? All of these thoughts flashed through my mind as our hosts looked blankly at me. My Japanese being so limited, so inadequate to explain the rush of memory, sentimentality, and fear, I took the rings off, placed them in an inside pouch of my purse, and zipped the whole contraption shut. This is one of the things that I enjoy most about my time in Japan, the communication gap, the foreignness of the culture, and how it forces me to act decisively: to eat here or there, to take this subway exit or that one. There's no room for waffling, at least for me, when my brain is being flooded with the crisp rhythym of Japanese words in my ear, the visual rush of being surrounded by the kanji letters that I can hardly begin to understand.

After taking off our jewelry, Michelle and I put on simple cotton slips. The slip feels good against my skin, like the nightgowns my grandmother used to wear, soft from countless washings. I put the slip on backward, tying it behind me like an apron. But Oriel tells me that it opens to the front, like a hospital gown. I notice she has three earrings in one ear.

In the makeup room, Michelle and I take our seats in front of a large, bright mirror. I look over at her and imagine us in a parallel universe, one where we are stage actresses and this is our nightly ritual, getting our makeup done in our cotton gowns. This makes me smile and Michelle smiles back at me. Our hair: my dreads and Michelle's braids, are pulled back in a tight hair net; another cloth headband protects our hairlines from the makeup that is coming. Then like a cold bath, I feel it, a thick brush of white paint comes down and across my face. Izumi continues like this, up and down, over my eyes, dotting my ears, completely covering my lips. I am startled and maybe a little scared by the sight and feel of thick, cold white paint on an industrial-size paintbrush, going up and down, up and down, as if my face were a picket fence. When I open my eyes, my vision is cloudy, as if I were looking at the world through talcum lenses.

Izumi does a trick with my eyes, a series of red dots and pink swirls designed to almond-ize the shape of my eyes. My lashes are still white; the face paint was rolled right across them. I look around for mascara, taking furtive, powdery glances at the pictures of geishas taped to the big mirror. The geishas in the picture have jet black curly lashes. Then Izumi tells me to close my eyes for five minutes. All at once, I am on a *shinkansen,* a bullet train, to childhood when five minutes of my favorite TV show went by in the blink of an eye and five minutes in punishment were an eternity. Then I see that she is opening the black liquid eyeliner. "Close your eyes, please," she reminds me. So I do. Then I feel that she has taken the liquid eyeliner, thick and wet and cold, and is carefully dabbing each eyelash. All of a sudden, I am still and mesmerized. I did not know I had so many lashes. My eyes are closed, but I can feel each one, as strong and powerful as my legs the first time that I ran a ten-minute mile. But here, in this traditional form in the middle of Tokyo's busiest and most fashion-conscious district, I have reconnected with a slower form of Japanese life that has eluded me for months. In one of my favorite books, Anne Lamott says that you become a writer bird by bird. Is it possible, I wonder, that I might become a woman at peace with myself, eyelash by eyelash?

My experiences dressing as a geisha helped open my eyes to the strong currents of traditional femininity that still course through Japanese culture. The glaring wildness of the new costuming of the Harajuku girls sometimes masks the more profound changes going on in the lives of Japanese women we don't see in the media glare. The schoolgirls with their Hello Kitty obsession may dominate our view of Japan today, but the hip-hop girls are a force of their own. And more telling still are the legions of women finding ways to change their lives, and push their culture forward, in more subtle but powerful fashion. These women are choosing many different ways to live, some quite traditional, as mothers and housewives, and some utterly unconventional, like Miss Monday, Trish, and Naomi. Still others are finding middle ground. It's a struggle, but they are forging ahead. For all of the costuming that goes on in Japan, ultimately, I think a kickboxing geisha isn't easily distinguished by what she wears. Her independence is more in how she moves than in how she dresses, and the ways in which she boldly blends the old and the new.

3

TEA AND SYMPATHY

Working Women in Japan

The thing about Japan is that it's a developed country and a developing country all in the same breath. It's such a contradiction. Nowhere is this more true than in women's lives and the tensions therein. Like their American counterparts, Japanese women struggle to balance traditional business careers with pursuits of married life and motherhood. In Japan, however, the difficulties of being a woman in a man's corporate world has its own distinctive colorings. The most glaring difference is how few women occupy professional positions. The Equal Oppportunity Act of 1985, later revised in 1997, is still considered to be largely cosmetic. Although five million women joined the workforce since the enactment of the EOA in 1985, the number of women in management positions remains virtually unchanged. In an article titled "The New Lifestyles of Japanese Women," Dr. Sumiko Iwao cited a Ministry of Labor study that found that, "Forty-eight percent of business leaders felt that women do not have the necessary knowledge, experience or judgement to serve as senior executives. The second most popular response, chosen by 35 percent of the respondents, was that women don't stay with the company long enough to justify a senior position." Another survey, this one by the Japan Federation of Economic Organizations, cited "the possibilities of giving birth" and "lack of professionalism" as reasons why women were not promoted to senior positions. Exactly the kind of sweeping chauvinism that the EOA was supposed to protect women from. A 2005 Cabinet Office survey found that more than 63 percent of Japanese companies have no intention to hire more women. This begs the question whenever I meet a successful woman in Japan: is there an actual movement or is it just a few women getting ahead, on their own terms, in their own way?

It is the quintessential experience of anyone who has done business in Japan. You sit down in a room full of men, and before the meeting commences, as you are making your introductions, a young woman comes in and pours you tea. While the Japanese term for "businessman" is the English-inspired salaryman, there is no equivalent for a businesswoman. Women who work in Japanese companies are called, with few exceptions, office ladies and the term implies that even though many of them have degrees from reputable universities, their roles are limited: they make copies, they clean the kitchen, they pour tea. Even in creative fields, like film and television, the old values still exist. Miho Shimizu is thirty, works in film distribution, and loves her job. "Society is getting better and better for women," Miho says. "I'm quite comfortable with my work, but there are still some issues. Some jobs are expected to be done by women, like serving tea when guests come. Even if you have a career, if you're a woman, you're expected to serve tea. It might differ from company to company, but at my company, that's a woman's job."

Japan's costume culture also works against women with corner office ambitions. Rochelle Kopp, author of *The Rice Paper Ceiling* points out that there is no such thing as an Ann Taylor in Japan, "There are no career clothes. The clothes are either for the ladies who lunch or the first blue suit for the post-university job interview." She says that sometimes when she is in Japan on a business trip, she sees that the younger career women are wearing twin sets and slacks while the young men are in suits. "I want to tell them, you need a jacket," Kopp says. "You need to be more conscious of the image you're putting across."

Similarly Kopp points out that if the Japanese wardrobe is limited in its offerings for the ambitious career woman, the language is even more so. Recently, she went to a conference where a Japanese linguist pointed out the limits of the language for Japanese women in management. "There is no good way for a Japanese woman to speak to a male subordinate," says Kopp. "Just as in the Meiji era when the introduction of Western ideas meant the creation of all new words, Japan is going to have to be just as creative about language and women's roles in the workplace."

Even getting to work can be a sexual minefield for women. Groping on the subways is epidemic. Commutes of one to two hours each way are common. The trains are packed to the gills. Pornographic magazines are sold at newsstands throughout the stations, right next to issues of the Japanese news weeklies and international editions of *Newsweek* and *Time*. Add this to the fact that after work drinking with clients or the boss is still considered a de rigeur extension of your workday. What you've got are: long commutes, crowded trains, drunk men reading pornographic magazines, add to this a certain repressed element of Japanese sexuality and you get a very common practice of men reaching out to fondle women on the train. The *Time Out* guide recommends that if a female visitor feels a hand groping her on the train, the best method of action is to get a firm grip on the hand, hold it up and yell *Chikan!,* the Japanese word for pervert.

This year, in response to women's complaints, the East Japan Rail Company (JR East) began offering female-only cars on popular rush hour lines. JR East has now been flooded with calls requesting female-only cars on its other train lines, a possibility the company is investigating. In 2004, 2,201 men were arrested for assaulting women on trains; this was up from 778 in 1996. In London, in comparison, there were 352 arrests for sexual assaults on the subways for the same year. A twenty-three-year-old woman named Yasue Ikeda was interviewed by a Bloomberg reporter, waiting at the far end of the platform for the female-only car. "The daily stress of possibly encountering gropers in a crowded train is just too much. I've had enough," says Ikeda. "I still feel a sense of rage about [being groped]."

One women who forged her own way in Japanese business and has found great success is Yasuko Nakamura. Now forty-five years old, she is the president of Boom, Inc., a marketing research firm that has interviewed over 100,000 teenage girls in the twenty years since she first founded it.

It actually took eleven years for Yasuko to make teenage girls her full-time job. After graduating from university, Yasuko worked as an office lady at an insurance company from the age of twenty-two to age thirty-three. "I actually had two businesses," Yasuko explains, "I left the insurance office around five o'clock, then I started to work for my own company,

Boom, right after. Because I was researching teenage girls being able to spend time with them in the early evening worked out perfectly."

Way before international news crews and photographers became obsessed with *joshi kosei,* way before Gwen Stefani built her multiplatinum solo album on the ultracool style of Japan's Harajuku girls, Yasuko had a feeling that girls were going to drive the economy. In the late 1980s, there was a popular television program called *Onyanko Club.* Onyanko was a cute, mischievous cat and the show was something of a cross between the *New Mickey Mouse Club* and *American Bandstand.* The show featured many high school girls—they were scouted and if they were selected to be a member of the Onyanko Club, they could be on TV. These high school girls were considered the ultimate *joshi kosei* and the success of the show created tremendous media hype over teenage girls. "Even before the Onyanko Club I was interested in these girls," Yasuko explains, "because they were so powerful and interesting and so much fun to know." What she noticed was that although the girls were popular, no one was taking them seriously. "People were still mean to them," she says, "and treated them like toys." She made sure that within the offices of Boom, Inc., things were different.

Boom's offices are strategically located in Shibuya, a stone's throw away from the teenage girls mother ship of Shibuya 109. Now that the entire country realizes that teenage girls are the ones who are driving the GNC, business at Boom, Inc., is indeed booming.

"*Joshi kosei* are voracious shoppers with a quirky eye for fashion and an uncanny ability to start trends," Yasuko explains. "They have come up with eye-opening ideas such as the tamagotchi, a virtual pet shaped like an egg. That was a huge craze. The girls also created a sassy lingo, just by doing the fun stuff that teenage girls do." Yasuko used to write a bimonthly column for the *Asahi Shimbun* newspaper called *"Uchira no Hayarimon,"* "What we girls like right now." Recently, she published a book, *The* Uchira *and* Osoro *Generation: Unadorned High School Girls of Tokyo.* The *Uchira* in the title refers to the way Shibuya's masses of teenage girls like to refer to themselves—a posse called "us." *Osoro* is short for *osoroi* meaning that the girls like to dress the same. Currently eight thousand of these girls are on the Boom, Inc., payroll, just a phone call away if Yasuko needs them. Companies rely on her and her teen experts to help develop products such as soft drinks and cosmetics.

Yasuko herself is a teen girl fact factory. The girls exchange between thirty and one hundred e-mails a day, before school, at school, and as Yasuko explains, "heavy e-mailing goes on at night." Karaoke became more popular with teen girls ten years ago when the shops began to slash their prices. The trademark of schoolgirl style are slouchy white socks, somewhere between tube socks and Flashdance-like leg warmers. Like a minister recounting a favorite piece of scripture, Yasuko can speak book, chapter, and verse on the "loose socks." She'll tell you that they appeared more than ten years ago, and after going up and down in length, they finally settled into their current one meter length. She'll also tell you about a phenomenon called the "just joking uniform" in which a girl might wear a uniform from another school or carry a bag from a boys school.

Perhaps because she takes them so seriously, she has developed deep friendships with the girls who call her *Yakko-san* and confide in her about everything from grades to boyfriends. In turn, she worries about them. The girls often have such high cell phone bills that they have to take on part-time jobs. She's concerned about the *Mean Girls* element of their friendships. The girls drop their friends quickly, and unceremoniously,

changing their e-mail addresses to freeze out the new outsiders. Eating disorders are also on the rise in Japan. "A lot of
the girls go on crash diets," she says. "Sometimes losing five to
ten kilos. But they are still growing. I worry about their health."

Originally from the Yamaguchi Prefecture, Yasuko came to
Tokyo to go to college. She had the a-ha moment about her
professional future when she saw a long line of teenage girls
waiting outside a Shibuya boutique to meet a popular celebrity.
Part of the uniqueness of her vision is that she sensed these
girls were as smart as they are fashionable. "In Yamaguchi,
where I grew up, the people are so soft and warm and kind,"
she says. "It's a different lifestyle, kind of slow, sluggish. They
are relaxed and don't talk that fast. They are not quite crazy
about what's new and the latest." When she came up to Tokyo
and began meeting the high school girls, she was surprised that
they spoke so fast, "like machine guns. They are so powerful
and they talk a lot. I was so overwhelmed and I always wondered where their power comes from." This was when she was
eighteen or nineteen, as a university student. In 1986, Yasuko
convened her first teenage girl focus group. She founded
Boom, Inc., when she graduated college in 1988.

I ask if she ever faced any obstacles as a woman, either at
the insurance company or in setting up her own company. "I
often get asked this question but I've never had any bad experience because I am a woman," she says. "People around me—
my clients, for example—always tell me that I don't act like a
typical woman. Sometimes, the men who work for me say, as a
joke, that I'm more likely to sexually harass them."

Her company is still quite small. She depends on freelancers and part-time workers to manage the vast amount of
research that she provides. "I've been doing this for over
twenty years and now this kind of business is really worth
doing. Everybody knows the *joshi kosei* are the really interesting

consumers. Twenty years ago, nobody thought this kind of thing could be a business." Now, when businesses contact her, she dives into her vast database to pull out the proper teen experts. "They are registered so that any time the condition of the research matches, they participate in my research," she says. "Once I make the choice of who I'm going to use, I try to contact them as many times as possible before we meet via emails, phone calls, whatever." Establishing a fresh rapport with the girls, she believes, is critical to getting the best research. She calls it, "the research full of real blood" and says she has to put herself out there for the girls to supply her with their honest responses. Now that teenage girls are so critical to Japan's GNC, Yasuko has to compete with some of the big advertising and PR firms in Japan. She still thinks they can never replicate the giant slumber party atmosphere that is Boom, Inc. "Sometimes I have the chance to see the results of their research," she says. "I always think it's full of numbers and figures without an actual voice." Yasuko is a striking example of how Japanese women are finding creative ways to make room for the women's voice within the still heavily male-dominated world of Japanese business.

Yoshitaka Yano is forty years old and a producer, director, and writer. Dressed in a cream turtleneck and jeans, he's sitting next to his wife, Akiko Oku. Akiko is wearing pearls, a light gray cardigan, and jeans. She is thirty-seven. Akiko is also a writer and together they have a media content business that they run out of a home office. They hope to also write television scripts one day.

Yoshitaka is frank about just how far women have come in Japanese society and how far they have to go. "This is probably a typical comment about the difference between our generation and our parents'," he says. "Our generation has more freedom in doing anything, but also I also think that even though we have more freedom, if women want to survive in a career they have to work hard—probably twice as hard as the men. Only the strongest can survive in this society."

Akiko explains that she was working for a labor division of the government. "I was so fed up after four months that I quit," she says. "It wasn't that my job was so different from the regular work most people do. But during those four months I kept feeling like I was just being discriminated against because I am a woman." Being asked to do menial tasks really grated on her. "Like serving tea?" I ask. "Like serving tea," she says, and there are daggers in her eyes when she says it. Her goal was to find a way to express herself without being part of a mainstream institution. "That is why I've worked so hard to find a place for myself in the creative industry," she says.

Akiko categorizes women into three fields: career women who have a high position in a company and women who have established their own companies; office ladies working for the company without too much hope of gaining higher positions; and freelancers like her, who as she says, "are outsiders doing as we wish." As a former office lady, she has a tremendous amount of respect for the women who stuck it out. "I think the so-called office ladies are one of the most powerful groups of people now," she says. "People think most women can be office ladies if they work for a company, but staying there is much harder than people think. For me, it would be one of the most difficult things in the world." Even if they aren't climbing the corporate ladder, she believes their very presence has an impact. "Twenty or thirty years ago, women just quit once they got married or had children," she says. "The office ladies are powerful because they continue to work and figure out how to have both a career and a family."

Both Akiko and Yokiko ask if I've seen a television drama whose title translates, roughly, as *The Course of Your Life Will Be Very Difficult Because There Are Many Evil Spirits.* The title comes from an old proverb that suggests that you won't be plagued by evil spirits if you live your own life. The problem is that the show, about five sisters and the ins and outs of family life, doesn't really encourage women to live their own life. It was written by a woman, Nakoshi Hashita, who is, Akiko says, "almost eighty years old now." The dialogue, Yokiko points out, reflects the writer's age. Just like when a grandmother tells the sisters, "You shouldn't even think about having a career or working too hard because you are a woman. You should just focus on having your own family."

Still the Evil Spirits program is the top rated TV drama in the country and hundreds of thousands of women in their thirties tune in weekly. Most of them are housewives. "They think they enjoy this show because it is for them and it agrees with what they are doing," Akiko says, "but in general it's so discriminating."

Akiko says she is so interested in the office ladies, despite being unable to take their lifestyle, because she thinks their lives would make a powerful TV drama. She wants to observe them and make something that reflects their attitude about themselves, not like something created by the media that is so dominated by men (and eighty-year-old female screenwriters). She mentions another popular television show, this one featuring a fortune teller. "She actually says things like 'women should use their wombs and not their brain'—on TV!" Akiko says. Her husband wonders why women put up with it, "It's like most audiences want to be scolded," he says.

That said, housewives don't fare much better in television dramas—or in the arena of public opinion. "If you end up being a housewife, they say, it's because you don't struggle, you didn't work hard enough to choose a different path," Yokiko says. "All women are in the most complicated situation now. People think they have much more freedom but the reality is different. You actually hear people say: 'If you are a housewife it's because you are lazy,' but it's not true because making up the house is very hard."

The interesting thing is that there's been a sort of collective amnesia, especially in Tokyo, about the role of the housewife in the Japanese household. The belief is that Japanese women have always played the role of *okusan,* the Japanese word for housewife, the literal translation being "person in the back of the house." But the truth is that Japanese women have always been very productive, especially in farming communities. The history of this country is an agricultural one. It wasn't until the 1920s, when men started to become salaried workers on a national scale, that a woman were able to tend to the domain of the home without needing to work a wage job.

It turns out that the old stale Christmas cake routine that has been fed to Japanese girls since at least the 1950s, has roots in the country's agricultural past. Given the historically high infant mortality rate, and a life expectancy as low as fifty, it made sense that women needed to have many babies for any one farm to survive. As early as the seventeenth century, farmers in Japan were advised that in order to create enough of a workforce to man the farm, their wives needed to start having children by twenty-four, twenty-five at the latest. Voila, a Christmas cake metaphor is born.

The prosperity of the postwar economic boom in Japan further adds to this amnesia; in the sixties, seventies, and eighties, the image of the Japanese "housewife" begins to really take hold. These women enjoyed real wealth even if their husbands were not high on the totem pole and they are the mothers of the young men and women who are in their twenties and thirties today. As is so often the case, when we think of young Japanese women tearing the "rice paper ceiling" we'd do well to remember the adage that certain qualities skip a generation. Today's young career women—entrepreneurial, independent—have more in common with their hard-working grandmothers than they do with their bubble economy house-wife mothers.

Masako Nara, who works at the copier giant, Canon, is one of the few women in Japan who is a senior executive at a traditional company. When I arrive at her office, I feel certain that I have stepped back in time to a 1960s film such as *The Apartment*. I am greeted at the desk by young women in bright pink skirt suits, wearing white shirts with floppy blouses (think Renée Zellweger in *Down with Love*). It's not just subversive street culture like the Lolitas in Harajuku, clearly the powers that be at Canon are invested in making sure these women look like little girls. Forget about pouring tea, when you come to work dressed like Minnie Mouse, there's no question as to whether or not you're on the career track.

I meet Masako Nara (and her corporate minder from the company's publicity and marketing department) and she told me about her extraordinary rise at Canon. She does not speak to the "girls" at the reception, nor does she acknowledge them. It is not so much rudeness as it is clear that Nara and these young women operate on different planes. She is dressed in a pink and white pinstriped shirt, a navy blue pant-suit, and ivory, stylish frames shape her face. She loves her work—and it shows. She has an easy rapport with the fellow from publicity and she seems as at home in the boardroom where we meet as some people are in their living room. At forty-five, Masako is a pioneer—one of the first, if not *the* first,

Japanese women to reach the executive ranks at a Japanese company.

When I press her about her past, she says that her initial interview at Canon went something like this:

"Do you think you will be interested in quality management?" the interviewer asked.

"No, I don't," she said.

"How about software design?"

"No, I don't think so, either."

"Then what do you want to do?"

"I would like to be placed in one of those divisions where I can develop data and help make management decisions."

It helped that she had a degree in science from Tokyo University, the Harvard of Japan. But these days Masako Nara laughs at the chutzpah with which she asserted herself in that interview. "I feel so bad for him now," she says. "He must have been so annoyed and he was not sure where to place me."

She took a job in quality control, and in her division of six, there was one other woman. This woman was two years older than Masako and had a master's degree (a power move that Masako eventually emulated). Even now she looks back on this opportunity to work with a slightly older female as a rare opportunity in Japanese corporate culture. Few of the women I've interviewed talk about having female mentors in the workplace: there are still so few women in any given sector and hardly any who get on the lifetime employment track at a major company. Masako's mentor gave her many tips and one absolute request: "I really need to ask you this. You will not serve tea. Ever. Because once someone starts it, everybody will take it for granted. So we (meaning the female employees) have strictly agreed and are determined to cut this task. We need you to be with us." Masako laughs as she relays the story; she understood well the subversiveness and importance of the request and has, in all her years at Canon, never served tea.

Having overcome the tea challenge, Masako faced another hurdle when she got married in 1986. She wanted to keep her maiden name but was aware that women who kept their own names were looked down upon. She returned the day after her honeymoon to find that everything in her office had been changed to her husband's name: the company phone list, her payroll, her insurance. She felt like she never even had a chance to take this stand at work; the decision was made—and swiftly—for her. In her private life, however, she continued to use her maiden name. And when she switched divisions in 1996 to Canon Sales, she decided to use her maiden name again. For this, she enlisted the help of a female friend who had faced a similar predicament. "My coworker who used her own maiden name told me that she would use my maiden name whenever she called me or sent me a document. I would do the same for her. At the time, that was how we made sure people used our maiden names."

When she was made manager in 1996, promoted at the same pace as her peers, she had the benefit of seeing how other female managers handled their roles. "I was not really worried as I was not the first one," she says. "There had been some female managers before me and they already made a path for me. Plus, I was able to be free of any pressures because my division was new and has no predecessor to compare against me. I just went with the flow. Starting from scratch can either be very hard or challenging and rewarding."

Although it is true that many Japanese companies state they have no interest in or intention in hiring more female employees, for an international company like Canon, in recent years, the female role has become increasingly important. The way to distinguish yourself from old-line Japanese companies is by putting your female employees front and center. Nissan Motors, for example, made international news and the front page of every Japanese paper when they announced in late 2005 that they were going to double the percentage of women in their Japanese sales force and raise the percentage of female technical advisers from 11 percent to 20 percent. Chief executive of the Tokyo-based company, Carlos Ghosn, stated: "The bottom line is that—statistically—more than half the public say that they would prefer to have a woman sell them a car." This is especially key because you can't make it to the top ranks of the Japanese auto industry without a stint on the company's sales floor. Adding women to the sales force so dramatically not only changes their immediate circumstances, but literally props the ladder of opportunity against the wall for them. No one thought Carlos Ghosn would last as the CEO of Nissan. He's a foreigner—born in Brazil to Lebanese parents, educated in France—but by 2001, Japan had named him "Father of the Year." (The Japanese equivalent to *Time*'s "Man of the Year.") Ghosn's promotion of so many women in one fell swoop attracted attention because he's a rainmaker. Before his arrival in 1999, the car company had lost money for years. He returned it to profitability. "Ghosn-san really appreciates the female employees," says feminist writer Yoko Tajima. "It's always the outsider's influence that changes Japanese society."

As a female manager, Masako Nara is often cited as Canon's answer to those who believe that Japanese women are the nation's most precious wasted asset. Yet she is only one woman. Even in the company of the corporate publicist, Masako admits that she doesn't mind talking to me as a woman; what makes her uncomfortable is speaking to me as a representative of all Canon women. While youth is often prized both in Japan and in the U.S., in a company like Canon, it takes a long time to get a seat at the power table. At forty-five, Masako is reaching the sprint stage of her corporate career—she's got a good ten more years to scale the company's corporate ladder, show them what she's capable of. This time between forty-five and fifty-five can be the most satisfying: where the long hours and sacrifices begin to pay off. Masako is quick to point out, however, that she never saw herself as a trailblazer, just someone who was committed to doing the kind of work she was trained to do. "We were very innocent, weren't we?" she says. "We neither fought amongst ourselves, nor were we bullied by the female seniors. Oh, but let's face it. Now I am old enough to be called a scary senior by the younger employees!"

Satoko Seki could be Masako Nara's younger sister. Certainly, she aspires to climb the same career path. At twenty-nine, Satoko is part of the next generation of women trying to make it in a world where there is literally no name for her. She is more than an office lady—she is not there to pour tea and make copies, but she is most assuredly not a salaryman. Her boyfriend is a salaryman at the same company, and because they spend so much time together, it is easy for her to cite the differences.

We are having dinner at T.Y. Harbor. Satoko is straightforward about her work life, her love life, her ambition. She is pretty, but not at all *kawaii* in the childish way of the young women her age who hang out in Harajuku. Dressed in a slim-fitting black turtleneck and charcoal gray cardigan, she reminds me of the Japanese obsession with Audrey Hepburn. So many Japanese women possess her easy elegance. I think about how few women like Satoko I met during my first visit to Japan. As a visitor to Japan, it was easy to get swept away in Japan's costume culture: the *yamamba* girls and *kawaii* girls and the Lolitas. Not only did I not really "see" women like Satoko, but I had no occasion to meet them. This book gave me a tremendous opportunity to knock on doors that might have otherwise been closed to me as a foreigner.

Satoko works at IBM Japan. She heard about her job from an alumni at her college, a guy who had worked at IBM in Japan, then left to form his own company. Alumni connections are a common way for any young university graduate to land a foot in the industry. But in Japan, favors are not asked nor granted in a straightforward way. There are three top universities in Tokyo. Tokyo University, where Masako Nara graduated from, is the Harvard of Japan. This isn't to say it's the best, you'll meet many people who will tell you otherwise, it means simply that the name of the university and its long association with old Japanese families, including the Imperial family, means that the name alone opens doors. Keio is a conservative university, also known for its highly placed connections. As Satoko says, "Keio alumni rule Japan." Graduates of Waseda University, where Satoko attended, are highly regarded movers and shakers—at least among the men. Even when she graduated in 2000, Satoko's professors were "not encouraging." She had to work hard to figure out a way for herself, to make the old boys' network work for her.

"When I graduated from university, Internet companies were very popular in Japan," says Satoko. "It was an exciting option, but I thought that in a big company, the system would be more stable." Although IBM Japan is technically an American company, the company's history in Japan is so long that many consider the company to be really "half-Japanese." Still, Satoko knew that a "global" company and one invested in marketing itself as such, would be a better environment for a young woman. At IBM Japan, there aren't any office ladies. "All the women are fully employed career-track women. It's kind of special, being in an international company," she says. Satoko's not surprised that the Canon marketing department pushes women like Masako Nara front and center. After only six years at the company, Satoko's been the recipient of some plum assignments because of her gender. She also knows that this is a recent development, "I compare my work with women who are ten years older and they are in a more difficult situation."

I mentioned that Satoko's boyfriend also works at IBM Japan. His situation is patently different from Satoko's. If you asked the higher-ups at the company who has more potential, Satoko or her boyfriend, they would pick her boyfriend. He's a young man with a bright future; lifetime employment is his for the asking. But if you ask Satoko, who has the better quality of life, she would say most assuredly that she does. She and her boyfriend both wake at 6 A.M. and begin their work at 8:30 A.M. Her day ends, with the exception of the end-of-quarter crunches, at 7 or 8 P.M. Because she has international clients (the plum assignments I mentioned earlier) most of the time she has lunch meetings. Her evenings are her own. When she is in charge of Japanese clients, she sometimes plays golf with them on a Saturday afternoon. (A woman who plays golf well is a valuable commodity in Japan. Knowing this, Satoko's father taught her when she was at university.)

Satoko's boyfriend, by comparison, rarely ends his days before midnight. He has to entertain clients at night—when all the real work of a Japanese company gets done. When there are not clients, he must go out drinking with the senior staff. In Japan, weekday evenings are when you really build your relationships. From 8 P.M. to midnight on a weekday evening is not your time to do as you please, it's part of the workday. "He is the youngest member of his team, so he can't say no," Satoko explains. She too had to do her share of drinking, especially in the early days before she proved herself and landed the foreign clients who prefer lunch to late night debauchery.

"More than going out with clients, I didn't like drinking with colleagues," Satoko says. "This used to cause me a lot of stress." Although she is sympathetic to her boyfriend's situation, she's not in love with the idea of being with a man who wakes at six and doesn't return home until after midnight. "It's a big issue in our relationship," she explains. "We lived together, but we didn't see each other." She uses the past tense because this past weekend, Satoko moved out and got her own apartment. She loves her boyfriend dearly, but she'd rather have her own place and see him on the weekends. It seems like a small thing, but I recognize it to be another example of the Waseda University grad's determination to make her own way. There would be no shame at all in Satoko's moving back in with her parents. In Japan, girls are expected to live at home until they get married. She, however, has no interest in being a parasite single or any of its more polite facsimiles. She doesn't need to spend her disposable income on high-end luxury goods. She would much rather be one of the few twentysomething women in Japan in possession of the rarest luxury of all, a room of her own with a lock and a key.

Fumie Shibata is also on the vanguard of Japanese working women. At forty, she is CEO of her own design firm and is largely regarded as one of the leading industrial designers in the world. Her work includes such award-winning items as a baby product series, a cell phone, electric thermometers, a rice cooker, and other kitchen appliances. When we meet at her office, she is wearing a light-gray turtleneck with a slate blue shawl and jeans. She's the only CEO I've interviewed so far—and the only woman—dressed for work in jeans. Everyone in the office wears slippers, as is the custom in smaller companies and everyone looks to be about forty or younger.

Fumie Shibata became interested in design as a teenager. At her university, her industrial design class had thirty-five students (five were female) in the major. Only two students from her year actually became industrial designers. "From my class, I'm the only female who is doing this so far," she explains. "This tendency is not limited to this country. In the world, there is a small number of women who are dedicated to industrial design; it is the universal tendency."

Her parents were craftsmen, working in traditional Japanese woodmaking. "But they could not imagine how a woman can survive as an industrial designer in this country," she says. "They are very conservative. They denied me support at first but now they accept and encourage me. But this is only as of five or six years ago."

Fumie began her career at Toshiba, where she worked as an in-house designer for three years. Her life there wasn't subject to the tea-pouring, office lady stereotypes nor does industrial design require the late night drinking that more typical corporate jobs do. Perhaps this is why she's so much more upfront about how good she is and what she deserves than many women who've been beaten down by corporate Japan. "I've just been through so much of the hard work and so much of the typical experiences," she says. "Now I'm forty years old and I have a major career. I've won the trust of the customers and people in this industry. I have the rare experience of someone who has had a major career for so long. It's kind of easy for me to get orders and jobs in the industry but I had to go through so many hardships at first."

While women are a rare force in industrial design, she's used her gender to inform her work. "A lot of what we do as industrial designers is design home appliances," Fumie explains. "Usually women mainly use those appliances and so they need some attention to a woman's point of view. At the same time, when a company develops a product, they can put ten or twenty or thirty million into development for one product. The men from this industry do not even think about trusting a woman who is in her twenties or early thirties with such a huge project. So that is why it is so difficult for young women to survive in this industry. Now I have the trust and I'm doing good business, but it was a matter of waiting out the difficult period when I was too young to command authority."

Even as an entrepreneur, she still has to face the limited thinking of what a woman can and cannot do in Japan. "Since 1994, I've been the CEO of this company, but when customers visit, some people ask to meet the CEO—that happens a lot," she says. One way she built her reputation was by entering competitions and submitting projects. She used her own time and labor to build a name through competitions, rather than courting clients who may not want a female designer. "I won many awards so they know I'm capable," she says. "That is why some companies make orders through me, but even now there is a very long waiting period in which all the top people have to decide." This stage can be very long because she is a woman. "It happens a lot," she explains. "I'm often told that I'm the first female designer that a particular company is going to use."

Like hip-hop DJ Naomi, Fumie's parents wanted her to go to junior college. In Japan, junior college is usually aimed at girls, the most popular "major" being domestic science. "After graduation, they wanted me to just marry and dedicate my life to being a housewife and have children," she says with a slight roll of her eyes. "I chose to go to the four-year university and that was quite controversial for my parents because they thought that women should go to junior college and that four-year university is mainly for men." She has two older sisters and they followed her parents' instructions to a tee. "So they are married and have children and have the typical married life,"

Fumie says. "Growing up in that kind of environment, I strongly hoped that I would not have that kind of life."

When I ask if she is married and has children, she hesitates. "I do not have children," she says quickly. "I am married, but . . ." I learn that she is married but they are separated. Her husband is one of her business partners and the company is doing very well. "My primary focus is business," she says, "and I just want to dedicate my life as an industrial designer so that is why we chose to be business partners but not life partners." Mixing work and romance is more complicated than it can seem. "We are probably getting divorced in the future but we are not quite sure about that," she says. I am surprised and intrigued by her frankness. "There is a small percentage that we could get together again, so right now there are those two possibilities. All I know is that my primary focus is business . . . because design is my life."

She knows that a career can't take the place of family, friends, and community. At the same time, she knows from her own experience, and from observing others around her, that marriage alone wouldn't make her feel complete. "People have always told me that I'm lucky that I've found something that I love to do and that I can achieve so well at," she says. "Nothing can change what I'm doing or what my job is. People around me are sometimes envious of that."

Fumie also believes that Japan's herd mentality can only hold women back. The nail that stands out may get hammered down, but ultimately women have to believe they are more, much more, than nails. "Especially in this country people are so afraid of having a different opinion or different kinds of values," she says. "So people feel safe if they find out that they have the same sense of value as others. I strongly believe that people should be aware of what the most important thing is in their own lives. For me, it's design. If they find out their own sense of value and what is so important to them, they need to be responsible for it and they need to have enough effort to make it happen. Women, in particular, should be fully aware of the responsibility and effort it takes to make everything come true if they really want it. If they believe it, it can really happen." If you believe it, it can really happen. It's the sort of thing that sounds pat when it comes out of a lot of people's mouths, but when Fumie Shibata speaks—her voice is a powerful mixture of industrial designer logic, individuality, and frankness—you believe her.

I am sitting in the lobby of my Shinagawa apartment building with Rochelle Kopp, author of *The Rice Paper Ceiling: Breaking Through Japanese Corporate Culture*. Rochelle is also the Managing Principle of Japan Intercultural Consulting, a Chicago- and Tokyo-based company whose clients include Sony, Honda, Panasonic, and Toyota. We are having tea, so it's only natural that we come back to the idea of Japanese women, business, and the perils of pouring tea. When Rochelle was a first-year business student at the University of Chicago, she already had an impressive list of credits: she was fluent in Japanese, had started writing a book, and had worked for two years in Tokyo at a Japanese bank. However, she found that in one interview with a major consulting firm, that the recruiter seemed underwhelmed. "What did you *really* do in Japan? Did you do any real work?" Rochelle learned that this man had taken a two-week trip to Japan when he was in business school; two weeks in which the only women he saw in a professional setting were pouring tea.

It didn't matter that she'd been in charge of international public relations at the bank: writing the company's annual report, press releases, interviewing securities analysts, and managing internal communications for all the overseas branches. She had been a woman working in Japan, and that could only mean one thing. Even now, Rochelle says, there is a rumor that many American consulting firms won't staff women on their Japanese accounts. "It's a big pet peeve for me," says Rochelle. "Occasionally, some American clients will say, 'Are you sure Japanese male executives will listen to females?' I think, 'You're in Human Resources, you should know better than to say something like that to me.'"

What comes first? The promotion or the confidence to get the promotion? It never occurs to me that the paucity of top-ranked executive women in Japan is at all self-selecting. Then I read a *Wall Street Journal* article about Hewlett Packard, the U.S.-based computer company. A global company, HP boasts women in 20 percent of its managerial posts worldwide. Women in the U.S. occupy more than 25 percent of all managerial posts. In Japan, that figure is less than 4 percent. A new program has been initiated to up those numbers. But Motoko Honma, a forty-four-year-old HP marketing specialist, isn't interested in a corner office. "Women in Japan," she believes, "tend to see management work as a risk to their personal lives and are dogged by the old-fashioned notion that aggressive behavior is unattractive." She goes on to say, "Doing support-type work is somehow psychologically easier." Honma isn't pouring tea in a bright pink skirt suit, but the dangers of climbing too high on the corporate ladder are still clear.

Those women who do make it to the ranks of a Masako Nara are highly vulnerable to the cry of tokenism, always an effective strategy for stripping an outsider of respect, but perhaps especially effective in a country like Japan where honor is such an important thing. At HP, one Japanese woman who was promoted to the ranks of manager didn't take well to the company's desire to promote her as a role model. She eventually quit. "She misunderstood and thought that she'd gotten there just because she was a woman," says Akiko Kawai, an HP manager in charge of a new program focused on promoting Japanese women. "This became stressful to her."

What is interesting about the daughters of Japan's pre-bubble economic boom is that their career ambitions are directly linked to how they read their mothers' situations. If they saw their mothers' lives as happy, then they too would like to be housewives. If they saw their mothers' lives as limited, then a career becomes crucial. Take for example, Yuki Yamashiro, who works in foreign relations. She says: "My mother is a housewife, but that's why she pushes me to have a career. My mother dreamed of independence, but she had a very severe situation with her mother-in-law. My grandmother still lives in my mother's house."

This may seem familiar, merely a Japanese remix of Alice Walker's *In Search of Our Mothers' Gardens,* but these decisions take place in a context very different from our own. In the twenty-first-century U.S., some women may choose to stay at home, but generally they are expected to share the economic burden of the household. In Japan, a man who proposes marriage is making an overt, not tacit, economic offer to fully take care of the household. As psychologist Rika Kayama explained it to me, "Marriage is one kind of employment for women, lifetime employment for women." Lifetime employment being the Japanese term for a job that you can't be fired from, a bottomless rice bowl, the job that will take care of you forever. A tall order for something as complicated as marriage, but one that is honored in Japan nonetheless.

One December afternoon, I visited Sacred Heart University, Japan's top women's college, alma mater of the Empress and her ilk, to talk to young women about what they see as their prospects for the future. These women, as I saw it, were Japan's third wave: after Masako Nara's generation, following in the footsteps of Satoko and her rapid rise at IBM. Certainly, these young women would feel even more entitlement and confidence about their future careers. I was interested in how the college girls viewed the trailblazers I was interviewing as well as whether they felt a prevailing ambition to follow their model or not.

My friend, Marsha Krakower, a Sacred Heart alum who grew up in Japan, is a professor there. She invited me to visit her media class. One student, named Mariko says, "My mother is a housewife. My grandmother is too. I'm thinking about having a career, maybe working with older people." This seems like an especially smart idea in a country with the largest elderly population and lowest birth rate among all industrialized nations. A girl named Kanae says: "My grandmother was a very independent woman. When my grandfather passed away, she supported the whole family. She calls all the time. We're very close. She wants me to have a career." Another girl named Rinna says, "I want to be a mother, like my mother. She's an artist. She's planning to exhibit her own works at the Palace Hotel in January. She's shown me how to balance work and family."

The most obvious question to ask, when you are reporting on women and their changing roles in society, is: Who are your role models? Even if the answer is pat—"my mother," "Hilary Clinton," "Maya Angelou"—it tells you something about the woman and how she thinks of herself. Perhaps because Japan is not, by nature, a country of individualists, the role model question gets a lot of blank stares. "I don't have any role models," a girl named Gaga tells me at Sacred Heart. "My parents taught me when I was small, you can choose your own way." Akiko, another student, says, "I think I don't have a certain person, but an image: someone who's independent, strong, and caring." I wonder, too, if it is because the national culture is so private, that it is hard to develop the kind of admiration and deep-seated affiliation that one feels for a role model: be it a senior employee at your company or someone you see on TV.

I wonder how many women at Masako Nara's company know how important it was for her to be called by her maiden name and the deal she struck with a coworker to make it happen. How many of Satoko's female coworkers know how uncomfortable she was at the late night drinking parties that were once part of her job, and how relieved she was to get more international clients who prefer lunch to dinner for work-related socializing? My sense, again and again, was that women told me stories they did not share with their colleagues, or even sometimes with their friends. It occurs to me that in order for someone to be a role model, they must reveal not only their strengths, but their vulnerabilities. It's in the interplay between the two, and how they overcome the latter, that we find something worthy of admiring.

Roppongi Hills is the hot new development in Tokyo. A fiercely ambitious sprawling complex built by developer Minoru Mori, it features a Virgin movie theater, a Grand Hyatt hotel, fitness clubs, dozens of restaurants, and the Mori Art Museum. The Mori Art Museum specializes in contemporary exhibits (recent offers included a panoramic perspective on Brit fashion designer Vivienne Westwood, to the first career retrospective of photographer Hiroshi Sugimoto.) But it is also a kind of cultural lounge, open from 10 A.M. to 10 P.M. In the evenings, you can find literally hundreds of young people on the Tokyo City View floor (there's an extra fee), looking out onto the city, listening to DJs and slouching on the modern furniture in the lounge areas.

Mina Takahashi has been with the Mori Art Museum since its inception. She joined in September 2000, three years before the museum and the complex opened. It was a small team at the museum, just eight people to start with, and Mina was able to be privy to not only the creative side of opening a museum, but the architectural and operational planning. About her job, she says, "I guess I was lucky to get in." When I ask Mina who her role models are, she says, "There aren't any. I read about some big names at new companies and some of them are actually women. A lot of the newspapers have a weekly column about women and work. I read it but I feel like it doesn't really include me, myself."

Later, she sent me an e-mail, trying to clarify her position on the matter: "I've thought a little about your interview . . . Career is, of course, an important aspect of many women's minds, but it is not something we talk about amongst each other, or at least, people around me. People talk of dreams down the road, but not immediate ones. Nor do we talk about role models. There aren't any that I aspire to in my immediate surroundings. Maybe I'm just unlucky and I haven't met anyone who could become a role model for me. I don't aspire to famous women because, really, I don't know their lives or how they really work or what they really are like as bosses." This last part of Mina's e-mail strikes me as very insightful and I see a relation between her comment and the Japanese idea of trust: how it takes a very long time to build. It only makes sense that you don't elevate someone to the level of role model so easily. At the same time, it also helps explain why this "revolution" of women in Japan is at once so strong—the dropping birth rate!

The growing numbers of Japanese career women and entre-preneurs! The nation's most wasted asset!—and yet at the same time, so diffused. When flesh and blood role models are so lacking, when you don't have women like Rosa Parks and Gloria Steinem willing to stand up and be the face of a move-ment, then sometimes, it can be quite confusing.

Women like Mina, women who are doing interesting, engaging work, are in a vacuum. It's not just that it is hard for Mina to get to know someone who might provide the next aspirational step. It's not likely that the girls at Sacred Heart University will, at least while they are still undergrads, get to know someone like Mina. I think of her job in the public rela-tions department at the Mori Art Museum: how her life is a flurry of meeting artists, entertaining journalists on press vis-its, opening receptions at the museum, and opening recep-tions of the other art museums in town. It's so easy to take for granted all the things we have in the U.S., even at the most dis-advantaged schools, you have career days and take-your-daughter-to-work days. I think of the girls I met at Sacred Heart University, the ones who are "media majors," but really have no idea what that means, and I think of what a good role model Mina Takahashi would be to them.

My friend, Karen Hill Anton, who has lived in rural Japan for more than thirty years now, really brought home for me all the competing tensions in Japanese women's lives—the desire for more opportunity that is so deeply married to the respect and appreciation for traditional Japanese culture. Karen, who now works as a diversity consultant for Citibank, is a very popular speaker on the lecture circuit: both in Japan and abroad. Three of her four children were born in Japan and she raised them in a traditional Japanese farmhouse (without indoor plumbing, for seven years!) on a mountain top, amidst some of the most beautiful tea farms you have ever seen. Her experience was so unusual, that Japanese public television commissioned a documentary about her and her family called "Karen's Country Diary." Karen's perspective, her years of experience and deep friendship with women in rural Japan, gave me a level of sympathy for working women that I might not have had before. Climbing the corporate ladder is not as simple as whether or not you pour tea; it never has been.

"What I saw and knew and observed when I first came here and what I see and know and observe now are worlds apart," Karen says, as we sat in her house, overlooking the mountains of Hamamatsu. Karen's house, which she and her husband Bill designed themselves, is an interesting mix of Western and Eastern styles. Traditional calligraphy abounds: Karen is a master calligrapher, reaching a level few foreigners ever have. But then there's this glorious wood-burning stove, imported from New England, that fills her great room with an all-enveloping warmth.

We come back to the matter of tea. I say, quite brashly, that in order for a woman to be taken seriously in Japan, she must not pour tea. It's what I've heard, again and again, and like a true believer, I now preach the gospel. Karen offers up a different perspective. Karen and Bill first came to Japan in the early seventies, for Bill to study traditional Japanese arts at a dojo. "Outside the dojo, whenever we were invited to anyone's house, there was always the matter of women serving tea." It was the mid-seventies and Karen, who'd come to Japan from New York, by way of forward-thinking Scandanavia, was appalled. It wasn't until much later that she learned that the women she consciously separated herself from, the women pouring tea, had rich intellectual and social lives: they were academics, mathematicians, dentists. It would take years for the women to pour out the story of their own accomplishments, along with that tea. These days Karen considers her friendships among these women invaluable. "In America, it cracks me up, people start talking about the most personal things," Karen says. "It can be charming, the kind of things Americans find to be worthy of conversation with a near stranger. But living in Japan has taught me that it takes time to have real intimacy; it takes time, patience, and investment."

For years, Karen wrote a nationally renowned column called "Crossing Cultures" for the *Japan Times*. In one of her columns, she relays the story of giving a lecture to a group of American women. Karen, at the time, was raising three daughters and a son in rural Japan. One young women asked, "Aren't you worried your daughters will become like Japanese women?" The implication, of course, being that a Japanese woman is one who walks two steps behind her man and is a meek, voiceless creature who pours tea. In response, Karen wrote: "I suppose if I wanted to say what I thought characterized the Japanese women I know, what they have that I value, it would be such qualities as selflessness, grace, forbearance, perservance, generosity, modest and humility. My daughter could have worse examples to emulate. So could I."

Despite the challenges of navigating corporate Japan, more and more young women are pursuing careers. In her paper, "The New Lifestyles of Japanese Women," Sumiko Iwao notes that part of the trouble with integrating women into the workplace is how they are perceived: "A Japan Labor Institute survey of men conducted in 1991 revealed that the most common view of women colleagues is as "considerate supporters." The same survey showed that only 26 percent of men regard women as "able partners." An amazing 15 percent said they have no particular impression of women whatsoever." This lag in the attitude toward women in the country has a lot to do with why so many Japanese women are deciding to pursue careers abroad, rather than struggle with the structures at home. As any resident of a U.S. or European city knows, Japanese women have begun traveling the world en force, and many of those who have lived abroad or traveled extensively are returning home with new expectations. These women who have experienced the wider world are having a profound effect on the culture back home.

4

BANANAS

How Travel and Life Abroad
Liberates Japanese Women

The Japanese woman shopping abroad is as universal an urban scene as the street corner vendor or the subway busker, playing his horn or guitar. You can see the Japanese woman spending her still powerful yen from New York to Milan, from Capetown to Prague, and back again. But it wasn't until I began to interview Japanese women that I realized that they are shopping for more than retail goods. In a country that keeps one foot firmly planted in its feudal past, any woman who does not want to suffocate under the weight of so much traditionalism eventually makes her way abroad. Many of them stay abroad, for a university semester or longer if they can manage it. Others use their parasite single incomes to take several trips abroad a year, shopping yes, but also learning foreign languages, soaking up experience and knowledge. They pick up more than French perfume and trendy American jeans as they course through duty-free; they are picking up samples of independence, which they pack away and bring back home.

A 2000 census found that of the 16,516 foreign-born Japanese living in New York City, more than 63 percent are women, more than 64 percent of these women are between twenty and thirty-nine years old, a much younger demographic than can be found in Chinese and Korean immigrant groups in the city. They are called Big Apple *issei* and at many of the city's universities and language schools, they make up 30 percent of the foreign-born population. Caitlin Morgan, an assistant director of English language studies at The New School, told a reporter from *The New York Times* that the changes in the young Japanese women she sees in New York are monumental. This speaks to the point several of the women I've interviewed have made about how important travel abroad has been in this cultural revolution that Japanese women are experiencing. For Morgan, the first thing she notices about the Japanese women in New York are the physical changes: "they change their hair color, get tattoos, acquire multiple piercings, use hair extensions, and grow dreadlocks." But the bigger changes are in direct contrast to the Lolitas flopped across Harajuku. "The women especially," says Morgan, "their voices seem to get deeper, they put on a little weight and become fitter, they use less makeup, they become a little realer."

For a very long time, the working title of this book was *A Girl Called Banana*. As I faxed my interview requests to people, it became obvious that some people's minds weren't going to Banana Yoshimoto at all. They thought I was talking about banana as a cultural term, for someone who, as one girl put it, is "Asian on the outside and western on the inside." In the U.S., every racial minority has a term for someone they consider to be "white on the inside." For African-Americans, the term is Oreo. For Native-Americans, it's apples. For Asian-Americans, it's banana or Twinkie. For the most part, these terms are considered derogatory. In Japan where Asians are the majority, I found that people had a different attitude toward the term "banana"—one that opened up a completely different dialogue about race, culture, and belonging than I had ever had in the country before.

The fact that Japanese women tend to change in so many ways when they move abroad highlights just how confining the culture still is for women in general. For some, once they've lived overseas, they never again feel like they quite fit into the culture or even want to readjust to its demands. Others make the transition back, but it is rarely easy. For Kazumi Hasegawa, finding her place in Japanese culture has been like Goldilocks trying to find a place in the home of the three bears. Except in Kazumi's case, nothing ever felt just right—except for life in the U.S., which is ironic, because as a teenager in Yokohama, Kazumi says, "I hated English and the U.S. so much. I tried not to buy U.S. things. I didn't understand why the movies were so popular. I thought it was a waste of money." It seems like an especially strong case of xenophobia, for a teenage girl to hate American movies. Kazumi tries to explain: "Here movies are so expensive. Tickets cost twenty dollars. Even with a student discount, it was ten dollars. In high school, when I didn't have a lot of money, I wanted to feel that a movie made my ten dollars worthwhile."

At university, Kazumi had initially planned to study French literature and sociology. A professor pointed her in the direction of the international department. For Kazumi when she opened the department door, she literally stepped into a new life. "When I went to the international department, there were Japanese kids who had grown up in Africa, the U.S., India, Thailand," she says. "They were speaking French and English to each other. At the time, I didn't speak English. These kids could speak Japanese, but they didn't write it. They asked questions I would have never thought of. They had such a diverse perspective. It was very shocking to me."

At the same time, Kazumi sensed that this was where she belonged. Two years into the program, she was still struggling with her English. "I was very shy," she explains. "I was intimidated, just being across from these Japanese students having serious conversations in English." Kazumi began to read Japanese translations of black women's literature: *Their Eyes Were Watching God, The Bluest Eye,* and *Playing in the Dark.* "I started to think if I read these books in English, I could understand more," she says. "These books were very powerful. I often had to stop reading because I was crying so much."

Kazumi's university had an exchange program with Hope College in Michigan. Kazumi dreamed of going there, but an oral exam was required and she was confident she would fail. She was in the throes of an endless cycle, familiar to anyone who tries to master a foreign language: she did not speak because her English wasn't very good, but her English never improved because she did not speak. Finally she decided she had to put her courage to the sticking place and *gambate.* "My teacher was really surprised because I didn't speak at all in English class," she says. "On the day of the interview, I passed the written exam, no problem. But when I saw his face, at the beginning of the oral exam, I thought there's no way I'm going to pass this test. Somehow I made it."

She spent three weeks in Michigan and then, as part of the program, she was given one week to travel anywhere she wanted. Influenced by the literature she had read in Japan, she decided to go to New Orleans and Atlanta. "I wanted to see how black women pray in real churches," she says. "It was fantastic. I had read about black churches in Japan, but experiencing it was completely different." Kazumi's words come fast and furiously when she describes the sense of community she felt in the churches, the vibrant colors that shone through the stained glass windows, the richly textured folds of the choir robes. "The gospel . . ." she pauses, to catch her breath, "was just great. Beyond words. We sing karaoke in Japan, but it's an artifical experience. You're crowded in these small rooms and everyone gets drunk first. I'm not a Christian, but gospel has come to mean a lot to me."

Kazumi returned to Japan filled with purpose and passion. She decided to spend her senior year abroad. Most of her fellow students who did American exchange programs went to West Coast schools with high Asian enrollment, like UCLA and UC Berkeley. Kazumi wanted to go to Howard, a historically black university in Washington, D.C. "I wanted to have a very direct experience," she says. "I wanted to jump into the black community." Frederick Douglass' slave narrative, she tells me, was the first book she read in English. At Howard, she became captivated by the story of a Japanese man named Zenichiro Oyabe, who graduated from Howard in the late nineteenth century. I find it interesting how Kazumi landed on this path, so similar and yet so different from the Japanese hip-hop girls like Miss Monday and DJ Naomi. The hip-hop girls in Japan are driven by an affinity for the music, but for Kazumi there was a direct connection. She felt at home in the black American community because as a Japanese woman she understood on a very deep level, what it felt like to be oppressed by one's own culture.

She spent a year at Howard and then completed her master's degree at Ohio State. Her plan was to live in the U.S. and she was working for the Japanese consulate in New York on September 11, 2001. "I had heard that if you were at the consulate, you automatically got a working visa. But after September 11, the policy changed. That's why I had to come back to Tokyo. My visa expired."

Now living in Tokyo, she finds that the language she once clung to does not work for her at all. "When you speak Japanese, you have to follow the cultural codes," she says. "You have to bow. You have to follow these invisible rules. My voice is very loud. Japanese women traditionally speak softly. The Japanese language is very soft, very indirect. English is very direct. Even simple sentences are very powerful in English. Even though my English is not very good, I can say strong things. I feel powerful when I speak English."

She tells me that her father was a salaryman, but "he was adopted when he was three years old. We don't know who his parents were." Her mother was a homemaker, "but she was very interested in American literature. She graduated from college with a degree in English literature." I notice that while many of the women I've interviewed give me a rote answer—salaryman father, housewife mother—Kazumi has added a lot of details to her "buts." She tells me that growing up, "I didn't have any kind of dream. Girls in Japan want to get married and have a happy family. I never thought about having kids or a husband. That's not me."

Leaning in closer, we are on a subway in Tokyo, sitting side by side, Kazumi tells me: "My body is kind of big by Japanese standards. Growing up, I had to wear men's clothes and men's shoes. My mother didn't know what else to put me in. I read men's magazines and tried to imitate men's fashions. When I was small, I had no choice but to wear men's clothes." My heart just breaks for her. She is not overweight, by any stretch of the imagination. But she is what used to be called "husky"—broad shoulders, solid build. In the U.S., she would blend in perfectly. But she is, by far, the largest woman on our crowded subway car. She is also wearing what may well be a man's oxford shirt and belted pants.

Kazumi says, "When I went to the U.S., women's clothes

were a revelation. It wasn't until I got to the U.S. that I realized how light female shoes are. Men's shoes are very heavy and that's all I could wear in Japan. In the U.S., I learned how light my step could be." I try to keep the expression out of my face, but it's all I could do not to grab Kazumi into a hug. I restrained myself, but barely. "I think I've always been a weird person in Japan," she says. "I have some difficulty in being adapted into Japanese society. Being in the U.S. means freedom to me."

The more I talk to Kazumi, the more I understand her passion for black women's literature and gospel. Gospel, and the literature that grows out that vernacular, is about putting together what's been broken by forces outside of your control. Certainly, it's a type of soul-crushing experience for a little Japanese girl, to be forced to go to school in boys' clothing and shoes. For days after our conversation, I will picture a scene she never described; I see Kazumi walking, almost skipping, across New York's Fifth Avenue, wearing women's shoes for the very first time.

Though many women find the return home quite difficult, the culture is awakening to the value of the experience outside Japan that they are bringing back. The remarkable success of one woman I interviewed speaks to how receptive the Japanese are becoming to experience from abroad. Catherine is the host of "Better English with Catherine," a radio show that appears four times a day, Monday through Friday, on Tokyo's most popular radio station, InterFM. She goes by her first name only, because her Western first name sets her apart. She also explains that her last name, "Kobayashi," is the Japanese equivalent of "Smith"—too common to stand out. The author of a bestselling book, Catherine has hundreds of thousands of listeners in Tokyo. More than 50,000 Tokyoites download her podcasts daily.

Sitting in the popular L'Atelier de Joël Robuchon restaurant, Tokyo's beautiful people line the long sushi-bar-like counter that snakes throughout the restaurant. Dressed in a pink V-neck sweater and gold raindrop earrings, thirty-year-old Catherine fits in perfectly. At least visually. "I'm like a banana," Catherine says to me, with no prompting on the subject at all, "I look like everybody else here, but inside I'm very Canadian."

She grew up in Vancouver, the oldest child in a family of four. Her mother she tells me was *kyoiku* Mama, the education-minded mother. "She was always very strict with me," Catherine remembers. Far away from home, her mother who had immigrated to Canada, tried to raise her first child as if they had never left Japan. "When I was just a baby, she tried so hard to instill Japanese in me," Catherine remembers. "She pounded the kanji characters into me from birth." As a kid, she couldn't stand it. She never understood why her family was different. Like the typical Japanese parents, her parents did not show their emotions and were never physically affectionate. "I would see my friends being kissed by their fathers or hugged by their mothers and wondered what was wrong," she says. "My Mom put sushi in my lunchbox when all I wanted was an apple and a peanut butter sandwich." Her childhood was a series of tug-of-wars between her and her mother, who remained so steadfastly Japanese. "It wasn't until I was an adult," Catherine says, "that I could see she put a lot of love into everything she did."

The older she got, the more Catherine realized how being Japanese might limit her opportunities in Canada. "When I was a kid, I never really saw any Asians on television," she says. "Even on the local news, I never saw more than one. My dream, when I was a teenager, was to be an anchor on CNN

Asia. Even then, I thought I had to be realistic; and realistically, there was more opportunity for me in Asia."

After graduating from university in Vancouver, she was hired by NHK, Japan's public broadcasting network. For her parents, especially her *kyoiku* Mama, this was the kind of success they could understand.

When Catherine decided to move to Japan, her father told her never to try to pass for a local. "One thing my father told me many times before I came here was that I had to explain that I was born and raised in Canada, I'm *nissei Nikkei*, second generation Japanese," she says. "He said, 'Make sure you mention it right off the bat.'" At first, Catherine didn't get it. Now, she says: "He knew what would be expected of me in this world. If I say I'm Japanese and I give them my Japanese name, they wouldn't understand why I make so many mistakes with the language and the culture. Better to let them know beforehand, so they make allowances."

Her husband, who was raised in Hawaii by Japanese parents, shared a similar experience. "We were raised in the same way," Catherine says. "Our parents endured hard times, raising their kids in a foreign environment. Then we moved to Japan as adults and are trying to make a life here, where our parents left off."

As soon as she moved to Japan, Catherine began to attend Japanese school. Five years later, she still attends classes four times a week. She is fluent in Japanese, but in Japan where standards are so exacting, fluency is just a place to begin, not a place to end. "I'll probably always have to attend Japanese school as long as I live in Japan," Catherine says. "No matter how fluent I become, they're always going to be able to tell. I'm always going to have that little bit of an accent."

At the same time, she uses her accent, her foreignness, as a selling point. On her show, "Better English with Catherine," she teaches English expressions most Japanese wouldn't learn in school, phrases like "He's such a Mama's boy" and "Put your cell phone on vibe." Her show is broadcast during the morning rush hour, the evening rush hour, at lunchtime, and in the late afternoon. It's no wonder that it's so popular, in a country that can feel so isolated, where unworldly salarymen are left at the airport in the throes of a Narita divorce, Catherine brings the outside world to you. And because she is Japanese, you never have to worry about losing face. She's *nissei Nikkei,* but she's one of your own. "I'm a native speaker who blends in with everyone else. I need to think of everything that's different about me in a positive way. If I think of it is as a negative, then I would've never made it here in Japan."

Another banana who has adjusted to life in Japan quite well is Junko Watanabe. She was born in Tokyo, but grew up in the U.S., Switzerland, and the Phillipines. She's the director of the international program and membership at the Hara Contemporary Museum of Art. When I meet her she is dressed in a green mock turtleneck sweater, a long floral patterned skirt, and a truly fabulous pair of boots. Her life, as she describes it, is as glamorous as you imagine a post at a hip, young museum to be.

When I ask her to describe a typical day, she laughs, and then lets loose the following torrent: "Come in at 9:30 A.M. sharp, check all your e-mails, wait for responses for people you had been corresponding with the previous day—including international artists, studio people, museum people. Gallery people. Or embassy people in Tokyo, for example. During the day, many afternoons we have visitors—the museum opens at eleven. We might have guests visiting the museum for the first time or coming back to see a new show, so we might show them around—we, meaning myself and my colleague Vicki Naka-mura. The two of us are responsible for all the international communications. Then we have more people coming, we show them around, and then the day is over, so we come back to the office and send out some e-mails, chat, snack, and write some more. In the evening, we may go to the opening of an exhibition or to a reception hosted by some embassy people or a gallery for example. Other times we go to dinners that are related to the exhibitions that are here." Her downtime, when she has it, is also spent on cultural pursuits. She says, "I'm a Korean freak. I like going to Korea. I love Korean food. I go there every two months."

Ten years ago, Junko was doing an internship at the Museum of Fine Arts in Boston. She had just completed a degree program at Sotheby's in London, where her interest had always been classical Japanese art and antiquities. "During my course at Sotheby's, I met one of the curators at the MFA and she told me about an internship program where I could help catalogue," she says. "I thought it would be a very interesting way to come in touch with the actual work." She stayed in Boston for a few months, but eventually had to come back to Tokyo and find a job. "I started calling people up and saying, 'I'm back, is there anything?'" she remembers. "One of the first people I called was a lady I went to school with at Sotheby's. She had completed her course before me and she was back in Tokyo. She was working here. I had visited this museum once and I thought, 'It's nothing grand, but very homey and very friendly.' My friend said, 'Oh, do you want to come and interview with our boss?' and I said 'Hell no. I'm not qualified for this and contemporary art is not what I'm studying.' She told me to come and meet him anyway."

Junko came in for a meeting with the Hara's director, Toshio Hara. He founded the museum twenty-five years ago in a building that had belonged to his grandfather. It had always been used as a grand private residence. Toshio turned it into a museum. "He is a very unique man," Junko says. "I remember it so well. I thought, 'My gosh, what a gentleman.' He was just so easy to talk to and so open." Her comments stand out to me because she's the only woman I've interviewed who referred to a Japanese man as a gentleman. It's a big compliment.

Junko thanked him for the meeting, but explained again that her interest and expertise was in older Japanese art. Toshio told her, "Look, contemporary art is something that is happening every day. The artists are living at the same time we are, so we are learning as they create. Contemporary art is not something that you should have studied somewhere else. If you are interested in working with these artists, why don't you join us?" Junko was swayed. "I thought, 'Wow, that's interesting,'" she says. "Having studied antiques and older things, I'd come from an entirely different system. Most of the artworks already have the values set on them so it's very different. So I said, fine, I'll give it a try. That was ten years ago. And it was one of the best decisions I ever made in my life. I'm still very happy with where I am and what I do."

For Junko, returning to Japan proved to be a rather seamless transition. "I left when I was twelve and I returned when I was eighteen," she says. "Maybe it's my personality. Maybe it's the fact that in my house, my parents would always speak Japanese and they were constantly reminding us of the culture we come from; nothing was really alien to me when I came back. It was almost as if I knew it all and then I came back to it."

Yet Junko has had her own banana-like experience. As a woman who spent her formative years abroad, she is well aware that she grew up with a freedom that her peers simply didn't have. "Many of the women who grew up in Japan that I speak with or have become friends with say they envy me for what I have," Junko says. "The fact that I was away and I had all these great times in America in high school. I had *so* much fun. They think it was fantastic I was able to receive this."

Japanese men, however, have a different reaction. "Some men would look at me and they would feel intimidated," Junko says. "A few times, they would actually say it openly, 'Well, you scare me.' And I don't think, as a Japanese person, I'm outstandingly outspoken. Especially when I'm talking in Japanese, I make a point of making myself low-key. Yet these men—and I think it's also that I'm tall—say that I intimidate them. The first time I heard it, I was a bit hurt. But then you reach the point when you say, 'That's too bad for you.'"

Like Kazumi Hasegewa pointed out, Junko says that returning to Japan means being prepared to obey the rules. "The role that a young woman should play in this country is very different from that in America," she says. I was surprised to hear her say that when she speaks Japanese, she makes it a point to be low-key, for example. But one of the reasons that she's been able to make a life in Japan is that Junko knows how to play by the rules—and not take them personally. She has two sisters; the youngest is married to an American and lives in New York. "I think for her, she's more comfortable living in America," she says. "For me, either way is fine. I'm just what I am and I will make the best out of what I have. I think in my sister's case, that's not good enough."

Although she has her own career, is single at forty, and has studied and worked abroad, Junko is the product of her upbringing. Unlike Catherine, who felt trapped by her mother's Japanese-ness, for Junko, her mother's training laid the foundation for a harmonious reentry into Japanese society. "My mother's a very traditional Japanese woman and she grew up in a very traditional Japanese family," Junko says. "She made a very strong point of these things. It was her way of making sure that we didn't get lost when we came back."

This meant that when Junko was growing up, you ate Sunday dinner at home and you spent New Year's with your family—no matter how many fabulous invitations Junko and her sisters received. Her mother emphasized the art of conversation and the proper way to address people. "She made sure we knew the proper Japanese way to say something and how to pay respect to the elderly, you know, those kinds of things," Junko says. "She made sure that we spoke Japanese with her. That, in and of itself, I think was a huge thing."

Junko's mother passed away a year ago. But her lessons are still with her. Even though she knows she is a modern career woman, part of a new wave in Japan, old habits are hard to break. "The way I interact with my boss may be one example," she says. "Our director is a very atypical Japanese man who encourages us to be honest with him. He is open to debates and criticism and I appreciate this a lot, but from time to time my Japanese upbringing hinders me from speaking up to him. A part of me always believes that I should not speak back to an older person . . . This is not very easy, particularly in a work environment."

When I ask about Junko's personal life, she says: "No marriage, no children, no boyfriend. I'm interested in this one particular guy, but we'll see what happens. I've always had the attitude of 'Well, if somebody comes along . . .' It's not so much the marriage that I want, but you do want somebody with you, somebody to grow old with. I'm not looking, but then again, it was in this museum that I met this man that I'm currently interested in, so you never know what your job can bring you!"

Although she gets job offers to join museums all around the world, Junko says she has no plans to leave Japan. She is pleased with how things are changing, and she is aware that women like her, who've had the experience of living abroad, are moving the society forward. "Technically I am a banana," Junko says. "Half of my life was spent in the Western environment and along the way I must have accumulated habits and developed a value system that may appear unique or foreign to most Japanese. The idea of a banana, however, seems a bit outdated now, as the younger generation in Japan seems so much more exposed to the rest of the world through different media. Consequently many of them—even without realizing it—became bananas, or whatever term applies to those who are cosmopolitan." Ever the museum person, Junko says there must be a more visually accurate term for the kind of culture mixing that the term 'banana' is meant to describe. She smiles broadly, then says: "'Marbles' perhaps?"

Still, Junko has pressures on her that I find it hard to imagine. She is the oldest of three daughters. Her parents were afraid that this particular tribe of Watanabe, their family name, will die out unless measures are taken. "If I wanted to continue the Watanabe line, I would ideally find a man who would agree to marry into my family and take on the Watanabe name. The other sisters are already married so this would be my thing to do, the gift I would give my family. Unfortunately, I'm not particularly interested in it. For me, it's not very important whether I continue the name or not. I think it's more about the spirit."

Although she is particularly well assimilated into Japanese culture for a banana, Junko tells me she has dated only one Japanese man in her life, the rest were non-Japanese. "I think I'm more open to Japanese men than I was ten years ago," she says. "You know Japanese men are not very affectionate. Growing up with guys who would just hug you, and then you meet these guys who aren't as affectionate, I don't know what to do with them. But that's not my main reason for not dating Japanese guys. I think if I had met an interesting Japanese man, I would have been interested, but I just didn't. Now, however, I realize that there's so much more to a man than just what you see. Right now, I'm more interested in learning the inner workings of these men. Before, I always looked for somebody I could relate to, somebody I could kiss or hug or whatever. But those are very simple things. Now, it's the more mysterious elements of Japanese men that seem interesting to me." Junko may feel that she's ready to pursue a relationship with a Japanese man, but more and more Japanese women are disillusioned with the men at home, especially the women who have either lived abroad or traveled extensively and dated non-Japanese guys.

So the story goes something like this. A young woman meets a charming young man, through friends, in Tokyo. Courting leads to engagement and the engagement leads to a wedding, with all the bells and whistles, at Anniversaire, the glitzy department store in Ometesando. For their honeymoon, they decide to go to Hawaii. The first thing the man does when he checks into the hotel is call his mother. He wants to know what he should order from room service; it's his first trip abroad and he's a little overwhelmed by his options. Then he hangs up the phone and asks his bride to order the room service. She wonders, "Why can't you do it?" He lies back on the bed, "I'm very tired." But what he means is, "I'm self-conscious about my accent." She's not fluent in English either, but she's been to Italy on an art trip and to Hawaii with her sister. *"Gambate!"* she thinks. "You gotta go for it." She picks up the phone and orders the room service. For the next ten days, she finds that she's in charge of everything. Her new husband seemed like such an alpha male in Tokyo; he's a hotshot in sales, and the head of the division has singled him out personally. But abroad, he reveals himself to be both brash and incapable. It's up to her to plan their days, order the food, call for a taxi, sign them up for snorkeling. On the plane ride back, she barely speaks to him. When the plane touches down at Narita International Airport, she's already planning her escape. Once they clear customs, she tells him that she's leaving. She hops into a taxi and goes back to her parents. No papers have been served, but the groom knows it's over. He's standing in Japan's most famous airport and he's just another statistic, known across the country as *"Narita rikon"* or in English, "Narita divorce."

There were more than 16,000 cases of Narita divorce in 2003 and an additional 21,000 cases of divorce between couples who had been married for less than two years. These numbers may not seem especially high, but they represent a 300 percent increase from Japan's divorce rate in the 1970s.

Narita rikon is in part about the clash of experience—the cosmopolitan sophistication of young Japanese women who have the time and money to travel abroad, versus the parochialism of young salarymen who haven't seen much of the world outside their corporate offices and are whole-heartedly committed to not losing face. Travel agencies have even begun advertising male-oriented trips to help young Japanese men get up to speed before their honeymoon. One company called Keio advertised a series of tours to Hawaii, a popular honeymoon destination for Japanese couples. The tour cost $690 for the land portion, for which experienced travelers would guide young men to typical honeymoon destinations on the island including beaches and shopping centers. "The problems are not due to a lack of character among the bridegrooms, but simply a lack of experience," says a representative from the travel company. "We think one of these trips can help solve the problem."

I got some insight into the clash of culture between the more cosmopolitan young women and their salarymen peers when I got together with Erina Noda and a group of her friends. Erina spent a year of high school in Chicago and two years in Maine. Her English is very good, although the more animated she gets, the more words evade her. When she says something in Japanese that I don't understand, she writes it down. I'm glad to be able to talk to her without the filter of a translator. I also understand what she means when she says she's not a "typical" Japanese girl. For one, although she's in her late twenties, her parents aren't pressuring her or her sister to get married. She also introduces her boyfriends to her family. She says it's "unheard of" for a woman in her twenties to tell the family that she is dating. As most girls live at home, paying no rent and doing no housework, they also try to keep up a façade of being "good girls." That means no dating.

But Erina also doesn't live with her parents. She rents an apartment and, along with her sister, often throws dinner parties. It's very "un-Japanese" to entertain in your home, but Erina likes it. She throws "pasta parties" and invites ten to twelve friends over to her house. I ask her whether it's uncommon to invite people over to your house because the homes are so small in Japan. She pauses, and gives me a look that I'm not sure how to read. "They don't want to show their private stuff," she says. "You have to have an open heart to invite people into your home. I think for the Japanese, it's hard to have an open heart when you are so private."

Erina also goes to the gym, although most of her Japanese friends don't. This interests me because I've just recently seen my first Japanese diet commercial. I was standing in a subway car, watching the TV monitors over the door display a number of young women in bathing suits, holding flowers and bawling their eyes out. I assumed that it was a beauty pageant of some sorts. Then I saw that they were beginning to show "before" and "after" photos of the crying women. The women's testimonials were intercut with pictures of a meal replacement shake. The commercials now seem to be everywhere, but it takes a good deal of effort to find a gym.

Erina is the very antithesis to the type of Japanese twenty-something portrayed on magazines and TV. She's twenty-seven, has her own cosmetics company, and sells her products on a QVC-type show. At first Erina went on the program to hawk her creams and lotions, but the feedback was that she looked too young. Now she hires an actress to do it. I'm impressed.

Erina tells me that she tried Japanese corporate life. She used to work at Pioneer, the electronics giant. When she worked there she says she had no life. "I had to be at the company until twelve o'clock at night. It's a common thing. I got really sick because of all the hard work and the stress. That's why I decided to quit and start my own business."

She is stylish, but not shop-happy. She says, "I don't go shopping with my friends. I usually go by myself or with my sister. I'm a quick shopper so it's in and out." She's not enamored of her cell phone either. Hers is a classic Japanese phone, capable of games, e-mail, picture-taking, and Internet access. It's not uncommon to see whole subway cars full of people deeply involved with their phones. "I have it, but I don't like it," says Erina. And while I will eventually come to spend a good deal of time with Erina, I will never, ever hear her refer to anything or anyone as *kawaii*. She's also frank. There's no question that's too personal; I don't get the sense that I put her off or that there's a wall between us. I'm excited to meet her friends.

We meet up for drinks in the restaurant of my Shinagawa apartment building. During the day, the dining area is staid and quiet. At night, there's a DJ, spinning house tunes. The DJ is a slim woman in an Adidas jacket, brightly colored T-shirt, and jeans. She looks cool. I can't help but think that this couldn't be a better setting to talk about the changing roles of women in Japan. Erina has brought along her friends Ritsuka, Mako, and Kaori. I hit it off with Ritsuka and Kaori right away, but Mako is a little more reserved. When I ask them what kind of qualities they like in a guy, Ritsuka asks: "For a boyfriend or a husband?" I'm surprised, "Aren't they the same thing?" Everyone looks at me as if I just fell of the turnip truck. Right now, because of a popular Korean soap opera called *Winter Sonata,* its star, Bae Yong-jun (or Yon-Sama, to his fans), and other Korean guys are considered hot. Yon-Sama was swamped, Beatle-mania style, during a recent trip to Tokyo. In the same way Terry McMillan's novel *How Stella Got Her Groove Back* led to a spike in American women looking for love in Jamaica, *Winter Sonata* has launched a series of pilgrimages by Japanese women to visit the destinations featured in the show.

One newspaper report told of four wealthy women, wives of the chairman, president, and major shareholders of a real estate company, who chartered an eight-passenger Learjet to take them from Tokyo to Inchon International Airport in Korea. The women, all major Yon-Sama fans, all victims of "yon-fluenza," checked into luxury suites then spent the next day being chauffeured around Seoul visiting sites from the film, including notably the site where Yon-Sama first kisses his co-star, Choi Ji-woo.

When I ask the women at my table why Korean guys are so desirable, everyone tells me that they are strong and passionate. Japanese men? Too reserved. Kaori, who dates only foreigners, says: "American guys, they date by words: 'I love you,' and stuff like that. But Japanese men never do that. My friends and I talk about this all the time. In Japanese, there's a term that means mutual understanding. If you are involved with a Japanese man, then you have a mutual understanding and he never has to say the words."

The extent to which Japanese men exert their power and dominance over women can be hard to detect beyond the shiny façade of honor and respect that the country presents, both to its citizens and to the world. Tokyo is famously one of the safest cities in the world. I am shocked, again and again, to sit in the back of a taxi late at night and see a well-dressed woman walking alone down a dark alley. The streets are still very safe, but it has recently been reported that the rape figures might be deceptively low since date rapes are considered "sex" and women still bear the burden of shame and guilt for forced sexual encounters with people they know. As recent as the 1980s, a Diet member was quoted as saying, "In Japan, the men cannot rape the women because they do not have the energy."

The largely male majority government has no compunction about shrugging off such complaints. In response to a recent government draft report on gender equality, a popular Tokyo assemblyman, Minoru Nakamura, had this to say: "Pitiable women who direct their dissatisfaction at being ignored by men toward society . . . are truly laughable. It's also strange how these women, compared with their peers, are uglier."

Although there is a long tradition of loyalty and honor in Japan, chivalry as we know it in the West, is also not part of the culture. Japanese men don't hold doors or offer a woman a seat on the subway or pull out her chair at a table. It's not that they wouldn't do these things, it's just that it's never been a tradition. The tradition is—as Tiger Tanaka so gamely explained it to James Bond in *You Only Live Twice*—that the woman serves the man. Junko Sakamoto is a twenty-nine-year-old magazine advertising executive. She's lived abroad in both New York and Seattle, but says proudly, "No matter where I go, Japan is the best." But living back home in Japan reminds her how out of synch she is with the traditional values many of her male counterparts still espouse. Junko informs me that socially, whether or not to pour sake for a man, is as big a question. Although Junko lives in Shimokitazawa, a hip, cool area of Tokyo, she often goes home to Hiroshima. And when she goes home, she says, "Men never pour sake for me, and they look at me strange if I don't pour sake for them. My friend actually says something about it to me. I feel like I work, I work on the same level as men. I'm not any less hard working. Why should I be the only one to pour? Personally, it makes me feel like an object. That's the part of me that doesn't feel connected to Japan."

Erina and her friends have many complaints about Japanese men. Kaori says, "They only want a woman they can dominate; that is why they are obsessed with schoolgirls." Ritsuka tells us a story of another girlfriend whose boyfriend began to cry on the phone. Everyone squeals in disgust. No one wants a man who cries. I tell them I'm confused. You don't want a man who is overbearing, but you don't want a man who cries. They say, yes, both things are true. "Today's young woman is not satisfied with Japanese men," says sociologist Mami Iwakima. "They know something is missing, right from the very start. If you're satisfied being of a certain status, marrying into a good family, and that's all you're seeking, that's possible. But a lot of young women want more. If you're aspiring for communication and emotion, you can't get that from Japanese men, even in this day and age."

Erina's friend, Kaori, is similarly disenchanted with the notion of marriage. She grew up in Buenos Aires, Argentina.

I will eventually meet whole groups of Japanese who grew up in Latin America, whose families traveled there after the devastation of World War II. I learn that Sao Paolo, Brazil, has the biggest population of Japanese immigrants living outside of Japan. For me, Kaori's Argentinian heritage has another plus: when we cannot communicate in Japanese, we switch to Spanish. And Ritsuka is studying Spanish, so sometimes when my Japanese fails, I can ask her questions in that language as well.

Kaori attended an American high school in Buenos Aires, and then spent three years at the University of La Verne in southern California. Her brother had already been sent to Japan. Since he was a man with a future in the Japanese corporate culture, his parents had enrolled him in a Japanese university so he could have a Japanese education. Kaori, as a young woman, had been allowed to make her own choices— to a certain point. "My parents were in Argentina, my brother was in Japan," Kaori says. "And suddenly my father called and said, 'Please quit the college because you're a woman and you are supposed to get married; go back to your country.'" Her country being Japan, a place she had not lived in since she was a little girl.

It was at this moment when her life began to resemble those *Choose Your Own Adventure* books that we read when we were children. Kaori had a choice to: A) stand up to her parents, stay in the United States, and manage without her parents' financial support or B) trust that her parents knew best when they said she belonged in Japan. It's the kind of story you hear again and again if you spend any amount of time in Japan. We are all changed by our circumstances, our exposure, our efforts to make a different life for ourselves. But for Japanese women, and in particular those who have lived abroad, there is a very narrow window where they can come back home and once again become Japanese. If they miss that opening they remain forever an outsider in their own culture. For Kaori, fourteen years in Buenos Aires and three years in the U.S. slammed that window shut.

Still, she kept trying to find a way to fulfill both her parents' dreams and her own. "I grew up abroad and I have these ideas, but my parents kind of forced me and I had to go home." Home, for the first time since she was a toddler, was Japan. She went to Kyoto and worked in a hotel for five years, saving money to continue her education. By the time she got her bachelor's degree she was thirty—staler than a Christmas cake girl and too old for most starting positions as an office lady. This is something else I soon learn. When you are interviewed to be an office lady in a Japanese company, there is often an explicit understanding that you are also being hired as part of an eligible dating pool for the young salarymen in the company. At thirty, Kaori had a hard time finding a job because she was already being typecast as an inappropriate wife for rising young executives. It didn't help that she told her would-be employers that she hoped to complete a master's degree. "All the Japanese guys were saying to me, 'How many years are you going to study? How long are you going to master's school? You're not going to be an easy person to get married.'"

She completed her master's at Temple University in Japan and she hoped to get a job teaching English. This created other problems. Teaching English is one of the few consistent jobs that a foreigner can get in Japan. It doesn't matter so much what your credentials are: Japanese students want to learn the language from a native speaker. No one wants to learn English from another Japanese, not even a Japanese person who grew up abroad. "I am not a native speaker," Kaori says. "I don't look like a foreigner so I cannot get a job."

Kaori now works as a part-time accountant. She hates that as a grown woman in her late thirties, she can be classified as a parasite single. "It makes me feel silly," she says. It also doesn't tell the full scope of her story—how hard she has tried to both fit into the mold and to break it. Her brother, also raised in Argentina, has had a much easier time of it. He has a big job at a Japanese company. Recently married, he had no problem dating in Japan. Kaori, on the other hand, dates only American men. She qualifies this by saying that American men are the ones most interested in her, "I haven't had a Japanese boyfriend since I came back here." She has been back in Japan for more than a dozen years. At the same time, American men come with their own perils. She frequents clubs that cater to American servicemen, but the very nature of dating men in the military means that her relationships are built on transience. Moreover, she looks down on Japanese women who sleep with foreigners so casually; they set up expectations that are hard to avoid. Furthermore, she says, it's no good to sleep with an American man who has had sex with too many Asian girls. He starts to have sex "like a Japanese." When I ask her what this means, "to have sex like a Japanese," she says simply, "no good."

I think of my Japanese guy friends: the boys I met on my first trip and who I've stayed in touch with to this day: Haruki, Jun, Kazu. Then I look around at the group of Erina's friends who have gathered to talk to me: Kaori, Ritsuka, Mako. We have come to talk about how women's roles are changing, but inevitably we come back, again and again, to what is wrong with Japanese men. They are too bossy. They are too soft. They are not expressive enough. They aren't good lovers. They need to make a lot of money. If your husband works long hours it's okay to take a lover. I am speaking in generalities, but these women speak in generalities, too. I know that Japanese men enjoy a great deal of privilege. But I can't help but feeling just a little bit bad for them. This is a tough crowd.

The more I probed into the question of relationships between men and women in Japan today, the more stories of dissatisfaction and disconnect I heard. The fact is that the more a Japanese woman has seen of the world outside her traditional island country, the more likely she is to be unhappy with traditional Japanese men. But as I was to find out, the tensions in dating life and marriage are not only a function of the women's new cosmopolitanism.

5

LOVE, JAPANESE STYLE

In a 1993 report on Japanese single women, the Hakuhodo Institute of Life and Living wrote, "A Japanese single woman has more of everything today than at anytime in the history of Japan. She has received her education. She has greater opportunities to work. She earns a higher income. She can choose from an overwhelming selection of goods and services. She has traveled or lived in more countries of the world. She has greater flexibility in choosing a lifestyle and greater leeway in making up her mind. She even has more time to live, over eighty years in fact. And because she has more of everything, she has a hard time focusing on what she wants." Ten plus years later, these observations have never been more true.

In Japan, even this is more complicated than it seems. In 1955, 75 percent of all nuptials in Japan were arranged marriages. In 2005, less than 10 percent are. What young people who grew up in the seventies and early eighties saw was that their parents, who had been married through *omiai* or matchmaking, were economically satifisfied with their marriages, but not emotionally satisfied. It was around this time that the trend toward "love marriages" started to grow. The trouble is that so much freedom can be paralyzing. "The kids today have seen both cases, matchmaking and romantic matches," says Mami Iwakima, a sociologist who specializes in family issues. "They can't decide on their own which is better. They don't have a criterion for choosing a mate and they don't have any place to seek advice. The sad thing is that girls have high expectations to be married and the guys aren't living up to these expectations. They just can't. Young men in Japan today are suffering from low self-esteem. They don't have confidence and they can't make decisions."

On a deeper level than the question of the worldliness of Japanese men, *Narita rikon* is also about the fragile nature of "love marriages." This is one of the first generation of Japanese young people to not be subjected to the decisions of parents and matchmakers—for young women, especially, there's a real fear of making a terrible mistake. It's telling that the young women, and it is almost always the woman who initiates *Narita rikon,* gets in a taxi, bound for her parents' home. One begins to imagine that she is not so much leaving her husband as she is going back to Mommy and Daddy. The parents welcome the soon to be divorcées with open arms. In many cases, the young man and woman never bother to attend the court proceedings—the parents show up for them, letting the children continue to be just that, children. And for many parents, that's okay.

"My father says he would have no problem if I wanted to become a parasite single," a young woman at Sacred Heart University told me. Another friend described how she saw that women in her generation, women in their forties and fifties, the "dedicated housewives" and "charismatic housewives" were overly attached to their daughters. "They treat their daughters like girlfriends," my friend says. "They do everything together, shopping, eating out, traveling abroad. The husband is at work all day and most of the night. If the daughter goes out and gets a job, or gets married, the mothers are lonely and isolated." Japanese men may have a reputation for being Mama's boys, but in the parasite singles and Narita divorce, we can see how young Japanese women are being lured to Mama's apron strings as well. "I personally feel that parents are spoiling them," says Yukiko Oka, a thirty-one-year-old mother of two. "Psychologically, they are so attached to them. They don't like for the kids to be independent because they feel so lonely. And of course, it's easy for the daughters. They don't have to worry about money or food."

For all the ways in which things are changing in Japan, young Japanese men and women still adhere to a certain traditionalism: they do not live together before marriage and out-of-wedlock birth is still unheard of. "Most young people in Japan live with their parents," says Junko Sakamoto, twenty-nine. "They just don't know how life is going to be like together until they travel together. Women expect guys to be tough. Japanese guys really know how to portray the tough-guy image when they are in Japan. He's got his big company background. But abroad, without his *meishi*—his business card—you see parts you never saw." Sociologist Mami Iwakima says, "The law is a very important factor. Most people in Japan want a legal marriage. Having a child out of wedlock is still not desired and out-of-wedlock pregnancies account for fewer than 1 percent of all births in Japan. Being legal deters young people from even living together before marriage, which means that they often jump into marriage without really knowing each other."

Ai Fukasawa, twenty-six, sees it this way: "In Japan, there has always been this tradition and culture of men being above women, being superior to women. They're trying to stop that;

the men are trying to change. The problem is they're just not changing as fast as we are."

For Japanese men, quitting isn't so easy. The sexism of Japanese companies is a double-edged sword: in its own way, it's very liberating for women my age. Salaryman is the term used to describe a Japanese businessman. There is no equivalent for women. The parallel term is "office lady," which means anything from receptionist to secretary to account executive. Inherent in the term "office lady" is a kind of expendability. Women are expected to leave a company like Pioneer, if not for marriage, then for the lack of opportunity. For men, it's quite different. Even after the burst of the Japanese economic bubble, the idea of lifetime employment still lingers. There is no such thing as head-hunting. You can't leave Honda for a bigger job at Toyota. If you leave Honda and go to Toyota, they will want to know what's wrong with you. "Why aren't you loyal to Honda?" If they even consider giving you a job at Toyota, you couldn't possibly start at the same level and salary you were at when you left Honda, you have to start the bottom, prove your worthiness and loyalty all over again. For most young men, stepping off the Japanese corporate ladder to do anything different—much less start a business—with the prospect of starting at the bottom again just isn't worth it.

Similarly, while both young Japanese men and women tend to live at home until marriage, the popular term "parasite single" tends to apply more to women than to men. Young men who live at home have more pressure to save money and to build toward the kind of independence that will allow them to marry. Young women, in contrast, are free to spend their disposable income as they please. If they agree to marry, then it is expected that the man will earn enough money to take care of them both. It's the kind of fact taken for truth that continues to surprise me. It's 2006. Japan is a country of the future.

How can it be that women expect men to take care of them? Then I stop to think about my own friends back at home; roughly half of my married girlfriends are stay-at-home Moms. No one ever talks about where the money comes from for them to make this life choice, and no one ever says that a man who hopes to marry needs to be able to provide. But just because my American friends don't say it, doesn't mean that there isn't some expectation that this will be true.

Miho Shimizu is thirty, single, and works for a film distribution company. She's not willfully abstaining from having children. She would actually be glad to do her part in raising the Japanese birth rate. She has every intention of getting married, having children—and keeping her career. "I think women are becoming a workforce for Japanese society so I think it's really good," she says. "Women get married later and they don't have many children so it's getting to be a really big problem for society. This society is now looking for a way to make women have children while they keep pursuing their careers. I think I will keep my career when I get married. If I have a child, I want to stay with the child for about a year or two, and after that I can go back to my career." She knows what she wants. She's just not sure how to put all the pieces of the puzzle together.

Miho knows she is lucky. The executives in her company are all men, but she sees a future in her career. "It used to be more male-dominated, but I think women are getting stronger and women's opinions are becoming more and more important," she says. "Like in Japan most of the people who go to the movies are women. So women's opinions are strong because audiences are mostly women."

She has a job that she loves, so she's not looking to marriage as a way out. "In my mother's generation they didn't have any choice," she says. "When they got married, they had to quit their job." Her father worked for an airline company and her mother is a housewife. She's not feeling the heat from her parents yet. "In Japan, these days, women get married at thirty or even forty whereas my mother's generation got married at twenty." At the same time, she knows they would be happier if she settled down. "My family is very shy," she explains. "We don't talk straight. So I think they are very worried because I am still single but they never tell me."

This is actually a very important statement. It's hard to say exactly when Japanese parents stopped meddling in the love lives of their children, but it's a fairly recent phenomenon. 1977 was the first year that "love" marriages outnumbered "arranged" marriages. Professor Marsha Krakower, my friend at Sacred Heart University, explains to me that for Miho's parents generation, the last twenty years have been completely destabilizing. Between the bubble burst of the economy and the techno boom, Japanese baby boomers lost all confidence that they knew best. They gave their children a great deal of freedom and their children, young men and women like Miho, aren't quite sure what to do with it. They know that not having an arranged marriage is a step forward, but they don't know how to arrange the marriages themselves.

A dating company called O-net has just commissioned and published a report on the phenomena, "The White Study on Marriage" (so called because it's a white-covered volume). The bottom line of the report being that both Japanese men and women actually want to get married and want to have babies, but they don't know how to close the deal. But close the deal they must, if they want to be fully accepted into Japanese society. As Ian Buruma writes in *Behind the Mask*, "Marriage is the passport to respectability in most parts of the world, but the pressure is particularly relentless in Japan. To be fully regarded as a woman one has to be a married mother—no matter whether the husband is dead or alive—for only then can one be called *ichininmae,* a favorite expression meaning both "adult" and "respectable." The popular media—newspapers, comics, films, magazines, television—help to drive this message home."

Miho has been dating her boyfriend for five years. She has nothing but nice things to say about him. "He's very generous," she says. Then with a laugh, she adds, "He's not very active and I'm not very active so we just like to stay at home and do nothing! It's very comfortable for me to be with him. I don't have to pretend I'm someone else."

She says that so often, in Japan especially, there's a pressure to put on makeup and nice clothes. She tells a story: "My friend's husband was very glad when she started working again after she gave birth to their daughter because when she was staying home with the baby, she didn't have to wear makeup and nice clothes so she was quite different from the person he knew when they got married. Now she wears makeup and perfume; she looks beautiful."

I tell her that I don't think the phenomenon of the schlubby stay-at-home Mom versus the glamorous career woman is unique to Japan. She agrees. "In a way men, all men, expect women to to look beautiful," she says. "Sometimes you don't want to wear makeup, you don't want to look sexy, you want to stay in your pajamas." She values her boyfriend because he doesn't make her feel like less than perfect when she doesn't get dressed up. She laughs, "I think he's already comfortable with me not wearing makeup."

Miho lives at home, so when she stays over at her boyfriend's apartment, she lies and says that she is staying with a girlfriend. Even at thirty, decorum must be maintained. When I ask what her family thinks of her boyfriend, she admits that they have never met him. In fact, they don't even know he exists—and she's been dating him for five years! She assures me this is common practice. "For Japan, it is. It depends on the family, but when you are just dating, I don't think your parents want you to introduce your boyfriend to the family. To introduce a boyfriend or girlfriend to your family is to say, 'We're ready to get married.' It's kind of like an official announcement."

Miho is, in fact, ready to get married. "I turned thirty last year and for Japanese women, I think thirty is a big turning point," she says. "I started to think about marriage so I started to talk to my boyfriend and he says he's not ready yet, so . . ." So Miho is part of a statistic to which she really doesn't want to belong. Her boyfriend has his own reasoning. He's thinking about changing jobs and doesn't feel financially ready to take care of a family. Miho fully expects to contribute to the household, but her boyfriend wants to be professionally settled before taking the step. "For my generation, a lot of men cannot earn enough money," she says. "It's really important for their wives to work and earn some money. Everything is getting expensive. Nowadays, for working women like me, it's easy to take care of myself. I can go abroad or I can buy nice clothes, but if it's only your husband earning money, you can't maintain that standard of living. I think that's why women want to continue to work—to earn money, but also to keep their standard of life."

Miho's not sure how long she's willing to wait for her boyfriend. "Five years is a long time," she says. "I was ready to get married when I turned thirty and I asked him. If he's not ready to get married in a year or so, I have to think about changing to another man. After thirty, you have to be with someone who is thinking about getting married."

I ask Miho where she sees herself in ten years. "I keep asking myself that question," she says. "Ten years ago, when I was twenty, it was easy for me to imagine where I would be when I was thirty. I was supposed to get married and have a child and keep working. Now it's so different from my imagination." So what does she see for herself at forty? She smiles. "At forty, I hope I'm married and have at least two children and a career." I'm struck by how many women find themselves in Miho's position of making a ten-year plan and not having it come out the way they imagined. We tend to see it as failure, but is it really? I wonder why we can't see holding onto the same dreams within a new and changed timetable for what it is—a benchmark of our own growing clarity, maturity, and experience.

Whenever I mention the term "Christmas cake girls" to the young Japanese women I meet, they laugh. It's like calling someone a "spinster" or an "old maid"—the insult is of a pure sticks and stones variety: you can throw those words around, but they no longer hurt. There's a new phrase being tossed around—one with a whole lot more sting than stale Christmas cake. In 2004, Junko Sakai, a thirty-eight-year-old novelist published a book called *Howl of the Losing Dogs*. The book, which was actually a funny novel along the lines of *Bridget Jones's Diary,* described childless, unmarried women over thirty as "losing dogs." The book became an instant bestseller, with over 300,000 copies in print. But like *Bridget Jones,* the amount of copies sold hardly spoke to the influence on popular culture. Everyone in Japan—man, woman, young, old—was talking about the "losing dogs" and was familiar with the term. All of a sudden, there was a new benchmark and a new phrase to describe—and terrify—single women. The benchmark for acceptable marriage age had risen from twenty-five to thirty. In 2000, 25 percent of all Japanese women between the ages of thirty and thirty-four were single. In 1990, that figure was 13 percent. In 1970, that figure was 7.2 percent. Marriage these days is simply not that appealing.

My friend, Erina, mentions an acquaintance. The woman is

thirty-five, married to a doctor she never sees. (An oft-quoted Japanese survey determined that the average Japanese father spent seventeen minutes a day with his child. Although I haven't found the corollary for husband/wife quality time, one can imagine that the commonness of twelve-hour workdays and two-hour daily commutes doesn't leave much time for wives either.) Erina's acquaintance, whom she had drinks with the night before, has three cell phone numbers: one for her husband, one for her boyfriend, and one for "dating." Erina says, "I look at her and I can't understand what marriage is."

Mina Takahashi of the Mori Art Museum says that in some ways it's easy to remain single in Japan. "Marriage is always a topic that's talked about," Mina says. "But I think it's funny because it is such a noncouple-oriented country. Husbands or wives or any significant other are not required to attend any work or formal events. Only in the "upper societies" does that happen. It is so normal for a group of women to be doing everything together. Of course, that happens elsewhere, all over the world, but I think the Japanese do it more often, socializing in bigger groups."

The catch-phrase that has unseated "stale Christmas cake" seems even more cutting to me. Women over thirty are now called, by women and men alike, *make inu* or "losing dogs." All of the women I interviewed assured me that it's entirely possible to go to a party, meet a man, and for him to ask, "Are you a losing dog?"—not meaning, as I would imagine, "I'm a jerk and I really, really want you to throw a drink in my face," but meaning, "Are you over thirty and single?" No one I interviewed seemed to find the phrase offensive, although more than one woman admitted that as her thirtieth birthday approached she was anxious to join "the winning team." I believe that women say they are not offended by being called a "losing dog" because they buy into what it means. In Japan, you accept the cultural terms you are handed. I'm a foreigner, which means I am a *gaijin*. It doesn't matter that I feel so at home in Japan, that I've spent so much time there. *Gaijin* means foreigner and even if I lived in Japan for fifty years, I'd still be a *gaijin*. Similarly, "losing dog" means an unmarried, childless woman over thirty. It is not about feeling, whether you're happy to be unmarried, whether you have a boyfriend or not, whether you're pretty, smart, ambitious, successful. No husband and no child equals "losing dog."

Some suggest that despite the moniker, the "losing dogs" are the future of Japan. They know how to make their own living. They're independent and are more confident, and optimistic, about achieving their dreams. Thirty-five-year-old screenwriter Haruko Nagatsu puts it this way, "You must know *make inu*, right? So the media listens to it and says single women who are on the career path and are not married like men are the *make inu*. But hey, I want to say that *make inu* is a good word. Why? Because now I can say I'm a loser; it's unique, you know. 'Hey, I'm a loser!' So what? I can focus on my career. I can see it in this way so *make inu* is a very good word. Because *kachaiino* is the opposite meaning of *make inu*, it means winner. But the winner, cannot be a winner, a *kachaiino*, all the time. Sometimes they fall. But the loser can be a winner. There's always that potential and potential is a beautiful thing."

In a 2005 cover story on this very topic—how women are changing in Japan but the society, and the men, are changing at a much slower pace—*Time Asia* tells the story of a woman named Hitomi Asano who used to own her own casting agency in Tokyo. At the age of thirty-five, she married a doctor and moved to Sendai, a rice-growing community in northern Japan. Asano has tried to throw herself into the kind of activities that middle-class housewives in rural communities do: singing in the choir, planting orchids, studying calligraphy. Still, she longs for something more. "In Tokyo, I had a passion. In Sendai, I don't," Asano told the reporter. "Sometimes when I'm at home alone, I put on my fancy clothes from Tokyo and just walk around pretending that I'm at work." Asano knows that she is, by society's measure, a *kachaiino*—a winner. But surely, she's not alone in the many ways her victory rings hollow.

Yasuko Nakamura, the president of Boom, Inc., is a single, childless woman. She is a so-called *make inu*. She finds the term laughable. "Life without a husband or children gives me breathing space and is easy to carry," she says. "I feel so much freedom living my own life unlike society's idea." It probably doesn't hurt that her work enables her to interact with thousands of Japanese teens every year, creating a kind of *Facts of Life* atmosphere where she gets to be the cool older sister. Yasuko has a boyfriend. "Actually, I have many guy friends and a boyfriend," she says, clarifying the matter. Her boyfriend often asks her why she won't marry him and her answer is always the same. "No, I'm satisfied now. If we get married, we will always be thinking about having children. I don't think I want to have children, but I like you." On this note, she laughs again—a strong, delighted laugh that sounds absolutely nothing like the howl of a losing dog.

In Japan, there isn't really a history or culture of single bars or personals. The Japanese version of Match.com exists, but many Japanese women are reluctant to pursue this line of dating: there are consistent rumors that women have been murdered by men they meet on these sites and, probably truer to the point, married men are known to advertise on these sites posing as single men. In other words, nice girls don't go online. "Japan doesn't have this cultural background for dating," says Mami Iwakima. "The family—parents, aunts, uncles—created the environment for people to get married." Without this environment, many young people can't seal the deal. There are many opportunities for *gokon* or get-togethers. A young person will call their friends and get together a group of men and women to gather at a bar and a restaurant. "But it just looks like they go out as a group, have fun, but it never materializes to a real relationship," says Mami Iwakima.

Part of it is that something as simple as flirting, the getting-to-know-you, getting-to-know-all-about-you element of conversation doesn't jibe well with a culture where people still use honorifics to address their parents and discretion is still considered the better part of valor. You don't just come out and say, "Hi my name is Kimie and I live in Saitama. I used to play flute, but I dropped it when I realized that I wasn't good enough to make it into the top musical school. So now I work at Toyota and in my free time I love to ski." It just isn't done. "Young people don't have the communication skills for the dating environment," says Mami Iwakima. "Communication skills aren't really taught or practiced in schools." Yet, it's something that young Japanese women crave. "I want to marry someone who is understanding and can talk, *really* talk," says screenwriter Haruko Nagatsu. In a recent *Financial Times* article, Naohiro Ogawa, a demographer and economist at Tokyo's Nihon University, summed up all the awkwardness, all the non-starter relationships by saying, "Dating is fairly new to the culture." The *FT* took it one step further, half-joking that it is entirely possible that "the Japanese race will be the first to die out because it is too shy to reproduce."

As much as I applaud the women that I've interviewed, and am sympathetic to their struggles, I can't help but shake the feeling that Japanese men, at least when it comes to dating, are getting the short end of the stick. I have Japanese guy friends. They are not the oafish salaryman caricatures that the Japanese women I know describe. When I get back home to the U.S., after a month-long research trip, I send an e-mail to both Erina's friend, Ritsuka, and to my friend, Kazu. The subject of the e-mail is: "How do you say blind date in Japanese?" Kazu writes back right away and says the word I am searching for is *"gokon."* Then he writes back to say that he was confused:

> "I misunderstood the meaning of 'blind date,' it's different a little from *'gokon.' Gokon* is the party . . . I can't imagine the Japanese version of blind date."

"Gokon" is a matchmaking party, where young Japanese men and women interact as a group, but even among groups of people who know one another, the men and women rarely break off into separate pairs. Going out alone, with someone you've never met, is unheard of. Over the course of the next several days, I manage to explain to Kazu and Ritsuka that I think they are both good-looking, charming, interesting people and that I think they should meet. It is hard to convey amusement by e-mail, but I think that's what I'm reading as both Kazu and Ritsuka continue to *cc* me as they talk back and forth, in a mixture of English and Japanese. Finally, they agree to meet up for dinner. Like any matchmaker, I am on pins and needles. This is made both better and worse by the fact that I am over five thousand miles away. My main concern is that in trying to sell them on the notion of the blind date, I have overhyped them to each other. "But Ritsuka *is* very pretty!" I tell myself as I walk to the pharmacy. "Kazu *is* very handsome," I tell myself as I unload groceries from my car.

My second concern is that they are going to think that I'm

a busybody racist. There's a great scene in the movie *Grand Canyon* when Alfre Woodard and Danny Glover realize that the reason they've been set up on a blind date is that they are the only black people Kevin Kline knows. What if Ritsuka and Kazu think I am setting them up because they are the only Japanese people I know? This is categorically untrue. But what if they think that?

The reason I set them up is because I think they will like each other. Kazu, whom I've known for five years now, continues to surprise me. If you had asked me when I first visited Japan which one of the boys I correspond with the most, my first answer would have been Jun: who is smart, funny, charismatic. My second answer would have been Haruki: energetic, earnest, thoughtful. Kazu was always kind of a mystery. He spoke the least English out of all of the boys and seemed to be the most reserved. While Jun has gone back to school and Haruki has traveled some, Kazu is the one who has been on a straight salaryman path since he graduated from university. Every time I see him, he seems less like a university student and more like an older established businessman. At the same time, it's Kazu who does the best job of keeping in touch. Every three months, if not more often, I get e-mails from him. His English is still halting, and we spend a lot of time talking about the weather (cherry blossom season, the first snow, the humidity of the city, the cool breeze in the countryside), but there is also something else there. He reveals, in just a line or two, funny thoughts about his coworkers, his family, his own health, my well-being. He advises me, with a kind of little-brother tenderness, to take care of myself.

After he met my husband Jason for the second time, I received an e-mail that says: "It was good to see Jason again. It is very good that you are married. Though Jason seems more tall and more wide than I remembered." Jason *had* gained a little weight and for a long time, we called him "tall and wide" in honor of Kazu's observation. Sometimes I wonder if it's because he leads the most typical salaryman life that Kazu makes such an effort to keep in touch with me. Am I a reminder that his world is bigger than the corporate giant that rules his days and most of his nights?

I thought that the thoughtful, slightly sardonic nature of our correspondence might make Kazu a good match with Ritsuka. Perhaps at her job, where she is a young, eligible "office lady," the salarymen there all seem like reserved, gauche slobs who only let their guard down when they've had too much to drink. After our initial meeting, Ritsuka and I kept up a lively correspondence, driven by our common interests in salsa music and an English language Japanese comic strip called "Charisma Man." I wanted Ritsuka to meet Kazu, in part because I thought they shared a desire for a broader-than-mainstream Japanese life.

About a week after their first date, I stopped receiving third-party messages and I assumed that perhaps Ritsuka and Kazu had decided to drop this whole blind date notion. Then I received two e-mails. Kazu wrote to say thank you for introducing him to Ritsuka. She was all that I promised and he'd had a very nice time and was hoping to take her out again. Ritsuka wrote to say that Kazu was indeed handsome and that she had enjoyed herself. Ritsuka also says that Kazu seemed a little distracted, that dinner had lasted only two hours; perhaps he did not like her as much as she liked him?

I couldn't believe it. I wrote Ritsuka back right away. She, more than me, should know how far out the suburbs of Tokyo can be. It took Kazu more than two hours to get back home by train. A two-hour dinner was plenty long, especially for a blind date. She wrote back to say yes, of course, she understood. They were talking about going to see a sumo wrestling match.

That was more than two months ago. And even though I am quite the nosy Parker, I am doing my best to stay out of it. Though I can't help but think it would really be nice if I could find a nice American guy for Kaori. The more time I spend in Japan, the more it seems that for a woman who doesn't fit the traditional mode, a foreign boyfriend is the way to go.

That's been the case for Yuki Yamamato, a young woman who has a great deal of the grace and poise the Japanese call *karisma*. The first thing she tells me is that her husband has a mustache. I am not sure why this is such a big deal. Then she asks me how many men in Japan I've seen with a mustache. I do a visual catalogue: tweezed eyebrows are now the craze among teenage boys; I've seen lots of that on the train in the past few weeks. Hair coloring remains universally popular—there are always lots of guys with orangey red hair. I've seen guys with long hair and whole tribes of young men who seem to have a *There's Something About Mary* relationship with their hair gel. But I can't think of the last time I have seen a Japanese man with a mustache.

Yuki is an only child who grew up in Kanagawa prefecture, in the southern portion of Japan. Four years ago, she was working at an import/export company. She wanted to travel to Israel, but worried about the precariousness of the situation there. Her company did some business with another company in Syria, so she decided to go there instead. She was a twenty-four-year-old Japanese woman, who didn't speak any Arabic, but she took off on her own. Her itinerary was to spend five days in Syria, two days in Jordan, and three days in Lebanon.

When she arrived in Syria, she was introduced to the man who would become her future husband, a Japanese man with a mustache (the mustache being not such an unusual accessory in Damascus). He was a friend of one of her coworkers who frequently did business in Syria. The first day they met, he insisted that she check out of her hotel and move in with his closest Syrian friends. "He advised me to do a homestay with an ordinary Syrian family. I was very safe and it was an adventure. Living with this family, I understood the system between men and women in Syria."

Yuki left Syria, continuing onto Lebanon and Jordan. When she returned to Tokyo, her friendship with her future husband blossomed into love. There were problems, though. Her husband is sixteen years older than her, only nine years younger than her mother. Her parents were not happy with her choice: this strange Japanese man who has a mustache and speaks Arabic and is almost as old as they are. Eventually they relented.

For Yuki, her one-year-old marriage is all that she never imagined marriage to a Japanese man to be: full of adventure, constant learning experiences, a set of rules that are distinctly her and her husband's own. She has come to love the Middle East, dreams about becoming fluent in Arabic as her husband is.

Yuki initially used the occasion of her wedding to quit a job she wasn't crazy about. Then she realized the toll that being at home was taking on her marriage. "We were often quarreling," she says. "For almost one year, I had nothing. I wasn't proud of myself as a woman." Now, Yuki is working at the FPC. Naturally, she is most passionate about her work with journalists from the Middle East. "Now, I can come home and talk to him about my work with the Arabic journalists and I tell him great stories," Yuki says. "He really enjoys that. We both do."

One of the things that was so refreshing about Yuki is that it was really, really nice to meet a Japanese woman who was happy to be in a relationship with a Japanese man. In many ways, the more time I spent in Japan, the more I felt that this book was very much a companion volume to my previous book, *Having It All? Black Women and Success.* As distant as they might seem, Japanese women are undergoing massive changes that are not dissimilar from the changes black women have recently experienced: more education, more opportunity, more confidence, more success. When I was writing *Having It All?* my biggest concern was the fear of bashing black men. I felt it when I interviewed black women and heard them describe black men in lacerating terms. I feared it when I was writing and it began to seem that my material could easily be interpreted as a negative sum game: black women are succeeding, hence black men are falling behind. Once I came to Japan, I was surprised to find myself in the same situation once again. Some of my interviews with Japanese women consisted of hour after hour of them talking about Japanese men in the most scurrilous terms. They said that Japanese men were animals, who had no manners and grunted through their meals. They said that Japanese men were cavemen who wanted a woman to prepare his meals, meet his sexual needs, and be absolutely silent while doing both. They said again and again that Japanese men were not good lovers. I listened to these insults, wondering why a woman would tell me this, except for the fact that it's safer to confide in a foreigner than to someone who is part of your society, a society so much built on rules and polite mores. I vowed to myself that I would try to keep the balance in this book, to not repeat slurs and insults. But the reporter in me needs to make it clear, as I did in my book about black women and success, that Japanese men and women are at an impasse. The falling birthrate and the delay in marriage has as much to do with Japanese women's flat-out frustration with traditional Japanese men as it does with their quests for independence.

* * *

That frustration is one of the factors leading so many young Japanese women to move abroad, and also to turn to foreign men for relationships. Although hers was not a Narita divorce, Kazuko Koizumi's first marriage to a Japanese man ended. They met at university and she got married when she was twenty-six. It's hard to say why the marriage ended. "Maybe I was young; maybe I was more selfish." What Kazuko did know was that it wasn't working. "For my mother's generation divorce was fatal, a kind of sin." Now, she says, "We can restart our life."

Restarting her life is exactly what Kazuko did. A manager at the FPC, she has been married to her husband, French foreign correspondent Joel Legendre, since 1998. She had been working for the Japanese embassy in London and they decided to marry there before Kazuko's assignment was finished. "Coincidentally, a classmate who I had known since I was in junior high school was also living in London and was engaged to an English man," Kazuko explains. "I asked her and her fiancé to be our witnesses."

The question of whether the new couple might move to France never came up. "Joel has been based in Tokyo since 1988; his field of expertise is Asia," Kazuko says. "It only makes sense that we live here." Still, living in Japan when you are married to a non-Japanese changes the landscape of a country that prides itself on its monolithic, conservative nature. "My whole world has expanded since I met Joel," Kazuko says. "He's from a totally different culture. I can enjoy that world through my relationship with him."

Kazuko grew up in Tokyo, near the famous Nihonbashi Bridge, "the starting point of the old road to Tokkaido." This is the fabled road, consisting of fifty-three stations, that samurai, farmers, and merchants took between Tokyo and Kyoto. Telling me that she grew up there is a way of signaling how deep her family's Tokyo roots are. Her parents are retired. They were third-generation tofu makers; her mother and grandmother worked in the family business. Kazuko always wanted to work. "When I was very little, three or four, I wanted to be a bus driver," she says. "Many girls wanted to be a bride. I didn't think that was a dream. It's not an occupation. I wanted to have a profession. I don't remember if I ever told anyone my dreams at the time."

In high school, she dreamed of becoming an Olympic athlete. She was good at sports—volleyball and swimming. Her father was a strong swimmer and often took her to the pool during the summer. He had dreamed of being a P.E. teacher. After World War II, Kazuko says, "He abandoned his dream and joined the family business."

For Kazuko, the dreaming never ended. At twelve, she wanted to be a television news anchor because, she says sheepishly, "I enjoyed reading from the textbook in front of the class." After that, she wanted to be a screenwriter and threw herself into writing dramas for the school theater. During junior high and high school, she attended Miwata, a girls' private school. The teachers were mostly women, mostly conservative. "I was kind of a radical student," Kazuko says. "But not delinquent. I studied and practiced sports and enjoyed being with my classmates."

At the age of sixteen, a group of girls in her school formed a rock-and-roll band. It was the 1970s and J-Rock and J-Pop (as the Japanese versions of this music is called) had not been created yet. Rock music was strictly a *gaijin* thing. Kazuko took up electric bass and started learning how to play along to Led Zeppelin and Aerosmith. "My mother came to see me performing at the school festival," Kazuko remembers, with a laugh. "We played wearing tank tops and short pants. The teachers were so angry at us. After the performance, the teachers came to scold us: 'You are outrageous! You are rude! Next time you have to wear the school uniform when you perform!'"

Although I have known Kazuko for years now and am well aware of how highly she is regarded by women in the foreign ministry, I never knew such intimate details about her life. I think she has been pushing the boundaries all along; a woman like her was bound to be a success—even in a country like Japan where being an independent woman can be a difficult thing. I think about what someone once told me about the difference between women in Japan and women in the U.S. This woman, who was Japanese, said: "In the U.S., it is easy to be exceptional and hard to be average. In Japan, it is easy to be average and hard to be exceptional." Of course, this is relative. But it is easy to forget how much class mobility we experience in the U.S., how much we reward and prize individuality. In the U.S., a small town boy from Arkansas can become president and his outspoken, upstart wife can weather scandal and tragedy to become a prominent senator. In Japan, at every level, from elementary school through university, in marriage and in the workplace, you are expected to tow the line, not make waves, to work tirelessly at school and for your company, but to never, ever be ambitious for yourself.

Kazuko began attending cram school from the age of twelve. There was cram school to pass the entrance exam to her prestigious middle school. Then there was cram school again to pass the entrance exams to university. She went after school, two hours a day, twice a week and all morning on Sundays. "On weekdays, after school, we studied drills and textbooks," she explained. "On Sundays, we just took exams." Much has been made about the rote learning system of Japanese schools, how the emphasis on exams makes it impossible to do any real learning. The pressure of school life is said to be responsible for the high teenage suicide rate, especially among boys. But Kazuko never saw it that way. "It was good," she says. "I didn't feel any pressure. Maybe it was just me, as an individual. But I was really good at school. It was a pleasure to study."

She was accepted at Meiji University, one of the country's top six schools. Kazuko has one sister, who is younger. As she tells her story, about the pleasure of attending girls' private school, the joy she took in the cram school, and her success at landing a spot in a prestigious university, I wonder how might Kazuko's life have been different if she had an older brother—or any brother at all. When the rule of thumb is *ichi hime, ni taro*—first a princess, then a prince—is it easier to shine when there are no princes stealing your spotlight? Is it possible that part of the frustration young women are experiencing in Narita divorce is the realization that their new husbands are not so very different than the coddled princes they grew up with at home?

Kazuko's sister is her polar opposite. "Takako," Kazuko says, whispering her name with a kind of reverence, "she's really different from me. She's more quiet. She was born with a slight handicap. Her right leg and arm are partly paralyzed. She's done so well. I'm so proud of her." Kazuko's parents now live in the western suburbs of Tokyo, nearly two hours by train outside of the city. Her sister lives there too, a dedicated housewife. She has two children, ages nine and three. What does her family make of her dashing French husband? Kazuko laughs. She is every bit the chic Tokyoite with her short haircut and her confident voice. Dressed in a black turtleneck, long black skirt, she wears an exquisite Chanel necklace with an Eiffel Tower charm around her neck. The necklace is a small but important symbol of the break she made from traditional Japanese culture when she married her husband. "These days, more Japanese women are married to international men," she says. "My parents' generation can accept this kind of change."

For Kazuko, there is no comparison. "Japanese men are not so well-educated to go out with as foreign men," she says, bluntly. "They are much more inward looking; the majority of them are still very conservative." It's not so much that chivalry is dead in Japan, but it's just that it hasn't been born yet. "Foreign men are much more gentle," Kazuko says. "They respect women. In the U.S. or Europe they say, 'Ladies first.' We don't know such a concept in Japan. When we are in an elevator and the door opens, it's always the men who come out first. It really means something."

She points to the women-only subway cars and how uncomfortable a woman can feel in her daily commute. "When we're in the subway, the young guys are reading manga comics. Sometimes they are very dirty," she says, bringing up a point many women have raised to me. "When an old lady comes into the subway, the men don't give her a seat. It's always a woman who will give up her seat."

At the same time, Kazuko has traveled enough to know that outside of her country, "most men have no idea what Japanese women are really like." She still remembers an experience in London when she met a colleague, a diplomat, for dinner. Kazuko and the woman were waiting for a cab after dinner and an Englishman nearly knocked them over to get into the cab. She also knows that when she is not seen as meek and inconsequential, she is being described as the oh-so-sexy geisha. "We're still seen as exotic," she says. "They can make a story in an easy way if they describe Japanese women as exotic figures."

She doesn't identify with the young girls who are strutting their stuff around Tokyo. "I was surprised when I came back from London to see young women expressing themselves more than before," she says. "But they look like prostitutes. They think they look sexy and charming, but they look vulgar."

Now that she's in her forties, Kazuko is finding it's hard to be a grown-up woman in Japan. "In Japanese culture, there's such an emphasis on things that look childish," she says, talking about the culture of *kawaii*. "But in the end it affects your attitude and behavior. The more childish you dress, the more selfish and childish you become."

Sometimes, she says, older Japanese men are offended that she married a foreigner. "They have this feeling," she says. "I'm with Joel. I chose a Frenchman. Why not a Japanese man?"

In the case of Narita divorce, travel shuts you down. You go on honeymoon with your typical Japanese husband, and the world is a closed-off place that he doesn't know and doesn't want to know. For a woman like Kazuko, marrying a foreigner means just the opposite. "When I married Joel, I wanted to appreciate the difference between me and him," she says. "That's not pain to me. I can really enjoy the differences and the surprises. For one, I got more involved with the French community in Tokyo. There are over 50,000 French people living in Japan. Joel knows many of the big guys, like the president of Chanel. Luckily, I get the chance to meet with them, and sometimes we get together for dinner. I've learned a lot from them."

Marriage to a French man has also taught Kazuko a kind of joie de vivre she never expected to find. "Joel knows how to enjoy life," she says. "In my parent's generation, life was just work. It was very difficult for them after the war."

As for her first husband, Kazuko still sees him. "We're good friends still," she says. "He's remarried. He has two kids." Sometimes, her husband Joel meets her ex for drinks. It's an unusually amiable situation, but indicative of the ways in which Japanese women are both anxious for change and foreign influences—in Kazuko's case, marrying a French man—but also unwilling to completely give up their ties to traditional culture and community—in Kazuko's case, her first husband.

* * *

The rise of working women in Japan, and their dissatisfaction with dating traditional Japanese men, has brought about an interesting phenomenon: the host club. Typically, a hostess club is where Japanese businessmen take clients and colleagues to unwind at the end of the evening. The hostesses, dressed in modern clothes but seeking to emulate a geisha's charm, flatter the men while getting them to buy expensive drinks. Sex is officially not on the menu, but unofficially, it often is. One of the oldest host clubs, called The English Club, is more than thirty years old. It used to be an anomaly, but now that women are making more money and enjoying more independence in society, there are more than one hundred host clubs in Tokyo willing to offer women the same services men have enjoyed. The surprising thing is that business is booming. Usagi Nakamura, forty-seven, made national news when she wrote her bestselling book, *The Host Club Guide*.

Dressed in a black turtleneck, black leather skirt, and black knee-high leather spiked-heel boots, Usagi smokes like a chimney and manages to look half her age. She says her history with the host clubs is quite long and can be divided into two stages: early stage and late stage. When she first started "host clubbing," she thought that they could be quite boring. Her image of a host club was that it was a place full of quite ugly older hosts and customers like Kazuko Hotoki. When I ask who this person is, Usagi says, "A famous Japanese celebrity. She is, anyway, rich."

Eventually though, the club owners became aware of the fact that they needed a different brand of hosts to appeal to Japan's *Sex and the City* crowd. That's when, according to Usagi, the fun started. "Many of the younger hosts are quite good looking," she says. "The customers started to be quite a bit younger. I began to think, 'They are not just rich people. They go there to have fun, just like me.'" Then Usagi did the one thing you're never supposed to do—she fell in love with her host and it cost her a fortune. A truly popular host can make $50,000 a month. With bottles of high-end champagne going for more than one thousand dollars a pop, it's easy for a giddy woman to spend $10,000 in a single night. Half of her bar tab goes to her host, so it's in his interest to keep her drinking— and paying. Most hosts will do anything: flirt, cajole, touch, and even promise sex, to keep a woman drinking. First timers are lured in with discount rates: $50 or $100 for the first visit. During this first time, all of the hosts will come over to visit the newcomer with the hopes of becoming her favorite.

While the majority of Japanese young men rely on the old tradition of *sogo rikai,* mutual understanding, hosts understand that today's Japanese woman wants to hear words of affection and love. She may have grown up with a salaryman father who was the strong, silent type, but she sees that her mother is ready to kick him out of the house and she's not interested in following in their romantic footsteps. While *The Financial Times* might be right that Japan may be the only culture to watch its birthrate plummet because it was "too shy to reproduce," the hosts are ready and willing to step into the gap, whispering sweet nothings at the cost of thousands of yen a pour.

For Usagi, the liberation of being able to visit a host club, flirt shamelessly, and maybe even do more, came with a very steep price tag. She says she spent twenty million yen (roughly $180,000) in a two-year period at a single club. "Like I said, I was in love," she says. "I needed to make more money to go back to the host club." Hence the idea of writing *The Host Club Guide.* She quickly used up her advance to continue wooing her favorite hosts. She just couldn't stop going back. Along the way, you hear more sinister stories: girls who become so deeply in debt to a host club that they are forced into prostitution to pay it all off, which is a little like selling drugs to make money to buy drugs. It's not the way to get free. There are a couple of nasty terms for getting a good-girl office lady to turn tricks: one is called "growing a baby" because you are slowly leading a "baby" into the sex industry. Another term is "letting the woman drown slowly in the bathtub" so called because while the woman thinks she is having a nice, relaxing bath, she is really drowning.

"I got in so much in trouble," Usagi remembers. "As a professional writer, I wanted to have some sort of tangible thing to explain why I went as far as I did, why I became so crazy about going there." So she wrote her second book about host clubs. Her first book had focused on how host clubs helped abate loneliness, while her second book showed how falling in love with a host could cause you so much pain. Usagi says she herself knows many women who work for what she calls "risky businesses" because of their association with host clubs. "They are not necessarily prostitutes," she says. "But they work for some bar or a place where men can go and drink and if they are lucky, they can *buy* their women—that kind of place. Anyway, this is called risky business, so the women who work in risky business make kind of a lot of money, so they keep going to the host club and spending the money that they just made."

Usagi describes her typical reader as someone like her, women who are looking for something to fill the great big hole they feel inside. "There are certain women who have the shopping syndrome—shopaholics. They just go to the mall and they buy anything they want; they don't care about the costs," she says. "I used to be like that too. The main readers of my books have the same kind of tendency to be addicted to something. This can be shopping, host clubs, or stuff like that. Sometimes they are wrist-cutters or women with eating disorders."

Whatever you may think about the host club phenomenon, one thing is for sure: There's a double standard about women who go out for sexual/romantic entertainment and men who do the same thing. Women who go to a host club and spend a lot of money are just stupid. Everybody knows that the hosts are nice to the women because it's their job. "At the same time, for the men who go to hostess clubs—where employees always make sure to sit down next to them and serve them alcohol—society shows some kind of understanding for them," says Usagi. "Why? Because they are men and they work quite hard so they need some place to be relaxed."

As much as we want to talk about equality, when it comes to the experience of hosts versus hostesses, different sets of rules apply. When men visit a hostess club, the understanding is that he's not going to get laid. A hostess who gives into the pressure to have sex knows she has lost a customer. Once she's had sex with a client, he has no reason to continue frequenting the club and running up a huge bar tab. For men in these situations at least, sex is an end goal. It's the hostess' job to allow a man to think he's getting close, but never to actually let him have what he wants. At host clubs, it's just the opposite. "Women take sex as the starting point," says Usagi. "When the sex starts, they get more emotional about the man they are having sex with, so they spend a lot more money if they have sex. Hosts know about that kind of basic instinct, that kind of nature of women, so they want to encourage women to have sex with them so they keep coming back. I'm telling you because I experienced it."

Usagi says that in the host club there are no rooms designated for sex. When you decide to have sex with your host, you go to a hotel or to his apartment. She also says, "This kind of relationship is not necessarily encouraged by the owner of the host club even though everybody knows that something is happening outside the host club."

It is Saturday night at Club Impact, a host club in the Shinjuku area. You can't tell it's a host club by looking at the women; they are all dressed in casual sweaters and jeans. It's the men who give the trade away: they are all wearing fitted dark suits, like they're from Spandau Ballet or some eighties band. What sets them apart from one another is their hair: dyed in shades from blonde to orange, some sport spiky dos, some are more tousled, others are slightly long. They also all have fake names. Mr. Hiriki is twenty-three years old and runs the club. "I worked as a host and always had the idea to open my own club," he says. "So when my previous employer went under, I opened this place." That was a year ago. Aporo, Hiriki's deputy director, is twenty-six. He's been a host for three and a half years and he's got his routine down pact. He likes the ladies, he wants you to know. That's why he became a host. Hiriki puts his clientele in two categories. The first group consists of "the women who are so lonely they just want to meet people." The second group is more like Usagi Nakamura, "the women who have been through everything and know everything about clubbing." The latter group, maybe a little older, not necessarily wiser, thrives on host clubs because they're an extraordinary experience, one of the few remaining taboos. Aporo says, "The women who come to the club are curious about everything."

The busiest times for the club, Hiriki and Aporo tell me, are early in the week. Their average customer, they say, is in her mid-twenties. As for sleeping with customers, Hiriki says,

"We do not necessarily encourage it but we do not discourage it. If the hosts' relationship with women outside of the club can be deeply beneficial to the business in the host club, then it's encouraged."

One of the things I noticed when I visited the club early on in the evening, is that the guys huddle together, drinking up a storm before the women arrive. The more they drank, the "friendlier" they became. I also wondered how many of the hosts, pretty boys through and through, were actually gay. Hiriki says, "I'm not quite sure how often it happens. We had a coworker here who was gay and he did not come out by himself, even though it was obvious to us that he was a homosexual. So we asked him and he came out. Gay people want to work with the hosts because the guys here are handsome and they want to have some kind of relationship with them. They are not really interested in the customers."

Hiriki sees his job as club owner as, "providing a place for women to take a rest. We know how to treat women professionally so the women can get satisfaction from them. The regular men cannot do that. The negative side of the host club is that the women who choose to be here—it will be very difficult for them to find a regular relationship or loving partnership from regular men, not just hosts."

Most of the women are regulars; women like Usagi who fall in love with a host and keep returning with the hopes of making him fall in love with her, too, are the company's bread and butter. I ask Hiriki if he ever feels guilty for making money off of a women's loneliness—even though I know the answer before it comes. "No," he says. "Because it's just the way it is in this business. The women are getting what they want."

Still Hiriki says he would like to get out of the host club business. "I'm trying to start a new business this year that is a daytime business," he says. "As long as I work here I cannot think about marriage and family because this would not be something I could proudly say to my family that I do as a profession. That is why I want to start a new daytime business, so I can have a job I am proud of."

I meet a host club customer from Hokkaido who tells me that she goes by the name of "Mama." She is thirty-eight years old and she has been coming to host clubs for three years. She works in a night lounge and was introduced to the world of host clubs by a friend. "The first time, I thought everyone was so young!" she says. Despite the fact that the average host is in his early twenties, Mama kept coming back for more. "I like to have a relationship with the hosts, talk to the hosts," she says. "But the major reason is that I'm so lonely, I need some company."

Her favorite host is Mr. Hiriki. "He is so professional, his conversation is always quite mature and he knows how to entertain people," she says. She has met with hosts for dinner outside of the club. She says most women meet their favorite hosts outside of the club. It is common practice, especially for the younger women. Even when she has a boyfriend, Mama says that she doesn't stop coming to the host club—underscoring Hiriki's notion that with a bottle of Dom Perignon in one hand, and a silver platter of flattery and sexual favors in the other, the hosts create a kind of atmosphere in which the average Japanese man can't compete. Yet when I ask Mama about her ideal man, she says, "I want a masculine man who can guide a woman. My ideal man is more like the traditional Japanese man because they are strong enough."

Mama's family has no idea that she comes to host clubs. Because she is thirty-eight, they have stopped asking her when she is going to get married and have kids. Before she worked at a lounge, Mama says she was a career woman. "I was able to get quite high up," she says. The company she was working for went bankrupt and she didn't have the energy to start the climb anew. Now she works at the lounge and spends her free time, and her discretionary income, at host clubs. "All I'm hoping for is to have a nice life until I die," she says. Her tone of voice is not dramatic, simply matter of fact.

I meet another woman who declines to give me her name. She's twenty-three and a waitress. She's been coming to host clubs for seven months. Like Mama, she came the first time with a friend. Her family also has no idea that she visits host clubs. She says, "I keep coming because of the homey atmosphere. This is a place where I can relax." The entire time we are speaking, the waitress sits snuggled next to her favorite host. If you saw them on the street, you would think they were a newlywed couple. It's not until he gets up to refresh her drink that she admits that she did have a boyfriend, but he left her and she has no idea why. When I ask whether she minds that this romantic attention comes with such a high price tag, she says, "I don't care. If I didn't visit host clubs, I would spend the same amount elsewhere." I worry about girls like this, girls so susceptible to drowning in the bathtub. You almost wish they'd spend their money on a Louis Vuitton handbag because you get the feeling that once they fall in love, there's nothing they wouldn't do for the host who has captured their heart.

Meet Erika and Shinajane. They are both part-time workers. Erika is twenty. Shinajane is eighteen. They've been coming to host clubs for less than a year. Erika's a host's worst nightmare: she doesn't drink, so she says, "I just like to come and relax. I'm young and I feel that it's my privilege." Shinajane interjects that "Erika loves men." Which makes you wonder just how she gets away with not drinking at a club that makes its money on marked-up booze. Erika says her favorite host doesn't force her to drink and doesn't pressure her to do anything. Shinajane says she's not quite sure about that. Erika reveals that she does have a boyfriend; he's a host at another club. They met while she was a client. Now that the two are dating, she does her "relaxing" elsewhere.

Around 3 A.M., the off-duty hostesses start piling in. One, who declines to give her name, tells me she works in a cabaret and has been there for six years. "I got into hostessing when a friend recommended it. I did not really know the society. I have been able to meet many different kinds of people." She's been visiting clubs for three years now, and although she's not a regular customer at any one club, because she works in a cabaret she knows what places are hot and moves around often. I can't help but wonder why a woman, who does the same exact kind of work, who understands how false the flattery is, who knows how financially motivated the connections are, would spend her hard-earned money in a host club. The hostess shrugs, "At work, I have to cater to my customers. Here, I can be who I truly am." I think of the old saying, "The cobbler's children never have shoes." Is the hostess like the cobbler's children? Does she come to the host clubs because it's the equivalent of getting her own pair of shoes?

It's 4 A.M. now and I meet another woman who won't give me her name. She is twenty-one and when I ask her what she does for a living she tells me, "I work in the sex industry." She's been coming to host clubs since she turned eighteen. Rather quickly she realized she didn't have enough money to keep coming. Her host, however, was "growing a baby." When she turned twenty years old (the age of legal consent in Japan), she started turning tricks. As soon as she started making her own money, she began coming to host clubs again. Although she says, quite blithely, that she comes to host clubs to "relax when I get stressed out," her story is more complex. Her parents think she works at a cabaret. She has a four-year-old son.

"When I was pregnant I did not tell my parents the truth because I wanted to hide it from them," she says. "My parents didn't like it at first, but now my son lives with my parents and I've rebuilt my relationship with them." She's only twenty-one, but I can't imagine what kind of future she has, working as a prostitute and using the money she makes to pay for a host's insincere affection. It's 5 A.M. and after spending the entire night in a host club, I want a shower. More than a shower, I want to stop hearing the Beatles sing "Eleanor Rigby" in my head. All the lonely people, where do they all come from?

6

BLUSHING BRIDES AND
CHARISMATIC HOUSEWIVES

The More Traditional Route

It's easy to forget, with so many women delaying marriage and others opting out altogether, that the majority of women still prefer to go the more traditional route. If Japanese men are still bound—through their corporate life—by a kind of samurai code, women are bound—through marriage—to a similar code of honor and loyalty. Marriage affords a woman not only the security of a relationship, but a place in the community at large. "Japanese society regards marriage as very important," one woman tells me. "It's when you grow up, not when you hit the age of twenty. There are a lot of social customs you face, customs with your family, your friends, your neighbors. Even something as simple as how to present a gift to someone who's had a baby is so precise: you have to choose the right envelope, you have to give the right amount of cash. It's the same when someone gets married or is sick." In a society like Japan, so full of invisible locked doors, the only way to get into the portal of the accepted adult community—the all-important rituals of holidays, births, funerals—is to get married. Single people, regardless of age, are subtly, but powerfully, shut out.

You can't have breakfast at Tiffany's, but you can indulge in the same Audrey Hepburn–like fantasies—complete with breakfast, lunch, or dinner—at Anniversaire, a stylish boutique-style department store in the Harajuku district of Tokyo. Located on Ometesando, a long, extra-wide walking street that leads to a pretty park, Anniversaire is typically Japanese in that it is typically French. When I first visited Tokyo, it was simply an elegantly pared-down department store like Paris' Colette or New York's Henri Bendel: flowers and jewelry on the first floor, women's clothing on the second floor, men's clothing on the third floor, china and housewares on the third. Anniversaire also has the best people-watching café, complete with a red awning, rattan chairs, and little tables straight off of the Boulevard Saint-Germain. It's a great place to shake what Holly Golightly called "the mean reds," as I found out on a recent summer day after nearly losing it following hours of running errands in Tokyo's famous summer humidity. I arrived, ordered a glass of champagne, and suddenly all was right in the world.

Over the past few years, Anniversaire has transformed itself from a merely chic department store to a wedding emporium. There is an elaborate, Italianate "Chapelle d'Anniversaire" in the back of the store. This is where wedding ceremonies are carried out, Christian-style, with foreign actors dressed up as priests. Receptions are held on one of five floors: the first floor villa, complete with an original Marc Chagall painting of two lovers floating in the sky; the fifth floor salon; the sixth floor gallery; the seventh floor atrium; and the eighth floor garden, complete with an elaborate roof deck so your guests can toast to your union underneath the stars. But the real appeal of Anniversaire is the pageant walk. After you say your vows in the chapel, and the actor-priest declares you man and wife, you take a leisurely stroll along Ometesando. All the guests at the Anniversaire café are given little golden bells and as you walk out, they ring the bell for you, heralding your new status with their good wishes. It's the kind of movie-moment packaging— complete with a shower of rose petals—that Anniversaire specializes in.

I spent an evening talking to girls who were getting their gowns fitted at Anniversaire. There's a special by-appointment-only wedding gown floor and from the moment the elevator door opens, there is a kind of hush that doesn't fall on other areas of the department store. This is Tokyo's bridal dream factory and the women who work here take their job very seriously. Pixieish girls maneuver silently like gamine Secret Service men in black Armani-style pantsuits, fitted black T-shirts underneath their suits, and polished black pumps on their feet. It is so quiet it seems like their feet must barely touch the shining oak floor.

There is so much to take in that my eyes don't know where to go first. Pearl and diamond tiaras glimmer in glass cases. There are black kimonos for mothers of the bride. These, like the tuxedos, are for rent. But what catches your eye and your imagination are the dozens and dozens of white dresses. There is also a section of colored dresses, bright and rich, like scoops of ice cream. I learn that while Japanese brides may wear white to the ceremony, it's becoming increasingly popular to change into a bright color for the reception. All of the furniture is white: ivory nubuck, as soft as suede, covers all the slip chairs, princess-style sofas, and chaise lounges. There are six changing rooms, each as well lit and designed as the stage in a small and exquisite theater. Each changing room features a raised platform covered in blonde parquet wood, and each is cloaked by ivory and pale gold satin curtains. I take it all in and find it hard to believe that this is considered a middle-class wedding option. The truly rich favor the Park Hyatt or the Royal Hotel in Ginza where Princess Sayako was married.

The average Anniversaire wedding starts at about ten thousand dollars, including the purchase of the dress, the tux, the ceremony, and a sit-down dinner. Masami Ito's wedding, she tells me, will be typically Japanese: thirty-five or thirty-six people. Most of her friends live in Osaka and won't expect to be invited. Anniversaire charges $100 a head for guests, all-inclusive. I quickly do the math then I think of the catering bill at my own wedding and I am jealous. Why didn't I get married here? It would have been so much cheaper.

Behind the satin curtains, I hear a saleswoman and a bride to be giggling like schoolgirls. When they are ready, they open the curtain and I'm introduced to Masami Ito. She is so soft-spoken, I have to strain to hear her. She has reddish hair and the kind of extra-long rock-star extensions that are so popular right now. Her dress is off the shoulder, a pale cream and white, with embroidered roses across the bodice and the skirt. She is, like all the other women I will meet at Anniversaire, a vision.

She is from Osaka, the Chicago to Tokyo's New York. I've been hearing recently that Osaka women are noted for their style. Tokyo girls tend to be casual, but Osaka women really like to dress up. Masami has been to Anniversaire five times in the past six months to try on dresses. She started out with twenty, narrowed the field to fifteen, and then finally three before choosing this dress.

The salesgirl who is helping her is named Yamada-san. She is wearing the requisite black suit and with her little glasses, she bears more than a passing resemblance to the writer

Banana Yoshimoto. I am interested in the back and forth between Yamada-san and her client, Masami. They seem almost like sisters, the way they joke and finish each other's sentence. Yamada-san is protective of the bride to be, helping her to sit down, worried that she will get tired, standing and talking to me in her somewhat heavy dress. It's the full princess treatment for Masami, and Yamada-san is her lady-in-waiting.

I also think it's interesting that Masami, like all the other girls I meet at Anniversaire, has come to her fittings alone: no cloying mothers or mothers-in-law, no aunts, no cousins, no friends. This, I learn, is typical in Japan. The independence of making all of one's bridal gown arrangements alone adds a level of maturity to Masami with her very stereotypical baby-girl voice. She may talk like a child, but she's grown-up enough to make her own choices.

Masami is an office lady for a major company in Osaka. There is a branch in Tokyo and she's been offered a position here because she's considered very efficient. I look at the black-and-white photos that surround us: all images of 1950s American, Grace Kelly look-alike brides. I know the words Masami will say, before she says them. She will not take the transfer, she says, "Marriage is a good opportunity to quit."

It's a story that I'll hear over and over again, though the frankness of it will continue to catch me by surprise. It's not that women in the U.S. don't sometimes leave their jobs, but the impetus is usually motherhood, not marriage. It's also not seen as your birthright to quit. In Japan, a man does not ask you to marry him unless he's financially prepared to take care of you. What I learned in the course of interviewing so many women is that there is a narrow window of time within which a woman decides the course of her working life. The most important decision, of course, is going to university. As I learned from women like DJ Naomi, junior college with a domestic science major is still a choice that is foisted upon many bright, otherwise ambitious young women. If you get into university, then as Satoko from IBM explained, you must overcome your professors' lack of expectation for you, as a woman, and network your way into a strong postuniversity job. This is where a great deal of Japanese women begin to fall out of the race, before its even started. Remember that 63 percent of Japanese companies have no intention of hiring more women. If you want a place in corporate Japan, you have to hustle to get in. Then between twenty-five and thirty, one of two things happens. Either a woman finds a satisfying work life, in a big company or in a small business of her own, or she works a job she doesn't like much, knowing that when she gets married, she will quit.

"My sister went to one of the best universities in Japan, Keio University," says Mina Takahashi. "She hated work. She hated the idea of work. Now she's happy to be at home with the kids. I've heard her say, 'When the kids grow up, I might want to do something.' But I don't think it really occurs to her about her education and how she's not using it. It's interesting because your parents have put in a lot of money and invested in you. But that doesn't seem to cross a woman's mind. I know two friends from Smith who came back to Japan, worked for a year or two, got married, and quit. They had acceptances to great graduate programs at places like Stanford. They kept deferring until finally they said, 'I'm just not going.'"

"Whenever a woman hates her job, she says, "I wish I could marry now and quit," Kaori, the Argentinian-born accountant, says. "They use marriage as an excuse to quit." She pauses for a moment and adds, "It's a good excuse." When her brother and sister-in-law got married, her sister-in-law quit her job as soon as possible. "I asked her why and she says she doesn't want to work. She said it's much more pleasant just to stay at home, doing origami work, nursing the baby, and having gorgeous lunches with their friends." For days, that phrase will stay with me: "gorgeous lunches" like a phrase out of the British comedy *Absolutely Fabulous*. I can't help but think that even someone like Kaori is caught up in the fantasy of what it means to be a housewife. Is staying at home really "much more pleasant?" I've never nursed a baby, but I'm aware that a newborn infant requires a great deal of work and doesn't leave a lot of time for things like origami. Certainly there's got to be a wizard pulling the strings behind the curtains of this Oz, when we continue to imagine that women who work at home have it so easy.

In the U.S., I have just written an essay for a new anthology called *Mommy Wars: Stay-at-Home Moms and Career Moms Face Off on Their Choices, Their Lives, Their Families*. The editor of this collection, my friend Leslie Morgan Steiner, asked me to write about what it was like to view the arguments and assessments from the outside, as a woman who hasn't yet had to make the choice of what kind of mother I will be. I find it interesting that in Japan as in the U.S., there is the same amount of fantasizing (and subtle dissing) about the choices that other women have made with their lives.

In between fittings, I sit with one of the sales associates, a young woman named Takegawa-san. She is twenty-six years old. She has worked at Anniversaire for three and a half years. She says she likes working here because "the couples who get married here have a sort of vision about their marriage. It's my job to help make those dreams come true," she says. I wonder if it's the language barrier, or just the slipperiness of the business of wedding planning, that makes it sound as if a vision for a marriage and a vision for a wedding are two interchangeable things.

Takegawa-san tells me that she sees all kinds of brides, though the average age is mid-twenties to early thirties. She herself feels no pressure to get married. She says, "It helps that this is my job. I get to live in the world of weddings everyday." Recently, she had a client who was forty-three and her groom was ten years younger. "I was really excited about this," Takegawa-san tells me. When I asked her why this was so exciting, she says, "A lot of women over forty are ashamed to be getting married so late. Ordinarily, they wouldn't come here. They are more likely to do something private, like getting married overseas."

I meet another bride to be. Her name is Kaori Suzuki. She is twenty-nine years old and an accountant in Tokyo. She seems very conservative, in her black shift dress and Tiffany-blue cardigan. She tells me that wedding customs are changing. For one, she did not accept her husband's dowry. Again, I'm not sure that I heard her right. A dowry? In this day and age? But I learn that yes, the groom's family still often pays a dowry, anywhere from the equivalent of $20,000 to $30,000. If the woman takes the dowry, then she has to show how she used the money: on furniture, things for the house, things for the future. Kaori chose to have her wedding without a dowry. She also fully intends to keep working at her job.

My friend Manami has invited me to lunch with a coworker of hers, a recently engaged young woman named Mari Takebayashi. She tells me that Mari is more forward thinking than the brides I've met at Anniversaire. Mari is a career woman, with strong opinions on how she wants her marriage to be different than the ones of many of her peers. I'm excited to meet her and hear what she has to say. We meet up at their office, the FPC, and eat at one of the office restaurants. We all order the beef curry. I quickly learn that Mari and her fiancé have been dating for five years. He's a salesperson at a Japanese computer company. He's up at six A.M., at his desk by eight A.M. She's not exactly sure where the line is drawn between working late and socializing with his colleagues but he is typically home by eleven P.M.

Mari would like to have children. "I love kids," she says. "I want to have two or three." Her sister just had her first kid at thirty-five and tells her, "Mari, you don't know what I'm going through. You have to do it younger." She's not sure if she would like to continue working, but she is sure that she'd like a husband who would be understanding of her work schedule. "I want more equality in the household," she says, "someone who can cook, do chores, and help take care of the kids."

Like a lot of couples their age, this "equality conversation" is one that Mari and her fiancé have had often. "You talk about it," Mari says. "But once you get married, the situation is different. I think in the end, I'll do more of the housework and childcare. As long as my husband helps out, I don't mind."

What is important to Mari, and harder to get at is that she doesn't want to have a marriage built on the Japanese notion of "mutual understanding," meaning "I love you. You know I love you. I don't have to say it." When she was in high school, she visited an American friend's house and remembers how odd it was to see her friends' parents holding hands or kissing each other when they got home. "All this, 'Honey, how was your day?' stuff," she says. "It was nice, but it was shocking to me." This is a common thread among the younger women that I interview. They grew up in homes where the parents barely spoke to each other. The stereotype is that Japanese men aren't communicative. We complain a lot about American men, not talking about their feelings. But Japanese men are known, defined even, by their silences.

Just the week before, Mari attended a friend's wedding. Her friend asked Mari to look after two couples that were visiting from the United States. Both couples were in their late forties, early fifties. Mari saw in them the kind of marriage that she dreams about. "All weekend long, they were so affectionate," she says. "They were always giving each other sweet compliments. You don't hear that from Japanese men. It's not their way." I think back to my conversation at the Shinagawa restaurant with Erina, Ritsuka, Kaori, and Mako and how they went on and on about the passion of Korean soap stars, the appeal of forward-thinking American men. (I make a mental note to get all of my Japanese guy friends Otis Redding CDs for their birthdays. I'm convinced that there's nothing wrong with them that multiple listenings of "Try a Little Tenderness" couldn't cure.)

Although she has just begun her wedding plans, what Mari doesn't want is a hollow Christian ceremony with a foreigner-actor-priest. "I'm thinking of doing a Japanese-style wedding," she says. "Because I spent some years abroad, I've become more appreciative of Japanese things. I would like to wear a kimono and I think it would make my grandmother happy." Six months later, I return to Japan. Mari did indeed get married in a kimono, but she hasn't had to worry whether she has married a man who would be "understanding of her work schedule."

Mari—the forward-thinking career woman—has quit her job.

In the U.S., *Desperate Housewives* is a hit TV show. In Japan, the nation is captivated by "charismatic housewives." By definition, charismatic housewives live in rich neighborhoods, eat lunch at luxury restaurants, take expensive lessons in foreign languages, and travel abroad. When the charismatic housewife has a child, she devotes all her sartorial effort to what is called "park debut," the first time she and her little bundle of joy make their appearance at the neighborhood park. To be a charismatic housewife is the new fantasy. A young Japanese woman studies the business card of a potential suitor with the idea that maybe being a housewife won't be the life of self-sacrifice and loneliness that her mother's generation suffered. She could even, if she wants, take a lover.

It's important to explain that in Japan, the term "charismatic" is, at the most basic level, not considered an insult. It's hard to imagine it, for example, coming out of the mouth of *Daily Show* host Jon Stewart without the requisite titters and easy low-blow jokes. But Japan is a land of *miha,* extreme fanaticism, where people who display an unerring focus and skill at what they do are applauded, not mocked. So a charismatic housewife is seen as being the equivalent to the sexy model in those old Charlie perfume commercials: she brings home the bacon, she fries it up in a pan, she never, ever lets you forget you're a man. "I think Japanese women are changing in that way," one woman tells me. "They are becoming more beautiful. We were always looking at American dramas, where the mothers were beautiful, wore fashionable clothes, had manicured nails. Today, you see Japanese women with kids and they look like that—beautiful."

In 2004, Harumi Kurihara, one of Japan's famous "charismatic housewives" won the Best Cookbook award (known unofficially as "the Cookbook Oscar") at the Gourmand World Cookbook Awards in Sweden. There were 5,000 entries from 67 countries. Kurihara not only came out on top, but she was the first Asian to ever win the prize. In addition to her best-selling cookbooks, translated into five languages, and with more than six million copies in print, Kurihara is the owner of six restaurants and twenty-five department store outlets that sell cookery products bearing her name. Still, she shudders at the thought of anyone calling her a career woman. In Japan, housewife is an honorific title like "Mrs." It doesn't matter whether you are a stay-at-home mother or a vice president at an international bank; if you are married then you are a housewife. As Kurihara told a reporter, "I have this old-fashioned view that a woman should not work unless she can take care of the home as well. I have cooked dinners and prepared box lunches for my children. Homemaking, I think, is a great job for women. I enjoy being a *shufu* (housewife)." In response to media reports that she is too busy to fulfill her housewife duties, she says, "I clean up fast. I get up before six A.M. every day. Homemaking really suits me." Her comments are typically Japanese. Who would expect a major American woman CEO to explain that she does her own housekeeping, that she's able to run a global empire because she "cleans up fast"?

Like Kurihara, Makiko Fujino is as synonymous with the term "charismatic housewife" as Meryl Streep is to the term "award-winning actress." When I go to the Parliament members' office building to meet the newly elected Fujino, I'm filled with some trepidation. For days the interview has been dangled in front of me like a carrot on a stick. When I mention her name to other Japanese women there is a kind of audible wonder. There are, of course, many celebrities in Japan, but Makiko Fujino is a particularly intimate kind of heroine. As *the* charismatic housewife, she is more famous for being who she is, than for what she actually does. I've met the occasional woman who has tried Fujino's recipes, but for the most part what women talk about is how often they have seen her on TV. At fifty-six, she has been famous for more than twenty years. Her story—like a soap opera heroine whose travails you watch every afternoon—is well known. At twenty-four, she married Kimitaka Fujino, who at the time, held a high post in the ministry of trade. At thirty, she followed her husband to a diplomatic post in New York. It was there that Fujino found her calling. Bored in her adopted city, she began to take courses in pastry making.

In and of itself, this might not seem extraordinary. But

Japanese desserts, called *wagashi,* are very different from *yogashi,* Western-style desserts. Japanese desserts are a somewhat acquired taste of more savory flavor and gelatinous texture: made with rice flour, red beans (*azuki*), and sugar. In the late seventies and early eighties, when Fujino was studying pastry making in New York, you couldn't easily get a dessert like cheesecake or apple tart in Japan. You need only to see a picture of the young diplomat's wife on her Web site, her hair a dark spiral of eighties curls a la Gloria Estefan, to know that she was ahead of her time in Japan.

In the gospel according to Fujino, she returned to Japan and began to teach pastry making to other housewives in the neighborhood. Another diplomatic stint abroad, this time in Paris, gave Fujino, who calls herself a "cooking researcher," the opportunity to add French desserts to her repertoire. Well, before you could say *mille feuilles,* the popularity of these informal classes led to the television appearances, cookbooks, and magazine features that are at the heart of her sweets empire today.

Fujino has become popular, even among this generation of women who could care less about cooking and are avoiding marriage and motherhood, like, well, the plague, because she epitomizes the values that young urban women in Japan prize the most. She is *karisma,* as they say in Japanese, because she has impeccable style—well put together without being a label whore; she is self-deprecating while always appearing flawless and she is worldly. When she appears on television, speaking French as she sometimes does, talking about her stints in New York and Paris, she reinforces this generation's viewpoint that there is more to life than being married to a hard working salaryman and a 3LDK (living room/dining room/kitchen) apartment in the suburbs of Tokyo. Maybe, just maybe, if Fujino-san sprinkles some of her fairy powder (or powdered sugar) on you, then you too can wear beautiful clothes, bake beautiful pastries, and see some of the beautiful world that awaits beyond the island that is Japan. In the fairy-tale life that is Makiko Fujino's, you could even get a call from the prime minister, inviting you to run for a seat in Parliament and after six short months of campaigning, you could add a seat in the House of Representatives to your impressive list of accomplishments.

When I finally meet Makiko Fujino, after clearing security and accompanied by a high-placed minder from the FPC, she does not disappoint. She is as attractive as she appears in the countless photographs of her that I have scene. It is the end of the day, but she is runway ready in a black blazer with a large Art Deco brooch, a long wool skirt, and stylish black boots. Her office in the Parliament members' building is 1970s governmental, with standard issue furniture and florescent lights. Still, she has set the room like a soundstage for a cheery morning talk show. The window is lined with orchids: seven or eight large pots bloom with cymbidium blossoms of white and pink. On the low coffee table, there are three mason jars of Japanese peppers, labeled in what is presumably Fujino's own handwriting. She says, off-handedly, that she is always developing spices for her original cooking.

The peppers are soaking in olive oil, Japanese vinegar, and white wine vinegar. I myself, love to cook and I am impressed by her handiwork, but I wonder at the logic in emphasizing her cooking background during this, her freshman year in the House. Just the month before, she was roundly criticized in the press for missing a Parliamentary plenary session on the postal privatization bill, Prime Minister Koizumi's key issue. Fujino, the media reported, had skipped Parliament to tape a cooking show in Fukuoaka. The show, she argued, had been scheduled months before the election. Yoshihiko Noda, chair of the opposition Democratic Party, publicly mocked Fujino, "You are a political child."

There are eighty-three "children" in Parliament now—all first-time House representatives elected on the Liberal Democratic Party (LDP) ticket. Anxious to avoid another fallen soufflé by the likes of Fujino and her counterparts, the LDP issued a publicity manual to its freshman representatives. The manual was called "How To Prepare For Press Coverage." In order to win sympathy from the press, newly elected representatives were advised to respond to any difficult questions with "I feel tense" and "I will study with all my strength as I am still an amateur in the political world." I can report that I've often heard the phrase, "I feel tense," as an apology for a poorly done job or a careless error. Until the LDP released its manual, I had no idea that this was actually believed to be a serious, considered response. (Because I am as capable of being as obnoxious an American as the next gal, when someone I'm working with in Japan says, "I feel tense," I can't help but think "Well, damn. I feel hungry. But that's not going to make a burger magically appear now will it?")

Sitting in her interior office, her peppers marinating in their golden elixirs, Makiko Fujino does not feel tense. Her assistant brings in cups of coffees and a tray of butter almond cookies. The cookies, each a delicate galette that would make any pastry chef proud, were made by Fujino herself. "I'm pretty busy," Fujino says. "I'm not only one of the House of Representatives, but my husband is a member of the House of Counselors. I'm a wife, a mother, and a cooking researcher. Nowadays, I have a dilemma. I'm losing my family life. Some politicians have a family life, but the common belief is that you have to sacrifice your private life for Japanese politics."

She tells me that before she became a politician, she was a conscientious citizen. Although she famously ran on a platform that promised healthy food would decrease juvenile delinquency (neither issue a true major concern in Japan), Fujino speaks passionately about the kinds of issues that in the past were rarely discussed by Japanese government officials: the rights of the disabled, domestic violence, the growing instances of child abuse. "Running for office seemed like a very good opportunity to raise a voice for human rights," she says. "I thought this was a good chance for me."

Green as she may be in her newly elected post, it is too soon to dismiss Fujino. She is only a few months into her term and aware of her power, if unsure of how to wield it. "I can't enter into a debate on any subject like fiscal policy or foreign policy or really anything beyond what I know, which is food," Fujino famously commented the evening of her electoral victory. "But I think I could learn a lot from here in. Even current politicians do not know much about many issues because they are lazy and they do not study. At least I can study."

Fujino actually spent most of our meeting talking about how she has failed her daughters: she says this, although her two daughters are grown women with prestigious university degrees and children of their own. Guilt, one discovers, is the universal language of working mothers all around the world. "I thought I was the perfect mother," Fujino tells me. "I prepared these exquisite dinners for my daughters whenever I had to be away filming a television program. I found out later they didn't need a fancy dinner. They needed me to be home so they could talk to me. I didn't understand their anger for a long time."

You might think Makiko Fujino is being too hard on herself, but the charismatic housewife always values the latter portion of her job title over the former. I ask Mrs. Fujino what it means to her to be seen as a charismatic housewife. She smiles. She likes the term quite a bit. "I think it means that people trust me," she says. "Women say, 'My husband really praised me when I made your recipe.' Young girls tell me, 'It made my grandmother so happy when I made your soup.' To me, being a charismatic housewife is about doing what you can to bring joy to your family and being a figure of stability and warmth."

That is clearly her official answer. Then she says, "I'm not a 100 percent perfect person. When I work very hard, I can't do my house life very well. I can be completely focused, but only on one thing at a time." She gets up to show me, putting her arms out like Lady Justice. "I know I need balance, I just don't know how. I've had great experiences as a cooking researcher, but my children felt lonely. What can you do? Life is just once. We have our chances. We make our mistakes. If a younger woman gets married and becomes an expectant mother, I'd tell her have your children and have your career."

For many women in Japan, however, having both children and a career is something they can't do or don't want to do. I went to Yokohama, to talk to a group of housewives. They ranged in age from thirty-two to forty-nine; some were dressed up in the "charismatic housewife" fashion (think St. John or Eileen Fisher), while most were in fairly casual clothes. Megumi is forty-five, she's a housewife and works part-time. Yumiko is thirty-seven and works in an after-school program. Ikuko, forty-nine, Yaskuo, thirty-seven, Masami, forty-two, and Yamagoti, forty-eighty, all work at a community center. Ryoko is forty-nine and manages an after-school program. Junko is thirty, Ayumi is thirty-two and they are so-called "dedicated housewives." Their children are young and there's no time yet for the community work the other women are engaged in.

Masami, now in her forties, remembers that ever since she was a young woman, her concern has always been her younger brother. For her, motherhood, and the work she does at the community center, began with the maternal feelings she had toward her younger brother. When he was in fourth grade, he started being bullied and he didn't want to go to school. This bullying continued until he was a junior high school student. She says, "I always regretted that I could not help him in any way. He was a failure as a student so he didn't go to university or college. My parents encouraged him to go to technical school and get a license as a chef and he did it." Her brother worked at a hotel as a cook and in a few more stores. But he had back problems and he had to give up working for a hotel because the cook has to be on his feet all day. "Now he uses a wheelchair," Masami explains. "So it's not his own failure but he had to stop and think again about what he would do with his life." He now is married and lives in Hiroshima and he has children and a happy life. He is learning how to use the computer. "Still, I alway regret the outcome of his life and the fact that I didn't give him any support or assistance," she says. "Even now that he's having a good life."

For Ryoko, her younger brother was the competition in a big family where money was limited, in particular for education. "I grew up in an extended family household that included my parents, an older sister, a younger brother, my aunt, and my grandmother," Ryoko explains. "My parents and aunt were not the sort of people who would pressure you. Their policy in raising kids was quite relaxed and flexible. They always said, 'Everything is up to you. If you want to go to college, you can study hard.'"

At the same time, it was clear to Ryoko that she couldn't go to any college she chose. There were three children to send to university and private universities are very expensive. Her parents encouraged her to aim for the national university. "If you make it there, we can pay for the tuition," they told her. Her older sister "studied really hard and got into the national university." Her younger brother failed the entrance exam. Her parents paid for an extra year of special schooling so that he could pass the national university entrance exam and he did. But when he did enter the school, it took him five years to complete a three-year program. "He could spend two extra years finishing school because he is the successor," she explains. "That's why my parents were willing to pay more than they would spend on their daughters." Ryoko herself failed the entrance exam to the national university, despite studying hard. But for her, there was no money for special school. She never got a second shot at that exam. She describes this missed opportunity as a "regret I will have to carry until the end, my death." I think back to what Rika Kayama says about marriage being a "lifelong employment for women." For a woman like Ryoko, in a country like Japan, it certainly seems that getting married is at least, in part, a career decision.

Typically, a boy's education is valued because he is the one who will become the head of the household and care for his parents in their old age. Even though Ryoko's brother eventually graduated, he never tried to take over the family and the one who is actually taking care of her parents is her older sister. Even at the age of forty-nine, Ryoko feels the sting of her loss. "If I were a man it would have been different," she says. "I was the second child and they were expecting a boy." Remember the old phrase, *ichi hime, ni taro*—first a princess and then a prince. "They were quite disappointed so they tried again to get a son. In older generations, having too many daughters is not an important thing to do." She pauses and tries to explain, "It's not like I'm always so sad, but I always think that I'm not quite important."

Junko, another of the women in the group, recalls that her parents were quite education-oriented and she and her older brother were forced to go to cram school, a practice that is becoming less and less common with the declining birthrate. (Fewer childen means less competition for places at prestigious univeristies.) However, in the 1970s and 1980s, with so few spots at the nation's top universities, many children were forced to go to cram school: studying for hours into the evening and on weekends, in order to pass the university entrance exams. There's a term for the mothers who push their children's academic careers: *kyoiku* Mama, or "education minded Mama." Junko, age thirty, doesn't feel it helped her any. "I worked hard to get a better life and went to cram school every day. But I'm seen as some sort of failure." It's the classic damned if you do, damned if you don't scenario. Housewives think that career women see them as failures. Single career women think that the "smug marrieds," as Bridget Jones so memorably termed them, are looking down at them.

I think about the term *make inu*, the "losing dog" term that is applied to unmarried career women over thirty. Technically Junko and this group of women are *kachaiino*—winners. Sit with any group of unmarried single women in Japan and they will talk about the *kachaiinos* and how simple their lives are. Sit with a group of housewives and they will quickly disabuse you of the notion that marriage solves all of your problems.

I begin to understand that each woman's motivation in choosing life as a housewife is motivated by her home life growing up. Yasuko's ambition was to create the kind of home she never had. Her father was a violent person. She says, "It wasn't as bad as domestic violence, but his behavior was kind of rough. If something didn't go his way, he would get so violent and act roughly toward me and my mother . . . I think this behavior comes from his own lack of education." It's only over the last few years that domestic violence has become an issue that is being discussed openly in Japan.

Natsuo Kirino's *Out* is one of the first major novels to bring the issue of domestic violence to the fore. An international bestseller and the winner of several major literary awards here in Japan, *Out* tells the story of a young woman who works in a factory and is suffering silently in a violent marriage. When she strangles her abusive husband, the other women in the factory get involved in covering up the crime. I tried for over a year to get an interview with Natsuo Kirino, but she is refusing all interviews with the media because she finds it difficult to live in Japan and speak to the issues in the book. Read it. *Out* is part Susan Faludi's *Backlash,* part Margaret Atwood's *Handmaid Tale,* and one hundred percent proof that while so many people lose themselves in the easy and appealing comforts of a book like *Memoirs of a Geisha,* something deeper and darker is happening with contemporary Japanese women.

Like many children with difficult family situations, Yasuko took refuge in school. She says, "I liked to study a lot in elementary and junior high school. But I didn't have any clue that I wanted to go to college." It wasn't until she was accepted at a top high school, the kind of school where everyone continues onto university, did she realize that her path was clear. After college, she had no problem entering corporate Japan. "I was employed by a major company because I was a good student," she says. "I was not hired as an office lady or clerk; I was doing the same kind of work that men do." This was in the late 1980s when the bubble had yet to burst and, she says, "the atmosphere was prowomen. The equal opportunity law of 1985 had been passed and this had a huge impact on my career." But ever since she was a high school student, she wanted to have her own family—a second chance at making a home without the violent father she'd been subjected to. "I didn't have the strong willingness to keep working and gain a higher position," she says. "I quit when I was twenty-five and started having children." At thirty-seven, she has no regrets.

Megumi didn't quite realize that she wanted to become a housewife. Nor did she particularly want to be a career woman. "All I thought was that I would just go with the flow and do what I wanted," she says. So she does. Her passion is music and she plays guitar in a band. "Even after getting married, I still pursue my interest in music," she explains. "My husband is the main person who takes care of the family. I always do what I want to do." Megumi is interesting to me because she represents the kind of woman that it's hard to classify in news magazine cover stories or morning talk show discussions about the catfight between working Moms and stay-at-home Moms. How many hundreds of thousands of mothers are like Megumi? Women who are happy to have the flexibility to work part-time, be home with their children part-time, and do something fun, like play rock guitar, in between. The allure of being a charismatic housewife may be plenty for so many women in Japan today, but there's no doubt that women's ambitions are moving more and more into the American conundrum of "having it all."

7

DERAILING THE MOMMY TRACK

Women, Pregnancy, and Politics

The average Japanese woman has 1.3 children, the lowest in the developed world. (The average American woman, in comparison, has 2.1 children.) In a country as wealthy as Japan, a low birthrate means low economic growth. The government is panicking: one recent front-page proposal reported that Parliament members are discussing whether a $30,000 cash incentive for each baby born might be enough to sway Japan's women away from their single life and back into the baby-making business. It's the women who bear the brunt of the blame for the falling birthrate. Prime Minister Yoshiro Mori has been quoted as saying that women who do not have children do not deserve pensions: "It is truly strange to say that we have to use tax money to take care of women who don't even give birth once, who grow old living their lives selfishly." In other words, if you're Japanese, your ovaries belong to the government as much as you.

Diet member Makiko Fujino says that while many young Japanese women are delaying marriage, ultimately marriage is not the key issue—motherhood is. "In Japan, it's very difficult to raise children, so women have to give up their careers. It's a big problem."

Back home in the U.S., there is often a Roy Lichenstein cartoon-like moment among career women—"Oops, I forgot to have a baby" as evidenced by fortysomething Moms such as top handbag designer Kate Spade—and perhaps more telling, all the women who never have children at all. What is so different in Japan is that while a career is optional to young Japanese women, and their feelings on marriage can be vague, having a baby is the one nonnegotiable aspect of their lives. Only one woman, out of the seventy-five I interviewed, said to me outright, "I do not want children." At Sacred Heart University, one of the most outspoken young women, a girl named Akiko says, "I will work and I probably wouldn't quit my job for the reason of marriage. But if I have children, then I would need to nurture the children."

It may seem like the decision of whether to have children or a career is one that Japanese women share with their counterparts in the U.S., but the lines in Japan are much more rigid. There is no such thing as maternity leave. At major Japanese companies like electronics giant Matsushita, only 2 percent of all female employees are on a career track, while the rest are in dead-end positions where their job is to pour tea and make photocopies. Some of the women pouring tea and making photocopies may have master's degrees. When women still hold such a precarious position in the corporate world— the things we take for granted in the U.S.—the fact that you can't be fired for being visibly pregnant, taking a maternity leave, negotiating flex time to pick up the child from day-care—is not even part of the equation. The more I asked about the child issue, the more I learned that this is why so many young women who work quit after they get married. If they continue to work, they quit once they become pregnant with their first child. "The problem is that this society is being built by fifty- and sixty-year-old men," says Kanako Otsuji, an assemblywoman from Osaka. She feels strongly that things have to change. "For example, there's a higher rate of women doctors now as well as lawyers and civil servant/government employees. Many women in civil/government employment in Osaka are getting good records. When these women get married and have children, if they don't quit their jobs, they can be in administrative positions. In order to do so, there needs to be a better support system. I do feel that we are getting closer to where we need to be."

When it comes to the idea of having children, it can be hard to parse out desire from societal expectation. If a woman decides to have a child, when she was confident that she didn't want to, is she giving into pressure or evolving in a way that feels natural to her? After all, isn't it a woman's prerogative to change her mind? Akiko Oku, the thirty-seven-year-old writer who owns a media company with her husband, never wanted to have kids. "Before I got married, I said I didn't want to have a baby," she says. "I asked him if that was okay with him, and he agreed." Six years later, Akiko is trying to get pregnant.

I ask her if she felt any societal pressure. And the answer, of course, is yes. "After we got married, many people asked me when we were going to have a baby," she says. "I was so uncomfortable with those comments. In the beginning, I really didn't want to have a baby. Then Princess Masako gave birth at thirty-seven and the media started to report on fortysomething Moms. Akiko was inspired. Maybe it was possible to take the time to build her career and have kids, too. At thirty-seven she feels ready for motherhood in a way that she simply didn't in her late twenties and early thirties.

"If I can, I'd like to have twins," she says with a laugh. When

I ask her why she wants children now, she says simply, "I know they could bring so much joy to my life and my husband's as well. With children, we'll enjoy life even more. Is that a selfish motivation?"

It helps that Akiko and Yoshitaka have had time to build up their own marriage. Akiko still remembers when they were first dating and she met his parents. "His parents are so sweet, but they are so traditional!" she says. "His mother said something like, "This air conditioner is too cold and it's not good for you because you want to have a baby one day." It hit me then that I wasn't just Yoshitaka's girlfriend. I was expected to be *reproductive*." It's not that she didn't like kids. She simply didn't see that as her role. Perhaps for a generation of women raised by stay-at-home mothers, it's the natural course of things to delay motherhood, if only to differentiate your path from your mother's. Akiko hadn't even been particularly keen on marriage. "Then I did get married and I was so overwhelmed by the fact that I was expected to have children," she says. "I started to reject all the comments and I became even more uncomfortable with the idea of having children."

Memo to the Japanese parliament: you're freaking women out! It's hard to believe that the 300,000 yen "baby bonus" (roughly $30,000) the government is thinking of offering young women as an incentive to have more children, would have swayed someone like Akiko who simply shut down in the midst of all the pressure. Only time has given her the comfort level she needed to try to get pregnant. "It's been six years and not so many people are pressuring me now," she says. "I have a stable life with my husband and I feel like having a baby because the baby is going to add more to our life as a couple."

The question of maternity leave—the fact that the Japanese government has no such policy and pregnant women aren't expected to return to work—is also not an issue for her. "We established the business together, so when I get pregnant, I will not be able to do as much, at least for a few months," she says. "But since it is our business, I'll be able to get back to it quite fast. Most women in companies are not encouraged to go back to their positions once they have a baby. Even though those companies have maternity leave, most working mothers are put in an environment where they feel like quitting."

If some women are quitting their jobs because of marriage with the understanding that marriage is an easy way out, quitting because of children is quite another thing. There are no maternity leave laws in Japan. Day care can be expensive—and is often stigmatized. And in a work environment where women are still, sometimes, expected to pour tea and clean the company kitchen, a pregnant woman can find it hard, if not impossible, to command any authority. "Especially when it comes to women's position in society, this is still a developing country," says Osaka assemblywoman Kanako Otsuji. "The wage inequality between men and women in Japan is an issue. Nonregular employment for women is over 50 percent. More than half the women who work are working part-time or as a temp. It's because companies try to cut the labor cost to deal with globalization. That's why women and young people are being exploited. And if you are a nonregular employee, it's hard to take a maternity leave. It's hard to bring up topics like this in an assembly full of men. Even if I did, they can't understand how big of an issue it is. And they don't understand the connection between this issue and the falling birthrate."

"For example, a single mother's yearly salary is about 1.6 million yen (about $13,000 a year) in Osaka," says Otsuji. With benefits, it's about 2.1 million. It's less than half of what men make a year. It's the idea that having a child is a disadvantage.

If the child is sick the women have to take days off. Women have to go and pick up their kids from kindergarten. Single mothers and issues of women in poverty is a big problem in Japan but it's not considered a priority."

There are also real regional issues to be addressed. In Tokyo, young women will tell you that it takes ten million yen to raise a baby (roughly $100,000). Other women will tell you, it takes twenty million yen, from cradle to university graduation. Tokyo is the nation's capital, a global city, where both men and women come to be ambitious. Outside of Japan's big cities, in prefectures like Nagano, where there is still a strong agricultural culture such as rice farming, more young women work outside of the household and feel much less conflicted about the need to choose between marriage and motherhood and a career. One reason is that these young women still live in intergenerational households: with mothers and grand-mothers who worked if not on the farm, then locally. The intergenerational household also provides the opportunity for the kind of safe, convenient, and most importantly, free, child care that is missing for so many women in big cities like Tokyo.

That said, Japanese young women are devouring the HBO series *Sex and the City* on DVD. When Miranda, the only Mom on that series, had a baby, she didn't live in Shizuoka prefecture in a farmhouse with her mother and her grandmother. Go back even further. The theme song to *Mary Tyler Moore* isn't, "You're going to make it after all, if you live with your mother and grandmother as built-in baby-sitters." It makes sense that more and more Japanese women are moving to cities and wanting to live on their own, meaning alone with their husbands, once they get married. One can only imagine that intergenerational households—convenient baby-sitting aside—are fraught with their own set of problems. Still, it's a useful vantage point to remember that outside of big cities like

Tokyo, Osaka, Nagoya, and Kobe, young career women are enjoying longer, more continuous careers because of their more traditional living arrangements.

The tough question is: Are we as women our own worse enemy when it comes to the delicate balancing act between work and family? Mariko Fujiwara, a director of a sociology-focused think tank called Hakuhodo Institute for Life and Living, has a love/hate affair with Japan's young career women. She herself is in her sixties, well-dressed in the kind of loose Yohji Yamamato knits that are so universally stylish and flattering. Her hair is shoulder length, hints of gray peeking around the edges. This gray hair is a true rarity in Japan where everyone— and I do mean everyone—dyes their hair, especially older women. Fujiwara says, "In the last ten years, we have seen a totally different generation of women coming into the workplace. They don't feel like they have to give up anything." When she says this, there is genuine excitement and admiration in her voice.

At the same time, she warns that young women today can be victims of their own drive. "I've seen this among my own colleagues, as well as the women I've researched here at the Institute," Fujiwara says. "The more ambitious a woman is, the more ambitious she is for her children, which can create difficulty for her. You have to pick and choose the perfect baby-sitter. You have to choose the perfect school. You have to choose the perfect tutor for after school lessons."

I think of Yukiko Oka, the thirty-one-year-old tour guide and mother of two. Her mother-in-law, who had been a day care teacher, had some concerns about public day care. "In her time, some of the teachers were not very good," Yukiko explained. "Thirty years ago, for example, it was okay to spank the kids. Right now it's quite different. We have some old teachers, with outdated ideas. But basically they are well-trained." Yukiko and her husband went to a few different day care centers. They met with each principal and then they chose one. Never in her explanation of the process does she talk about a school being "perfect" or "the best." Inherent in her explanation, there's an understanding: sometimes good enough is good enough.

Fujiwara points to the working mothers in the prefectures as a point of comparison with the affluent, ambitious young mothers in a city like Tokyo. "If you live with or are close to your family, you can drop your kid off at Grandma's," she says. "She may not be the most learned person, but she will love the child and love is important. In the prefectures, a good school is nice, but love is the key. I can go to work, and enjoy my work, because I know my child is with my parents or my in-laws. Suddenly, if you are very ambitious, convenience is not enough. If you are a working woman, and you are earning a sizeable income, you think that your money can do anything: the perfect school, the perfect baby-sitter. I'm not saying these women shouldn't work; we need them to work, I want them to work. But to think that you can throw enough money at anything involving a child and think it's a solution is a trap."

She also takes a dim view of charismatic housewives. "I think it's a sort of illness. You've seen Japanese kids—how well-dressed they are, the kids could care less. But parents see the kids as extensions of themselves. Being a fashionable mother not only means being well-dressed yourself, but also having the fashionable attire and haircuts for the kids as well."

I know what she means. Just this morning, I had coffee with a young working mother. She was dressed casually, but stylishly, in a simple sweater and pants. She confessed relief that her daughter did not attend one of Tokyo's more high-end child care centers. "The mothers dress to the nines when they pick up their children from these schools," she tells me. "And they absolutely will talk about you if you're not dressed up as well. At my kids' school, all the Moms are too busy to care."

Many of the women who opt for the charismatic housewife life do so because they find the conditions of work life for women in Japan so appalling. Ryoko, one of the housewives from Yokohama that I wrote about earlier, tells me her story. After high school, she took the civil service entrance exam because she did not make it into university. She passed the test and landed a coveted government administrative job. Quickly, she realized that "It was quite hard to survive because our workload was huge." At the same time, the work scope is quite narrow because they were women. "The discrimination toward women is strong now, but it was even stronger back then," she says. "Women were regarded as a public relations tactic, so they were always fair, pretty. Even though we worked quite hard and many late nights, our overtime was illegal and somebody deleted the records showing that we worked at night. We worked hard but it was like we got no reward." When the equal opportunity law was enforced and women were legally allowed to work at night, she says, "That is when people started working us harder than ever." Around this time, Ryoko became pregnant. "The way we were used at work was harsh," she explains. "So I thought about giving up my job because I was scared that I would have a miscarriage." At the time she lived with her in-laws and they also encouraged her to quit. Eventually, she gave in and left her job.

It's a classic story, but one with modern reverberations. Even Erina, the cosmetics entrepreneur, spoke about her hours at Pioneer as being so demanding that she was beginning to get sick. The fact is however, that the times are a-changing. Satoko Seki, who works for IBM Japan, isn't worried about having to choose children over a career. She works for an American company, yes, but these ideas are beginning to permeate the general culture. "I think my company has a very good system for maternity leave," she says. "Many women come back to work after having their babies. We even have a system where after you come back, you can leave a little earlier in the evening. A lot of people I know have used the system, so we talk and exchange information."

If, at times, women feel awkward because they have to take time off to care for a sick baby or relative, this also has the effect of letting their male colleagues know that the world does not revolve around corporate Japan. "As more women come into the workplace, they come in with greater obligations than men," explains Mariko Fujiwara. "Men suddenly realized that the world doesn't stop if a woman takes a sick day. This new generation of women feel that they're entitled to their vacations. So they take vacations and they don't work weekends. They say, 'I don't want to go out drinking with my boss, I want to go out to lunch with my girlfriends.' Women in the workplace are liberating men in the workplace."

When you talk to young Japanese women, there seems to be no shortage of women who want to have children. What they want is a different environment in which to raise children. Mieko Kawamoto is thirty-four years old and lives in Nagoya. She's hoping to have a family with her boyfriend who is British. Where they will raise their children is a real concern. "I don't plan to raise my children in Japan," she begins. Then she takes a different track, "At the same time, Japan is starting to rely on foreign employees because there aren't many resources in Japan anymore. So when I think about it, I think Japan in the future will be a plus for mixed people. From now on, it will be hard for Japanese people who cannot follow that diversity."

*　*　*

She was supposed to be the one. In a country full of fairy-tale images of women, from geisha to Go-Go (the Japanese school-girl assassin in Quentin Tarantino's *Kill Bill,*), one woman was supposed to break through the barriers—and like Pinocchio abandoning his puppet status, become real. Masako Owada became a princess, but she, and the nation of women who looked to her for guidance, were denied the fairy-tale ending they had hoped for. "Princess Masako is almost the icon of courage in terms of career women," says psychologist Rika Kayama. "She had a good career, a high profile marriage. She was supposed to be the happiest woman in Japan. She studied hard. She played sports. She was almost perfect. She could do anything."

From childhood, Masako Owada seemed to be following the script to the movie of the modern Japanese woman. The eldest daughter of a Hisashi Owada, a senior diplomat, she was not stranded in (or strangled by) Japan's homogenous island culture. As a girl, she studied in Moscow, New York, and Boston, eventually earning a degree in economics from Harvard. More than just a big brain, Masako was athletic: she skied, she played tennis. The one-time coxswain of the Harvard rowing team had even once tried out for all-girl wrestling. As *Hello!* magazine reported, she had a "strong-willed nature, pals said they seldom saw her cry." Fluent in Russian, English, French, and German, she followed her illustrious stint at Harvard with a postgraduate degree in international relations at Oxford University. She quickly landed on the radar of the Japanese foreign ministry, and the diplomat's daughter was fast-tracked to become a diplomat herself.

Unbeknown to her, Masako's intellectual accomplishment, coupled with her beauty and solid family background, was gaining attention within the walls of the palace as well. The Imperial Household Agency (IHA) is an innocuous term for the government agency that is in charge of all state matters regarding the royals and who many consider the Darth Vader-like power behind the royal family in Japan. Beginning in the late eighties, the IHA began searching for a suitable bride for Crown Prince Naruhito. The qualities they were looking for? The bride to be had to be under 5'5" tall, under thirty, and free of surgery and any piercings. Naruhito was already in his early thirties, and not married. His younger brother had already been married three years before, the first time in the history of the Japanese royal family when a younger brother had beat the older brother to the altar. The pressure was on to find Naruhito a bride.

Masako Owada had other things on her mind. She was twenty-nine, already stale Christmas cake. But she didn't care. She had worked long and hard for her career. She wasn't interested in the lifetime employment of being a Japanese housewife, even if it came with a palace and a royal title. She had first met the prince when she was twenty-two, at a party in honor of a Spanish princess. He was twenty-six, unmarried, and rumored to be gay. Masako was invited to dinner with the imperial family. The Prince proposed marriage, but the budding young diplomat turned him down.

Like a brazen version of Cinderella, the commoner turned the Prince down three times, over the course of four years. Then one day in June of 1993, after being ritually cleansed, Masako Owada was wrapped in twelve layers of kimono, and behind a bamboo screen with only a Shinto priest as a witness, she and the Crown Prince toasted each other and after the first sip of sake from the royal cups, they were married. Before joining the eight hundred guests waiting at the palace banquet, there was literally a celebration in the streets, led by a convertible Rolls-Royce, so that the world could see the Crown Prince and Princess, dressed now in a Western-style morning coat and full-skirted wedding gown. Nearly two hundred thousand people followed the royal motorcade, and for millions more Japanese women, who watched from home, a new era was going to begin. Japan had found its Princess Diana, the woman who would step beyond the walls of the Imperial Palace and be the breath of fresh air, the role model, that modern Japanese women had longed for, for so long.

The understanding was that in exchange for giving up her career (only one in forty applicants passes Japan's notoriously rigorous foreign service exam) the IHA would find a diplomatic role for its well-trained, multilingual princess. The Prince reportedly wooed the ambitious Masako by telling her that "working as a diplomat and working as a member of the Imperial Family are the same thing." In the end it appeared that the IHA had no intention of keeping up its end of the bargain, and instead it began to exert an enormous pressure for Masako to produce an heir.

In a postengagement interview, she told charming stories of her courtship with the Crown Prince. When she laughed, reporters, who were not used to royals with a sense of humor, said that she did not cover her mouth, which is the traditional thing for a Japanese woman to do. The opportunity for missteps, however, were enormous and the IHA, as the power behind the world's oldest monarchy, had no qualms about putting the princess in her place. She was criticized, for example, for speaking in English to President Clinton instead of speaking through an interpreter. Imperial Household officials let it be known that they believed, all around, that the Crown Princess "talks too much." When Masako told reporters, "At times, I experience hardship in trying to find the proper point of balance between traditional things and my own personality," she could have been speaking for every woman under forty in Japan.

Yet, the woman who was to be the new face of Japanese women became more and more a mystery. After suffering a miscarriage in 1999, she began to show symptoms of depression. The woman the media had once dubbed "the Twenty-first Century Princess" took on a new moniker: "the Quiet Princess." The stylish clothes she wore as a young career woman were replaced by conservative suits and kimonos. The Prince who had promised to protect his bride from the palace minders "with all his might" issued an uncommonly candid statement that shocked the nation: "Princess Masako, in giving up her job as a diplomat to enter the imperial household, has worked hard to adapt to the environment for the past ten years, but from what I can see, she has completely exhausted herself in trying to do so."

You'd think that within the Imperial Family, Masako might have found a kindred spirit in her mother-in-law, Empress Michiko. Michiko was the first commoner to marry into the Japanese royal family, the pioneer who paved the way for the Crown Prince's own "love marriage." However, press reports that the two are not close and that the Empress thinks that Masako's well-known depression has cast a dim pallor on the palace. Describing her own wedding in 1959, Empress Michiko said in one interview, "During all the years since, a heavy responsibility has stayed with me that I should not disgrace the Imperial Family, with its long history, which accepted me, an ordinary citizen, as a Crown Princess. The various official duties I performed were certainly not easy for me, but now, as I look back, I realize that each one of them was a necessary experience for me."

The evening of her wedding, the royal couple was asked how many children they hoped to have. A brazen Masako joked, "I told him not to expect enough players to complete an orchestra." Seven years later, in 2000, she wasn't joking with the media anymore. The Crown Princess fell under national criticism for not bearing a child, although no one questioned whether the problem might lie with the Crown Prince. The palace announced that she suffered a miscarriage, although some reports indicate that she may have actually had three miscarriages. In 2001, allegedly with the help of fertility treatments, a thirty-seven-year-old Masako gave birth to a baby girl, Princess Aiko.

Remember the saying *ichi hime, ni taro?* First a princess, then a prince is supposed to be a harbinger of good luck. But in the royal family, like the rest of Japan, the birthrate hovers stubbornly at 1.3. The future Emperor and Empress of Japan have only one child: a princess. There is no *taro,* there is no prince. In fact, no boys have been born to the royal family since 1965—which kind of makes you wonder if God is a woman and trying to send the land of the rising sun a message that it should no longer consider itself the land of the rising *son.* For years, this has been the cause of much consternation. Although Japan once had a system that allowed for princesses to ascend to the Chrysanthemum throne, the last time a woman ruled Japan was Go-Sakuramachi who was empress between 1762 and 1771. The 1947 Imperial House law states that it is impossible for a woman to succeed to the throne. If the wife of a reigning prince is supposed to produce "an heir and a spare," then Masako, in the eyes of the Imperial Household Agency, has failed miserably.

Women all over the country felt sympathy for Masako's situation. When I ask Junko Watanabe, of the Hara Museum of Contemporary Art, what's the one thing she wishes she could change for Japanese women, she says, "Of course it's not possible, but I would want to make sure that both men and women could bear children, so it's not only the task of women to give birth to a child. Look at our Imperial Household, the Crown Princess is suffering right now because she doesn't have a boy. I feel bad for her that she would have to suffer. She's probably the only woman in this country who has to have a boy. I just hope that she is happy or that she regains her strength or that she finds meaning in her role."

Masako's daughter Aiko is only three years old, but in Japan, the training of a ruler begins at birth. If Aiko is to be Empress, the law must change. Prince Tomohito, the cousin of the current Emperor and fifth in line to the throne, raised hackles when he suggested that the royal family should revive the tradition of concubines. The practice, abolished in 1921, meant that the child of a Crown Prince and a concubine was the legal heir to the throne. Another suggestion has been that the Crown Prince's younger brother and his wife could produce a male heir, which the Crown Prince could adopt as his own. A male heir, by any means necessary, seemed to be the belief of the powers that be in Japan.

Then in November 2005, a government panel on Imperial succession concluded that female descendants should be allowed to ascend to the throne. Although it will take time for the ruling to officially be made into law, the intent of the ruling was clear: Princess Aiko will be Empress one day, let her royal training begin. As for her mother, there are those who speculate whether she ever was the über-career woman that the media held her up to be. Yukie Kudo, a classmate of Masako's at Tokyo University, told *People* magazine that "the media image of her is completely wrong. I've seldom met any woman our age who is so graceful and so Japanese." Those who know her say the Quiet Princess, while an intellectual force to be reckoned with, has been a quiet woman all along. In the end, it may just be that the most radical thing Masako Owada has ever done is given birth to the girl who will become the first female monarch in Japan since the eighteenth century. We can only imagine what it will mean to Aiko to have a mother who was, for a time anyway, a high-rising diplomat; who speaks four languages; and who graduated from Harvard and Oxford. Remember that before she became princess, Masako Owada had been the coxswain of her rowing team at Harvard. The cox is the person who faces forward, when all the rowers are seated backward. She steers the boat, directing the speed and rhythm of her team. If the hand that rocks the cradle rules the world, then the Crown Princess Masako may be having the kind of influence that even the IHA cannot deny.

Though they would never put themselves forward as women who've got the delicate work-family balance sussed out, there are women who are figuring out how to have kids and keep their careers going. At thirty-one, Yukiko Oka has worked hard to have a family and work outside of the home. An Audrey Tautou–like gamine, she is stylishly dressed in a Kelly-green sweater and slacks. She has two small children and her husband, like her father, works for an American company. On one hand, this means he works in a more enlightened environment than corporate Japan. On the other hand, Yukiko explains, "There are two time zones he's answerable to. He works around the clock." A graduate of the prestigious Waseda University, Yukiko had a double major, an unusual decision in career-minded Japan where there really is no such thing as "electives." She majored in gender and sociology, while also attending a rigorous translation school. As a student, she studied in New Zealand, a country that she loves. "I go back every five years," she says.

As graduation grew closer, she pursued her job options.

She thought about going into the travel industry, because she loved to go abroad. She also thought about becoming an interpreter, although she found the work of simultaneous translation both difficult and unsatisfying. Her professor suggested that since she was fluent in English and had an outgoing personality, she should consider a career as a tour guide operator. From an American perspective, it doesn't sound like a fast-track career job, but to become a licensed tour guide operator in Japan is to earn a credential that is as practical and valuable as a CPA. For Yukiko, there was an added bonus. Being a tour guide would fit in well with her desire to have children. "I was already going out with my husband," she says. "We knew we were going to get married right after college. Being a tour guide is a very hard job. The hours are long. But it can also be very flexible. When you have a family, you can take on less work. You can stop altogether and you can always go back because you have this license."

Although Yukiko had her first child in her late twenties, I'm curious about women who wait until they are older to have children. In the U.S., the fortysomething mother is no big deal. But in Japan, even thirty-five was traditionally considered too old to start a family. Yet this, like so many things in Japanese women's lives, is changing. One person I spoke to even says that she had American friends who were coming to Japan for fertility treatments, because such treatments are less common in Japan, and it's cheaper than it is in the U.S. Yukiko says that even in a ten-year span, she sees a huge difference between her friends in their early thirties and their "big sisters" in their early forties. "In that generation, closer to forty, they worked really hard to pursue a career. Then they thought, 'Where's my marriage? Where are my children?'" Yukiko says. "I'm part of the generation after that one. We knew we had to balance. Those women are so exhausted, they can't think of themselves."

She has five best friends from her university days. One of her friends has no children; she lives in Russia and is a "dedicated housewife." Another friend is a full-time mother; her other two friends, like her, balance motherhood and careers. "We studied gender sociology with the same professor, we learned the same things," Yukiko says. "If you want children, choose a career where you can make it work. That's the result."

It seems so simple. "If you want children, choose a career where you can make it work." At the same time, isn't it a little problematic? Shouldn't a woman be able to choose any career and have a family? And why is it just the woman's job to make it work? All I can think is that life just isn't fair. If it was, then I could eat French fries every day and fit into my skinny jeans.

I listen to Yukiko speak and I am in awe of both her practicality and her happiness quotient. She never says it's not fair that she can't work as a trader for a big Tokyo bank or as a research scientist at a major chemistry lab. What she says is that she wanted children—she decided that first—and then she chose her job path accordingly. The bubble burst forced her to plan her career prudently. "After the economy started to slow down, there were no exceptions," she says. "Anyone could be fired at any time. It's not stable, like it was in the sixties and seventies when most middle-class women had the opportunity to stay home. I talked to my husband and I said, 'We need to have two breadwinners, especially in a city like Tokyo.'"

Yukiko's son is five and a half. Her daughter is about to turn two. Her first maternity leave was scary, especially because Japan has no formal policy for maternity leaves and most women don't take them: they quit their jobs as if bowing out gracefully from a competition they know they cannot win. "When I found out I was expecting, I planned to take one year leave, but I was still a little bit afraid," Yukiko says. "I had to convince myself that I have my license and I can go back any-

191

time. The bus company provides regular jobs because there are tours operating everyday."

Yukiko's children are in public day care, a service you hardly ever hear about in Japan. What you hear about are the private day care centers that cost a fortune. Yukiko believes that all the headlines about how day care costs thousands of dollars *per month, per child* are part of the media hype to convince upstart young Japanese women to stay home. The nation's plummeting birthrate is evidence that it's having the exact opposite effect. While the national average is 1.3, the birthrate in Tokyo has actually dropped to .9. "In Japan, for a long time, a lot of full-time mothers and a lot of specialists said that mothers should be with their children, at least until they are three years old," Yukiko explains. "They said it would affect their minds, their health, their entire life. There's a big pressure imposed by society—some of it well beneath the surface—telling women they can't afford it as a way to get them to quit their jobs."

I think of a young, married woman I interviewed just the day before. "I can't have a baby," the woman tells me. "It costs 10 million yen a year! I read it in the *Asahi Shimbun*!" The figure is ludicrous. $85,000 a year for day care? Before I force myself to skirt Japanese propriety and ask Yukiko how much her day care costs, she tells me. "I personally pay about $450 for my two children—a month," she adds. "We have to pay quite a good amount until they are three. It's about $180 a month after that."

In Japan, there is also a big difference between day care and kindergarten. Day care is for working mothers and has all the stigma attached therein. Kindergarten, the same word used in Japanese as in the U.S., offers shorter hours and is geared toward "charismatic housewives"—affluent, well-heeled women who want a few hours to themselves each day.

(Which is not to say that *all* mothers don't deserve a few hours for themselves each day.) There is no nanny culture in Japan—with the declining birthrate and strict immigration laws—there's not enough people to fill all the jobs that are on the books, much less in the murkier areas of home service providers.

Yukiko knows that she is lucky, or perhaps I should say that she made her own luck in the motherhood department. Her hours as a tour guide are flexible; the day care operates between the hours of 9 A.M. and 5 P.M. The average person working in Tokyo commutes from somewhere outside of the city core. The average commute is one to one and a half hours. Even with the extended hours that the day care center offers for working parents, 7:30 to 9 A.M, or 5 to 6:30 P.M., a career woman with late-night meetings would find it hard to pick up her child up on time. Yukiko can plan her tours accordingly.

The truism that how a woman views her mother's happiness will effect how she plans for her own career holds doubly true in a place like Japan where, with few exceptions, a whole generation of women grew up with mothers who were housewives. Yukiko's mother was also a housewife. Her mother lives nearby and if Yukiko does not want to rush her children off to day care, her mother comes over so the children can eat a leisurely breakfast and Yukiko can go to work. "She's been so supportive of me," Yukiko says. "She's been telling me my whole life that I should have a good career so I can be independent. She never says it outright, but being dependent on my father's salary wasn't something she wanted to do." Yukiko thinks her mother has also considered leaving her father: "I can't ever divorce," says her mother. "I don't have the financial background."

I ask Yukiko the role model question. She says, simply, "I have to make my own role model. I was one of the first people in my company to take a maternity leave. I paved the way for younger women."

As for her children, she is raising them to be ready for the Japan of the future. Not the one with flying cars and talking robots that you see in animation, but the one where men and women are regarded as equal. She's very concerned that her son, Yoshiki, not grow up to be the stereotypical Japanese Mama's boy. She's happy that her husband is a strong role model: her husband does the cooking, because *his* mother taught him how. "My son gets a little lazy in the morning," Yukiko says. "Especially now because it's cold this time of year. I tell him, 'I can't live to put your clothes on for you or cook for you. No thanks. You better be able to cook and take care of yourself." At five, little Yoshiki is already getting lessons in manhood that will hold him in good stead. Although the housewives in Yokohama may not always feel it, by raising their kids to respect equality, they are also contributing to Japan's gender revolution.

She's only thirty-one, but Yukiko seems to have already achieved so much. She has two healthy children, a job she enjoys, a marriage with a husband who cooks, and a mom who lives nearby and is happy to pitch in. Sometimes, she thinks of how things might be if she had chosen a different path. "If I were single now, I'd probably be worried," she admits. "I'm thirty-one. My parents would be worried too. I never thought I'd get married so early." There's an independent streak in her voice—she didn't go to university looking for an M-R-S degree. At the same time, there's relief too. She got married. She's a grown-up. In Japanese society, she's in like Flynn.

It's refreshing to speak to a woman who is as happy with her work life as she is with her home life. But I'm well aware that a woman who wants to work and have kids in Japan still has one hell of a juggling act to manage. When Katherine Graham, the publisher of the *Washington Post* and *Newsweek,* died, Anna Quindlen wrote a tribute article. She described how women of Graham's generation, built their lives "layer, by layer, like a cake," moving from work to family and eventually to work again in transitions that were, if not entirely smooth, clear in their definitions. In comparison, Quindlen wrote, younger women today build their lives like a fruitcake: a glob of experience in which its hard to know where one element of life begins and another one ends. The more I talk to women who are balancing work and children in Japan, the more I feel that while their lives are not perfect, there's a certain kind of layer by layer experience that is evocative of the Japanese term *wa. Wa* being harmony, but also meaning beautifully imperfect.

8

OUTSIDE OF CORPORATE JAPAN

Women Entrepreneurs

I'm dining at the Park Hotel. From the twenty-fifth floor view, I can see the tracks of the JR, the commuter rail. The rooftops are punctuated with patches of green—even if they are situated next to a gigantic heating system or satellite dishes, there are park-like seating areas. I see swaths of Astroturf studded with magnolia trees, swirls of ficus arranged to make tiny rooftop arrangements.

My breakfast is a feast for the eyes. First, a small, white ceramic cup of brown tea—hot, but not too hot. There is a stroke of sky blue in the enamel and dots of green, like emerald clouds, hovering above the blue. The table is a dark, almost black, wood. It's now bare, except for a tiny container of soy. The soy container is like a teapot in a doll's set—white enamel with pale blue and gray stripes. A small, onyx square container that holds toothpicks.

Then two wooden boxes—caramel wood—arrive. They are nestled, one atop of each other. I know from experience that the bottom box holds dry seaweed in individual plastic sleeves—it is tasty and salty like a sliver of cracker. The top box holds two tiny bowls. One is white with a red wavy pattern that resembles coral, and the second is white with the same pattern in blue. The red holds sea kelp, while the blue holds pickled Japanese plums—they are sweet at the center but also unbelievably salty too. In a few minutes, the waitress will uncover the boxes with a flourish, like French waiters in movies carrying silver domed trays.

I open the box and steal a taste of seaweed when I think no one is looking. I sip my tea. I write in my journal. I stare out at office workers drinking hot coffee in rooftop gardens and in a few minutes—maybe five? maybe ten?—I am presented with the main event, a mahogany lacquered tray. On it, there are eight small dishes and a pair of chopsticks. There is a bowl of rice and a container of tiny, tiny fishes to sprinkle on top of the rice. They are delicious, so I try not to notice their little eyes. There is a red lacquered bowl of miso soup with tofu. The tofu is not the tasteless square white chunks that I've become used to in Japanese restaurants in the United States. These are discs, round like a spaceship, and they are crispy around the edges as if they have been seared, before being dropped into the hot soup.

In a white bowl with burnt gold enamel, there is a root mountain vegetable drenched in the gelatinous sauce that the Japanese are so fond of. I can't stomach the texture so I don't even try. There is a small serving of scrambled egg, shaped like a Twinkie. And on a traditional blue and white dish, served on an elegantly displayed bamboo leaf, there is a piece of grilled fish that I will eat between pecks of the Japanese pickles and greens that sit on another side dish.

I take a deep breath, inventory complete. As many times as I've had Japanese breakfast, I still begin by counting and marveling at its many pieces, like a kid with a box of Legos. No wonder Japanese women are so thin, I think. With so much to look at, eating seems almost beside the point, like munching Fritos in front of Picasso's *Les Demoiselles D'Avignon*.

My friend Manami is, in so many ways, my Japanese twin. We are both in our thirties, both married for three years, both equally fond of clothes, murder mysteries, and good wine. The other night over dinner at an adorable little tapas place in Ometosando called Red Pepper, Manami-san asked me what Jason and I have for breakfast on a typical morning. I tell her that Jason likes Cocoa Puffs, a happy holdover from his childhood. I like to have turkey bacon and grapefruit. I asked her, "Do you eat Japanese breakfast?" I tell her that Japanese breakfast is one of my favorite things about coming to Japan. No, she says, in the morning, she and her husband have toast and coffee. Immediately, I regret the question. Our lives are so similar, why would I imagine that she would have time, before work, to make miso soup, grilled fish, root vegetables, and scrambled eggs; to lay out pickles and seaweed and plums; not to mention to make the brewed brown tea?

The next day, as I sit in Hanasanshou, the Park Hotel Japanese restaurant where I have been coming for breakfast, I am especially aware of what a treat this meal is. When the plates are put before me and the wooden boxes are uncovered, I begin with the Japanese grace that my husband and I have taken to saying before every meal, whether we are in Japan or not. What we say is, *"Itadakimasu,"* which literally means "I gratefully accept." Then I add another silent prayer for the hands that have prepared this meal, for being able to to start my day in a place of such wonder and peace.

It's just breakfast. But the difference between traditional Japanese breakfast and a bowl of cornflakes is a telling metaphor for the breakneck speed with which the average Japanese city person now lives their life. If you're part of Generation Gamer, equally fluent in Xbox and anime, then life in Tokyo or Osaka and even Sapporo, is just what you'd expect: bullet trains, neon lights, crowds of people that will carry you along like you've just been tossed into a mosh pit at a rock concert. For those of us who grew up watching Kurosawa films in art houses, going to see the cherry blossoms in D.C. and eating sushi in quiet charming Japanese restaurants in the U.S., the expectation is that Japan will be a retreat, a variation on the old Club Med slogan: "the antidote to civilization." Even the Japanese crave this old feeling about Japan; they flock during their holidays to cities like Kyoto where quiet rivers, bonsai and sand gardens, and ancient temples are a salve to the spirit.

Inspired by the "Slow Food" movement that has become so popular internationally, a "Slow Life" movement has captivated Japan. The words are said in English, not translated into Japanese and "slow," in this movement, is a synonym for relaxed, thoughtful, pleasing. At Christmastime, shopkeepers wish me a "slow holiday," which sounds funny at first, but then starts to sound like a really nice idea. *Slow Work, Slow Life* magazine highlights how women can choose and pursue careers that are both interesting, but not stressful. The Victorians believed in the calming, civilizing influence of women. "Slow Work, Slow Life" is distinctly a women's driven movement. It's an effort to counterbalance the frantic, all-consuming pace that most working men deal with in corporate Japan.

Kakegawa City, a town with about 80,000 residents, south of Tokyo, has taken all of this one step further by designating itself a "Slow Life City." In November 2002, more than one hundred events were planned throughout the city to promote "a comfortable lifestyle and a relaxed state of mind." Even the city planners have gotten in on the act, holding referendums on such issues as: "How can we bring the concept of 'Slow Life' into shape in the context of the local adminstration? How can we get support from local businesses to cut working hours and increase holidays, both indispensable to achieve 'slower' lifestyles?" In 2003, Tajimi City, Yasuduka, and Gifu City also held "Slow Life" months.

The Kakegawa Slow Life Declaration is a good insight into the national passion for this movement:

> "In the late twentieth century, Japan valued and pursued the 'fast, cheap, convenient, and efficient' life that brought us economic prosperity. However, it also caused some problems such as dehumanization, social ills, and environmental pollution. We would like to move forward, with the slogan 'Slow Life' to achieve 'slow, relaxed and comfortable' lifestyles, and shift from a society of mass production and mass consumption, to a society that is not hectic and does cherish our possessions and things of the heart.
>
> "Humans live about 700,800 hours (assuming an average life expectancy of 80 years), of which we spend about 70,000 hours working (assuming we work for 40 years). The remaining 630,000 hours are spent on other activities, such as eating, studying, and leisure, including 230,000 hours sleeping. Until now, people often focused their lives on these 70,000 hours of labor, devoting their lives to their companies. However, with the 'Slow Life' principles, we would now like to pay more attention to the 630,000 hours outside of work to achieve true happiness and peace of mind.
>
> "The practice of the 'Slow Life' involves the following eight themes:

1. *Slow Pace:* We value the culture of walking, to be fit and to reduce traffic accidents.
2. *Slow Wear:* We respect and cherish our beautiful traditional costumes, including woven and dyed fabrics, Japanese kimonos, and Japanese night robes (*yukata*)
3. *Slow Food:* We enjoy Japanese food culture, such as Japanese dishes and tea ceremony, and safe local ingredients.
4. *Slow House:* We respect houses built with wood, bamboo, and paper, lasting over one hundred or two hundred years, and are careful to make things durably, and to ultimately conserve our environment.
5. *Slow Industry:* We take care of our forests, through our agriculture and forestry, conduct sustainable farming with human labor, and ultimately spread urban farms and green tourism.
6. *Slow Education:* We pay less attention to academic achievement, and create a society in which people can enjoy arts, hobbies, and sports throughout our lifetimes, and where all generations can communicate well with each other.
7. *Slow Aging:* We aim to age with grace and be self-reliant through our lifetimes.
8. *Slow Life:* Based on the philosophy of life stated above, we live our lives with nature and the seasons, saving our resources and energy."

It sounds wonderful, but how do you incorporate such ideals into contemporary life? When I ask Masako Nara, the manager at Canon, what she thinks about the "Slow Life" movement, she bursts out laughing. It's not that she doesn't find it appealing, it's just that it's hard to squeeze anything "slow" into her life. She then admits that the movement has had an impact on her. "I like walking and thinking," she says. "For relaxation, I sometimes take small trips and I walk a lot."

"In Japan there are roads that were established in ancient times. Tokkaido Road stretches from Tokyo to Kyoto. When I get the chance, I walk this road." Masako stops and thinks about "Slow Life" some more. "I am also learning to play the Japanese flute," she says. "I am forcing myself to take up a hobby because otherwise I would do nothing but work." I wonder how many of us think about a relaxing lifestyle in the same way: first the laughter, "Me? Relax? Who has the time!" then the quiet revelations of what we do and would like to do, if only we could find the time.

The offices of *Slow Work, Slow Life* magazine are situated in a sliver of a building in the Ginza section of Tokyo; it's an edifice so narrow that it seems like a pencil box wedged between the massive office buildings on either side. When I get up to the office of the editor, it is clear that there is no place for us to sit down. She leads me back to the pencil-box elevator, to the top floor, which is a small-size conference room and library. She returns with two cups of green tea, places one before me, and takes a seat.

At thirty-two, Kay Otsuka is almost as old as the publication she now edits. She tells me that the magazine first debuted in 1970 as *The Job Guide for Women*. Women weren't really in the workplace at this time, and the magazine was more of a statistical abstract of how many women worked in different fields. In the 1980s, the magazine was reborn again as *The Catalogue of Female Jobs*. The covers featured illustrations of women dressed as photographers, businesswomen, golfers. It had a very "You've come a long way, baby" feel to it. The magazine became more prescriptive: featuring articles on how women could get a job, how to choose a career field, and what women need to do to get ahead. This second stage of the magazine featured a sixteen-page color insert on career women of the day and maybe two hundred pages of newsprint. Now in its *Slow Work, Slow Life* incarnation, which debuted in 2005, the magazine is all color, all aspirational profiles. "The magazine now features famous women," Kay explains. "Our readers want to know how they got there, and what their lives are like." She says the magazine is called *Slow Work, Slow Life* because the emphasis isn't on corporate Japan. "The focus is on jobs which provide the opportunity for slow life, which is life as they wish."

Kay started working for this women's magazine when she was a university student. "I actually went to university at night," she says. "During the day, I worked here." She worked for the publishing house for four years and really loved her job, but there wasn't a position for her when she graduated. So she took a job with an ad agency. A year later, she saw in the classifieds that the publishing house had an opening for an editor. She applied, got the job, and has now been here for seven years.

She grew up in a family that owned a diner. She's one of the few women that I've interviewed whose father wasn't a salary-man. "My mother worked with my father, from early in the morning," Kay says. "I watched my mother work very hard when I was growing up. Most of my friends came from families with small businesses as well." Kay, who has the well-heeled wardrobe and countenance of a young *Vogue* staffer, says that she never imagined she could be an editor. "In the environment that I grew up in, I couldn't think about a career," she says. "My thought is 'this is work and will always be here.'" She says that ever since her university days, working at the magazine inspired her. "I've been enlightened by these women I read about in these articles," she says.

The quiet pace of a small publishing house suits her. *Slow Work, Slow Life* is published just once a year, in a volume as thick as a telephone book. "My idea about work is quite simple," Kay says. "It would be a joy if I could work all of my life. There are many women who change their careers to have more time, more quality. I've already found it."

As an editor at a magazine about women and work, Kay has been tracking the rumblings of this revolution for seven years. "In the early stages, it was just a small number of women who had careers at big companies. In the beginning, they got a lot of attention from the media," she explains. "Nowadays, women working for small and medium companies are quite active. The biggest growth is in women who have started their own businesses. They have chosen to have more time and a schedule they can arrange for themselves. Women are becoming more flexible and better at arranging their lives, so they can live as they wish."

The key for women around the world, of course, is how to balance the private and the professional life. Kay points out that there's somewhat of an answer in how we talk about our jobs. You may never meet a woman who says, "I've got a perfectly balanced life." But as in music, the true melody can be found in the silence between the notes. "The early career women pushed us to do what they did—work really really hard," Kay says. "Their motto was *"Gambate!"* or "Go for it!" Today, women are working hard, they are just not showing their sweat as a badge of honor."

While she says that more and more recent university graduates are finding a place in big companies, entrepreneurship is the most satisfying path for a smart, ambitious woman. "What editing this magazine has taught me is that women who have the power and energy to do it, choose to open their own businesses," she says. "These women are just not going to wait for corporate Japan to change. The crucial point is that women need to take care of themselves and they need to feel like they are most important. Traditionally, Japanese women don't really put their wishes ahead of a man's. You know the stereotype, not really outspoken, very obedient."

There's a term for the this kind of woman, *yamato-nodeshiko,* which means "nice, sensitive, polite woman who follows." Kay says, "That's the kind of women who was appreciated in Japan. I'm not sure when that tradition changed, or if it has really changed. But the women we feature in our magazine express what they want by speaking out. At first, women were afraid to speak out. If they wanted to do a job, they didn't know how to make their dreams come true. But they found that when they spoke out, they were guided onto the right track."

I ask Kay about her role models. She says that while she finds the Harvard- and Oxford-educated Crown Princess Masako to be an intriguing figure, ultimately, "Masako is too high. Her starting point is too different from mine for me to admire her." She mentions a couple of American actresses she likes: "Gwyneth Paltrow and Jodie Foster." She also mentions two Japanese actresses: Nanoko Hitoshima and Hitomi Kroker. Both women are married with children, and as such, they are seen as examples of how you can balance motherhood and a career. "They are beautiful, even moments after labor," Kay says, mimicking the media's breathless reportage of these actresses' lives. "The mass media wants to establish their status as the role models. And they are nice, but they are not my role models." She says, in general, she is disappointed by Japanese celebrities. "When they are young, they express strong opinions about many things," she says. "Suddenly, when they get popular and are being handled by producers and agents and marketers, they have nothing to say."

Jewelry designer Yoko Shimizu, however, has plenty to say. She's in her early forties, with rock-star hair, bright blue turquoise stone rings, a black leather jacket with asymmetrical lapels, and four long silver necklaces hanging from her delicate neck. Her company, Balance +, sells Yoko's designs, both as completed jewelry you can buy as is and as jewelry kits, which you can assemble yourself. This "do-it-yourself" idea is new to Japan and Yoko has come along with the right idea at the right time. Thirty-five thousand individual users visit her Web site every day. Her office in the chic Aoyama neighborhood is bustling with more than a dozen employees. And because she understands that trends move quickly in Japan, she puts new designs and new kits on her Web site every week. The inspiration for her business, she tells me, was simple. "I love jewelry. I love stones," she says. "In Japan, there are many kinds of jewelry shops. But the kind of jewelry that is sold in shops is too childish for women in their thirties and forties to wear. I felt like I could step into the gap."

She had the background to do it, having designed jewelry for a popular Japanese brand called 4° as well as for Sotheby's. She had also been a graphic designer as well as produced events for the Guggenheim Museum. "All along, jewelry has been my focus," she says. "I needed to work as an employee. But I was unsatisfied because I have my own ideas and my own creativity. I let people know about my ideas and I started to make jewelry. I have a lot of friends who are editors and stylists; they got my stuff out there. Then I just went with the flow." Four years ago, she launched her own company. Soon after she published her first book called *Beads and Accessories*.

"The term 'balance' is quite important to me," Yoko says. "Having dealt with major companies like Sotheby's and Agnes B, I know how jewelry comes to the market. I always wanted to do my own original brand, even if it's a small one. I know that a small-size business is quite important these days. But it means I have to deal with many things: finances, managing staff, being a mother. I have to make the most appropriate balance. Otherwise, this place will go bankrupt. The people here will lose their jobs if I lose the balance between my professional focus and my creativity."

Balance + employs twenty-four people over all, including several part-time workers, who work from home. "My husband handles the Web site," Yoko explains. "It's updated twice a week because I try to release a new series of jewelry twice a week. It gives the impression to the public that there is always something new." With the exception of her husband, the entire staff is female. Yoko says this is both exciting and sometimes frustrating. "The women who have families choose to be part-time workers," she explains. For a small company, these workers are a boon as "they tend to be highly qualified and trained in jewelry design. One of the part-time workers is a former general manager for 4°." As a mother, Yoko is sympathetic to the desire for a flexible schedule and allows the women to choose their own hours, and to choose whether they work at the office or at home. Yet, she wishes she could attract the best and the brightest of these women to work for her full-time, like the former general manager. "She is highly talented, but she's so busy with her family, she'd rather work from home," Yoko says. "She's not interested in being as deeply involved with the brand as I'd hoped."

That's the businesswoman speaking. As the mother of a six-year-old, Yoko would never tell a woman to choose working for her over spending time with her family. "For the first two years after my daughter was born, I had the hardest time I've ever had in my life," Yoko says. "I was at the office until 6 P.M. Then from 6 to 9 P.M., I spent time with my daughter. Once I got her to sleep, I started working again until two or three in the morning. Then I started back at the office at 7 A.M. Plus, I was making dinner for the family. I began to realize that I was becoming ill. My eyesight started to go. I just turned forty-four; age matters too. I had to change my lifestyle. The business is important, but the job of being a mother is important, too. My daughter and my job have to coexist. They are both indispensable to my life. Even if I want to work after 9 P.M., I don't now. I go to bed when my daughter goes to bed. I wake up at 5 A.M. and if necessary, earlier than that. But I go to bed at 9 P.M."

Yoko made even more changes. She hired a mother's helper who comes in three times a week—not an easy thing to do in a country where nannies and maids are not common, even among the elite. "In Japan, domesticity is important to the identity of a woman," Yoko says. "If you skip it, you get a bad reputation. But since I've outsourced my domestic work, I have more intimate time with my daughter because the helper cooks."

You'll recall that in Japan, there's a difference between day care, which is public and reasonably priced, versus kindergarten, which is private and expensive. When Yoko's daughter was five, she enrolled her in kindergarten. Her daughter, now six, attends a regular public school. From Yoko's perspective, the private school provided a better situation for working moms. "The kindergarten my daughter attended was attached to Tokyo University," Yoko explains. "It was quite elite. Almost all the mothers at that school have quite high positions. These mothers have the same kind of demanding lives and they are sympathetic to each other." In the elementary school, the situation is different. "At my daughter's elementary school, it's common practice that mothers do everything for the kids," Yoko says, voicing complaints that are universal to working mothers. "They have meetings in the daytime when I can't possibly attend. They don't care about your schedule. At the private school, the husbands were quite supportive and understanding; it's almost always the fathers who drop the kids off in the morning. At the public school, it's the mothers."

Public school has upset the delicate balance of Yoko's life. "I've been under some deep pressure because of the environment at the elementary school," Yoko says. "I can't provide the time the way the other mothers do and I feel really depressed sometimes, even self-hatred. I can't even name the feeling that comes from inside of me."

Yoko introduces me to her husband, Aki. He is tall, with a similar rock-star kind of haircut. He's wearing a black sweatshirt, square glasses, more SoHo than salaryman. He's sympathetic to Yoko's plight and actually takes the role of point person for their daughter, Rinna. It's Aki who manages the day-to-day needs of their daughter's life. "Even in the twenty-first century, in this society, the preference is for men to work and for women to take care of the family," he says. "I don't think that way because I manage this jewelry brand with my wife. The areas where we are strong are quite clear and well defined between us. I'm better at accounting and recruitment, so that's what I do. Yoko's genius is design and public relations. If two people can get together and create one thing, then isn't that better? At home, I don't do the cooking because I'm not good at it. But I can clean and I can be the nanny for my daughter, so that's what I do."

It's Aki who attends most of the parent-teacher conferences. He sits on the school committees and attends the majority of Rinna's events. But it's not easy for a man to step into these roles in Japan, even if they're something he really wants to do. "I have to face a lot of discrimination," Aki says. "It comes from the other mothers, but it's the teachers, too. When they call and I say that I'm the representative of the family, I'm always rejected. They say, 'Can I talk to the mother?' It's like Yoko doesn't have a name. She's just the mother. If they want cookies or something for school and I offer to bring them, they say, 'No thank you.' They want the mother to do it.

When I go to meetings and events at the school, I'm always isolated. Sometimes, it's really unbelievable the way things work."

Since Aki is in charge of recruitment for the company, women and work is something he's thought a lot about. "I want to give women opportunities," he says. "But at the same time, I need to hire people who are deeply committed to this industry. I shouldn't say this, but when I hire a young woman, I'm thinking, 'Does she really want a career? Or is she going to quit when she gets married?'"

Yoko says that she believes that young women today are more conservative than women who are in their seventies and eighties. "Our grandmother's generation really valued having their own work," Yoko says. "Women now are more conservative; when they have a child, they tend to quit. That is the trend these days." Aki says that because in a small company you can't afford the high turnover and training of a constantly changing workforce, sometimes they believe that the solution is to hire more men, which is of course its own form of discrimination.

Aki says that while many people are surprised that he chooses to work for his wife, in a company where she is the president and CEO, he is more concerned with the idea of partnership than he is with titles or status. "With Yoko and I, you get two for the price of one," he says. "The most basic instinct is to choose someone who has a different kind of nature so you can complement each other. That's what we've done, in our marriage and in our work."

Yoko believes that more men have the same kind of insight that her husband does, but as a woman, it's still difficult to reach for equality in a society that just doesn't support it. "Even if your ideas are perfectly in synch, and you're lucky enough to be married to a supportive husband, you have mixed feelings," Yoko says. "You deal with people like the mothers at Rinna's elementary school and you still feel that somehow, you're not performing the roles you are meant to perform. The thing about balance is that by nature it suggests a compromise. I called my company Balance+ because I'm seeking more than balance. I'm looking to achieve an environment where I can feel more successful than the term balance implies on its own."

Two hours outside of Tokyo, in a residential town called Saitama, there's a café called Choco Bagel shop. The owner is a young woman called Tomoko Yachi, and the café is located on the first floor of her hosue. Tomoko has auburn hair and she's dressed in the casual-but-funky style of a woman who does a lot of running around but really, really loves clothes. She is wearing a white lace shirt underneath a black cardigan. She's also wearing khaki pants with a long black skirt thrown over them. Her café, which she and her husband built all by themselves, including all the construction and painting, is an homage to shabby chic. It's more like the kind of place you'd find in a beachside community in the Hamptons than in a town so spread out that the taxi driver cannot find it amidst all the fields. Everything is decorated in shades of white from yellowish cream to the palest caramel: clapboard walls, muslin curtains, painted wooden floors, chairs, and tables. The café actually grew out of a small fancy-foods gift shop (the only place in Saitama, for example, where you can buy caviar and Sarabeth's jam) that Tomoko runs in the converted barn next to the house.

"After running the store next door for a year, I realized that many customers with kids wanted a comfortable place to sit and have a cup of tea," Tomoko says. "I myself was hesitant to go to cafés with my own daughter, so I wanted to provide a safe space for my customers and that's what this is." Tomoko's store has been open for four years, and the café has been open for three.

The main café room is off of Tomoko's kitchen; she knocked down a wall to open the space. Next to that is the children's room, filled with child-size desks, toys, and baskets of books. To the front of the house, there's an exhibition area where Tomoko shows local artists. "I wanted it to be comfortable," Tomoko says. "We take off our shoes here; this is, after all, my house." There is no formal distinction between the café and the rest of the house, just a staircase in the back that leads to the living quarters. "I wanted to provide a space where mothers would feel good about bringing their children," she says. "When children take off their shoes, they feel very safe; it's like they are visiting friends. The mothers can relax because they can look into the next room and see their children playing with toys and books."

As Tomoko pours me a cup of *yuzu* tea, Japanese citrus rinds steamed with honey, and pours herself a cup of coffee, I realize that she is living the *Slow Work, Slow Life* ideal that I have been longing for since I first came to Japan. She laughs when I tell her that I've completely changed my own life plan. I want to move to Saitama and open up a café. She goes into another room and returns with a stack of books that were her inspiration in opening up the shop and later, the café. The titles range from *The Relaxed Home* to *Family Living* to *At Peace at Home*. Tomoko says, "I thought a lot about the kind of environment I wanted to create for my work life. I have so many responsibilities. I'm married, I have a career, I have a child. I think it's very important for me to have fun while I'm doing my work. Taking care of my daughter, especially, is a lot of hard work and responsibility."

The café is open only three days a week, from 11 A.M. to 4 P.M. Tomoko planned the hours around her daughter's school schedule. As if on cue, seven-year-old Natsumi—whose name means "summer ocean" Tomoko tells me—comes bouncing in. One of the two employees at work in the café makes Natsumi a cup of hot chocolate and she happily starts on her homework. Tomoko still remembers the days when the café sat empty for days at a time. Now, she says, it's very successful. "I feel so sad because in the beginning, I could remember all the customers names and faces," Tomoko says. "Now I just smile because I have no idea who all of these women are."

Tomoko grew up in Saitama. Her parents owned a soba restaurant, not far from her own café. "When I was my daughter's age," she remembers fondly. "I was always talking to the customers and bringing them tea. I really liked the soba place. When I was a girl, on Saturdays, school finished at noon. The only thing I hated was that they served soba every Saturday at school. I was sick of soba!" Her whole family worked at the restaurant and her grandmother made tempura. "As a woman, I grew up knowing that my mother and grandmother were working, so for me it was very natural that I would one day work too," she says. "My husband does not have very conventional ideas about women staying home to do housework. He understands that I have to work outside of the home."

Tomoko's Choco Bagel Shop and Café has not only made her an entrepreneur, but created opportunities for other women in the community as well. The café has two employees and the shop employs one other full-time employee. "All of the employees are working mothers," Tomoko says. "If they have special events, sporting events, a meeting at the school, we discuss it among the workers and we adjust the schedule. I can understand their situation because I'm a mother, too. As a working mother, I'm really concerned about all of my employees' kids. If it were a regular company, it would be very hard to say, 'I've got to go home. I'm concerned because my kid is sick.'" Tomoko's daughter comes in and takes a seat on her lap. At the same time that Tomoko is understanding of her employees' situation as working mothers, she has no problem dealing with other management issues that may arise, be it tardiness or poor performance. "I'm very frank," Tomoko says. "I say what I need to say as a boss. I consider the staff to be not just employees, but my business partners. If something is hurting the business, I'm going to bring it up."

She says that having the café open three days a week, "is the perfect schedule for me. Because the café is open three days a week, I can concentrate on my work and give it my full focus." On Mondays, she prepares for the week. She spends a great deal of the day baking cakes and making lunches. The café is open Tuesdays, Wednesdays, and Thursdays. Fridays, she says, "are just for me. Sometimes I visit other cafés, sometimes I just stay at home and relax. Saturdays and Sundays are for my family." She admits that she doesn't manage to have every Friday to herself, but she makes it a priority, "at least twice a month." I know it's hard work, but it also sounds idyllic. The "Slow Life" movement comes to life.

9

MEN IN THE KITCHEN

How Japanese Male Roles Are Changing

I f the legions of Japanese women bucking tradition might be referred to as kickboxing geishas, what can we say about the men? Although easily grouped together as corporate samurai—the multitude of salarymen, young and old, who are still wedded to corporate Japan, don't study foreign languages and have little understanding, or use, for the world outside of their powerful island—the truth is much more complex. Women in the workplace liberate men in the workplace as researcher Mariko Fujiwara put it, and in the process, men are trying out new roles: from househusband to the increasingly popular male geisha.

I think of something that Rochelle Kopp, author of *The Rice Paper Ceiling*, told me. She says, "In Japanese opinion polls, most men want to be reborn as women or birds." It seems like an inconsequential thing, the kind of "research" you'd read in a tabloid, but you have to remember that Japan is a country where people answer questions carefully and thoughtfully. It's also a nation whose religion honors both Buddhism and

Shinto rites. The Buddhist nature of Japan means that one takes the question of reincarnation seriously. The symbolism of women with birds is more than an Austin Powers colloquialism. Ironically, in Japanese society women and birds are believed to be the most free. "Women have more power. Compared to before, we are more aggressive," says Etsuko Adachi, principal ballerina with the Tokyo City Ballet. "Now women have more energy than men. Maybe, before, we tried to hide our talent and ability. But now we're not interested in hiding. I think it's surprising to men."

Perhaps no group has been caught more off guard than middle-aged men. The twentysomethings who make up the majority of those seeking Narita rikon, or Narita divorce, have nothing on the divorce figures of their parents who are swelling the courtrooms seeking *jukunen rikon,* or mature-age divorce. The situation goes something like this. You are a Japanese housewife married for forty years to a hard-working salaryman. Every day of your entire adult life, he left for work before you woke up. When he came home late at night, his suit reeked of cigarettes and alcohol and maybe the perfume of the girls at the hostess clubs. Now he's retired. He sits around all day. There are a number of terms to describe a retired man in Japan, and none of them are nice. "Wet leaves" is the clingy kind of husband, named for the wet leaves that are notoriously hard to sweep from your doorstep. "Oversize trash" is another name for a husband who is a burden in retirement, so called because in Japan, you must pay extra to have heavy trash items hauled away. Your husband is a burden, but you on the other hand, are living in the prime of your life.

Inspired by the charismatic housewives you see on TV, you are sixty and sexy. You've studied French and take regular shopping trips abroad with your girlfriends. You've raised two kids—maybe one of them is a parasite single, but that's okay;

she's a good girl and a lot of fun to hang out with. You start to think, "Why do I need my husband?" In Japan, there's no such thing as joint ownership. If you own a house, or a car, it will most likely be in your husband's name. But if you've been a dutiful wife; if you've contributed to the birthrate by bearing children, the courts will take sympathy on you—they'll give you half of your husband's pension and half of the family's savings. If you're the average Japanese family, you've been salting away 25 percent of your husband's income for forty years. Even in these tough economic times, that's quite a gold mine. Plenty for a charismatic housewife to go out on her own and enjoy life. "The guys are paying the price because they didn't do anything in the house," explains Mami Iwakimi, the sociologist who specializes in family relations at Sacred Heart University. "They didn't take any domestic responsibility. They seldom had any communications with their wives. The wives have been patient all these years."

There's another way to look at it. You are a long-suffering salaryman. For forty years, you work, literally, from dusk to dawn. At the end of the week, you hand over your paycheck to your wife (as most salarymen do) as she manages the household budget. She gives you an allowance of 1,000 yen a day (about $10,000). There's even a name for your kind of man: a "thousand yen man," a term that implies a man who is henpecked; "you'll take your thousand yen a day and you'll like it!" At work, you don't take a proper lunch; you slop noodles quickly at a counter while standing in a nearby soba shop. On your way back to your office, you see the *yukan madamu*— ladies who lunch. At some of the finer restaurants in Japan, you'll see no men during lunchtime, only women who have the leisure and the means. You are filled with jealousy. You are working your tail off, while these women are enjoying a 5,000 yen lunch. You think one day, in the not too distant future, you'll be retired. You'll take your wife out to a 5,000 yen lunch, or maybe you'll go on a weekend trip to the hot springs town she's been dropping hints about for years. Finally, the day of your retirement arrives. Your wife announces that she is leaving you. You've heard her complaints for years, but you've had your complaints, too. You've sacrificed everything so you can enjoy your golden years together. You never expected what was waiting for you at the end of forty years of twelve-hour days and a three-hour daily commute was to grow old without your beloved by your side.

In 1963, the director Akira Kurosawa made a film called *High and Low*. In the picture, which paired the director with his long-time colleague, movie star Toshiro Mifune, a man is in the midst of a high-stakes bid to take over the shoe company he worked for since he was sixteen years old. On the eve of the takeover, the man, Kingo Gondo (played by Mifune) receives a phone call: His son is being held ransom and will be killed unless Gondo pays an enormous ransom. (The film was actually remade in the nineties as *Ransom* starring Mel Gibson.) There is no question that Gondo will pay the money. Then he finds out the crooks have botched the job. They have kidnapped the chauffeur's son instead and so the drama begins. Does Gondo choose his financial future or the old ways of moral integrity and honor? It's a film that symbolizes Japan at a crossroads, between becoming a fast-paced world power and being a nation of emperors, samurai and geishas. Contemporary men are at a similar crossroads. They can hang on stubbornly to the old ways, or they can follow the women down a new path. Whether you see the old ways as heaven and the new way as hell, depends a lot on each individual man and his willingness to embrace change.

* * *

In 2000, close to 42,000 couples who had been married more than twenty years divorced. This is more than double the figures for 1985, when 20,000 such couples divorced. The numbers themselves don't seem startling by U.S. standards, but they reflect a huge shift for Japan where divorce, especially among older couples, has always been low. With seven million salarymen expected to retire between 2007 and 2009, it's understandable why the *jukunen rikon* has caused such a panic. If the numbers continue to increase, more and more Japanese men who might have fantasized about spending their golden years with their wives are going to be left out in the cold.

Jukunen rikon, or mature-age divorce, has become such a phenomenon that it is even the subject of a sexy nighttime soap opera. Think *Desperate Housewives* meets *Dynasty.* In these frothy divertimentos, the long-suffering housewife blossoms like Cinderella after the ball: she has her own money, she can see the world, and she has her friends and her hobbies. She's kicked loose of the ball and chain that was weighing her down. All over the country, women are following suit. The *Shukan Post* reported, "Growing numbers of middle-aged Japanese men, unceremoniously dumped by long suffering wives, are discovering that what they had believed were old nags are actually thoroughbreds."

These numbers are expected to increase in 2007, when the government will ensure that divorcing wives of retirees not only receive half of their basic pension, but also half of the man's retirement payout bonus: a figure that can be much greater than the pension alone. The National Institute of Population and Social Security worries about these men, not only emotionally but physically. Their studies show that the average sixty-year-old retiree in Japan can expect to live an additional twenty-five years. But a man who is left by his wife, at age sixty, can expect to only live an additional twenty years.

Tsugaya Araki, from the Family Counseling Service in Japan, explained it to reporters this way: "Women tend to have a well-balanced, nutritious diet. When left alone guys are more inclined to eat what they like and in large quantities. They also tend to drink more, often through loneliness brought on by the end of their marriage. This can create problems with internal organs like the liver. Many older men fall into depression following a divorce. This can lead to suicide. Even mild depression can prompt them to stop looking after themselves and invite all sorts of other health problems."

Hoping to stave off *jukunen rikon,* and maybe just a little fearing for their lives, a group of retired businessmen meet in Tokyo for cooking lessons. They call themselves "Men in the Kitchen" and members don burgundy aprons with their logo, a grinning little boy with a chef's toque on his head. The logo makes me think of what Professor Iwakima told me about these Japanese men whose wives leave them: "The guys never really mature." I went to a meeting of "Men in the Kitchen" to talk to them about the tremendous changes in their lives.

It's Friday night at a community center in western Tokyo, and the men in the kitchen are raring to go. They are all in their fifties and sixties and they get together like this once a month. At first, there are no more than a dozen men, but little by little more arrive; some of the ones wearing business suits and carrying briefcases have not quite hit retirement age. Others are dressed in a kind of formal casual wear—shirts, ties, and sweater vests—very Fred MacMurray in *My Three Sons.* Mr. Kondo, one of the group's founders, is giving the lesson tonight, although he explains to me that typically the group is instructed by a professional chef. Mr. Kondo is sixty-nine and has been retired for nine years. He worked for an electronics company, and from

1970 to 1975, he was posted in Taiwan. It was there that he developed a passion for Chinese food. He'll be instructing the group on how to make three Chinese dishes tonight.

The men settle down around a U-shaped formation of tables. They work in groups of three and take their work very seriously, studying the instruction sheets Mr. Kondo has passed out, carefully arranging the plates of squid, red peppers, pork, and bok choy as if they were preparing for a photo shoot for *Food & Wine* magazine. Even before the first ingredient hits the pan, there's a swarm of picture-taking of the raw ingredients, of the men in their aprons. A large element of *jukunen rikon* is that the retired salaryman has little or no social network; the colleagues and clients that he spent his days, nights, and even vacations with were a function of his job, not his personal life. It's easy to see, after only a few minutes, what a huge social refuge the "Men in the Kitchen" group is. The group is markedly different from the flower-arranging courses I've attended in Japan, where the women listen in respectful silence. Among this group of men, there is much calling out and confirming of directions, ingredients, nicknames, and playful name-calling. I notice that they welcome newcomers like long-lost friends— or perhaps, it's even deeper. They recognize one another as refugees from an older time, in this new and confusing world in which women are running their own businesses, aren't having babies, and don't care if they are stale Christmas cake.

The surprising thing is that there are actually a couple of women who are members of "Men in the Kitchen." Mr. Kondo tells me that the group is open to everybody and that women are welcome to come. I have a hard time getting anybody to comment on the women beyond this general comment: "The group is open to everybody." But I will tell you this: both of the women were in their late fifties, early sixties. They were impeccably dressed and in full makeup for the evening course. Both of them were single and they made a point of not being in the same group. It's my own personal opinion that they were two of the smartest women in Japan. In this age of *jukunen rikon*, what better place to suss out what type of fish other women had tossed back in than a place like "Men in the Kitchen"?

Kyosuke Shimeda is, at forty-three, a little young for "Men in the Kitchen." I learn that he works for a manufacturing company that builds kitchen equipment. "I'm here to do research on what sort of kitchen would be suitable for men who cook," he says. "I assume that more men will be cooking in the future, for fun. Not because it's a duty or a chore." If this group of men is part of a larger trend, then Shimeda wants to be able to help his company cash in on it. Although he admits that he doesn't actually cook at home, this first-time "Men in the Kitchen" visitor looks like he's having a good time.

Akimasa Asahitani is a sixty-three-year-old retired salesman. He's sharply dressed in a crisp white shirt and a gray sweater vest. A member of the group for four years, he says, "My work was quite hard, selling products. After retirement, I can enjoy a relaxing time. I liked having my own life. But I didn't know what to do with all the time. Now I can come here and cook." He tells me that he used to be a Boy Scout: "I've always enjoyed cooking." He feels that in retirement, he's finally beginning to get in synch with his wife. "Generally speaking, in my generation, salarymen work late and they have drinking parties they have to attend," Akimasa tells me. "My wife, generally speaking, has more time. She makes clothes for my granddaughter. She has her gardening and volunteer work." Now he has something to add to the mix: his cooking, in particular, "I like to grill vegetables and meat."

Yagi's life is different. As an architect, he's a freelance worker. He's in his mid-fifties, but he doesn't plan on retiring anytime soon. His passion is designing restaurants. Most recently, he designed a soba noodle shop in Ueno. Before he designed that shop, he visited more than fifty noodle restaurants across Japan so he could figure out the best design. Yagi has been coming to "Men in the Kitchen" for four months. Like most of the other men in the group, he doesn't cook very much at home. But he's happy to be learning and his wife is happy that he comes here. "My wife says that when she cooks every day, there's no diversity," Yagi explains. "She wants me to learn some special dishes that she can try, things she might have never learned otherwise."

I talk to Ms. Fumie Okamato, who is one of the assistant teachers for "Men in the Kitchen." She's a big supporter of the group and has been coming for more than eight years. When she first came, it was originally to accompany her son, who she thought might benefit from learning how to cook. "He was single then, but he's married now," she says, with a sly grin. She's a smart woman: a man who can cook, and is willing to do it, becomes a very desirable bachelor in Japan. "He left the group, but I kept staying. It's a good place to make friends who like to eat and who like to cook. Everybody can improve their lives. It's a good opportunity for men to be more liberal, have more freedom, be less traditional."

"I was almost the first member of this group," Mr. Kondo tells me. He is the instructor for the evening. He is also, I notice, the only man who wears a chef's toque. "It is unavoidable for men to be interested in cooking. Japan is getting into a period of long-life expectancy. Men are exploring more opportunities to have fun in their life, and part of that is cooking." As if on cue, when Mr. Kondo says "fun," a guy in a black turtleneck wheels in a shopping basket with two of the biggest bottles of sake I have ever seen in my life. I learn that the group publishes a newsletter, and that many members write stories and draw cartoons for the publication. Mr. Kondo tells me that he understands the phenomenon of *jukunen rikon* and the ways things are changing for men in Japan. This group, he insists, is not merely composed of men who are afraid of the statistics. "It's not just what you read in the papers," he says. "These are men who are exploring the new opportunities for men; these are men who welcome diversity."

Takeo Kami is twenty-six and works in finance. Today, though, he's casually dressed in a gray turtleneck, jeans, and gray sneakers. Although he's young, he's no fan of the way things were in Japan before women started kicking up dust. "My dad was a normal salaryman and he worked really late hours," Takeo says. "So my mom was the one who nurtured me. I lived in New York and Switzerland as a child and even on the weekends my dad played golf with clients, so I was pretty much raised by a single mother."

Takeo met his wife in graduate school. She's from a rural area of Japan. Her father is in agriculture and her mother was a housewife. One of the things he found so attractive about his wife, Takeo says, is that "she just grew up without caring really about money or materialistic things. But her parents taught her very well to be motivated, to be ambitious in life. She went to one of the best undergraduate schools in Japan, and then went to graduate school where we met, and now she's also in finance." Takeo says that from the beginning, he encouraged his wife to look beyond the traditional roles. Having lived abroad, he had an appreciation for having a partner who's an equal that even young men in Japan still haven't recognized. "She is really smart and talented," Takeo explains. "I said it's okay not to be the Japanese conventional role. It's better for the whole world if she uses her talents and adds that value."

He says he can see a marked difference between his wife

and other female friends he made in graduate school. "All of the female friends I made in Japan are still very subordinate," he says. "Even in the media or just in normal soap operas. You have the strong Japanese woman role, like the career woman role, but for the most part, they're still in the household. I think that's why I respect and married my wife. She got out of that box and did what she wanted to do. I respect women— even housewives—it's awesome that they do what they do, but I think it's very respectable for someone to do just what they want to do rather than what society tells them to do."

Not to say that the life of a liberated man in a liberated marriage is easy. Takeo says, "I think she has it really easy. She can be dominant when she wants to be dominant, she can be subordinate when she wants to be subordinate. Usually she becomes subordinate when the going gets rough, so I have to take it up the ass instead." Meaning? "The most clear example was when we were preparing for our wedding and she didn't want any children to be at our wedding. This occurred about a month before. She said, 'I want you to tell your dad that I don't want any kids there.' So I tell my father and he just starts yelling, 'What the fuck? Why are you saying that? You don't show any appreciation toward anything.' If I had said. 'No, it's my wife that wants it that way,' it would have made things worse. So I just had to say, 'I'm sorry, it was me, I was being immature.' I think those are the times that I have to stick up for her and defend her. So it's usually in times of hardship that I have to be the man."

So what do his parents think about his career woman wife? "Oh, they love her," Takeo says. "They love the fact that she's very opinionated, she has a goal that she's always working hard toward. I think those are the attributes that they really enjoy about her."

It used to be that from cradle to career, boys in Japanese

society were protected. They were coddled simply because they were going to be men, and to be a man in Japanese society meant you were automatically granted a certain status. Now that things are changing, corporate Japan won't promise you lifetime employment, your parents are off worrying about middle-aged divorce, guys are much more on their own. In this sense, things are becoming increasingly equal. Takeo says he counts on his wife to inspire him, "I think one of the things that I like about my wife is that I'm lazy. I'm not very career oriented or goal oriented so when I have a woman like her, she lets me know that I have to be something more, that I have to do something more."

Shiya Aoki has also had the experience of becoming something more through his wife. A career diplomat, fifty-two-year-old Shiya grew up in the Shiga prefecture near Kyoto. He's spent his life traveling for the Japanese foreign ministry: ten years in Singapore, three years in Bangkok, three years in Sydney. Married for twenty-five years, he met his wife when she was in the Japanese version of the Peace Corps, teaching Japanese in Thailand. "At the time, I was a diplomat and third secretary at the Japanese embassy in Bangkok." After his marriage, Shiya was transferred to Houston, Texas, where his daughter was born. After the family returned to Japan, he and his wife had two more children, a girl and a boy. It was around this time that life for the globe-trotting young family really got interesting.

"The Gulf War broke out and the Japanese government announced the Japanese contribution to the Gulf War and said we were to support the American government," Shiya explains. "I worked until very late, until 3 or 4 A.M. and my wife had complaints; she says she felt like a single mother with three babies. So my wife suddenly decided to study, to continue as a career woman, to study at postgraduate school. She stayed with her father and mother, and then I had to go to Singapore."

In a move that would be unusual, even for the U.S., Shiya left his wife to continue with her studies and took his three children with him abroad. For the next ten years, his wife focused on her career in international development, moving from a post in India to South Africa, from South Africa to Laos, from Laos to Cambodia. Shiya says, "So I was a house-husband and I took care of three kids abroad."

At this time, Shiya was continuing his own career as a diplomat. He and the kids lived on their own in Singapore, Sydney, and Bangkok. "In the morning I was very busy," he says. "So I woke up at 5:30 A.M. and prepared three lunch boxes for my kids. I then made breakfast for the children and for myself. In the evenings, I often had dinner with the guests—ambassadors, presidents, etc., so before I left in the morning, I prepared dinner for the kids." He laughs, then just so that I'm clear he says, "Before leaving my home to work at the office I had to prepare lunch boxes, breakfast, and dinner for three kids—*and* clean up the dishes." By the time the family returned to Japan, his children—ages fifteen, fourteen, and twelve—thought having a Japanese dad who did all the cooking and cleaning was the most natural thing in the world.

While Shiya's life is different from his father's, in his family, change has been brewing for generations. "My parents had the experience of stay in Manchuria, China, before World War II, so my family always had an international atmosphere where the husband is helpful to the wife. But it was not the same case as me. I was the househusband taking care of three children." He speaks with an obvious pride of his own accomplishments. "My father never prepared meals for children."

As for his own family, the long separations brought on by

him and his wife pursuing their individual careers took a toll. He's very happy that they are both living and working in the same country again. "I saw the American movie *Kramer vs. Kramer*," Shiya says, referencing a film I haven't seen or thought of in ages. "It is not easy for a couple to work and I understand it is not easy for ladies to work in an office *and* look after the children. I think it's very important for husband and wife to have a sense of balance. But sometimes it is difficult to spare much time for family." He also sees more men following his example. "Actually my colleague and my friend, he divorced but he married a second time. He is at the ministry of foreign affairs but he put in, and was granted, a request for a one-year leave for his family for a baby. He is home and his wife is working outside the home."

I was perusing magazines in Shinagawa station when I saw an unusual image. On the cover of a magazine, there was a young Japanese guy, playing with his kid. No big deal in the States, but in five years of coming to Japan, I'd hardly ever seen any father-child images: not on television, not in magazines, not in subway advertisements or billboards. I bought the magazine, *Nikkei Kids,* and learned that this was the debut issue of the magazine, and the theme of the launch was fatherhood. Shiya Aoki, the career diplomat who took his three kids to Singapore so his wife could finish her postgraduate degree, is the exception to a very hard and fast rule in Japan. The average Japanese man, the statistics say, spends ten minutes a day on housework and seventeen minutes a day with his children. When I told people about *Nikkei Kids,* they were unimpressed. It's one thing to put out a special issue of a magazine about fathers spending time with their kids, but it's a whole other thing to make Japanese men actually do it.

Kazuo Ojima is the editor-in-chief of *Nikkei Kids*. He's forty-three, dressed in a cashmere blazer, khakis, and a white shirt, no tie. Before launching *Nikkei Kids* in October 2005, he spent six years as the editor of *Nikkei Trendy*. Parenting magazines are a new phenomenon in Japan. Ojima focused on fatherhood to make waves. "I wanted to provide a message that is more entertaining for the readers," he says. "We wanted to send the message to men that raising kids can be more fun, unlike the traditional ideas that raising kids can be a burden or some kind of job that has to be split by the married couple. The idea is that they should share this work by distributing it bit by bit," Kazuo says. "Housework and childcare. This magazine is going to introduce a new idea about raising kids—that it can be fun and parents and kids can enjoy many things together."

"In this country so far there have not been specific magazines targeting men, at least that we can think of," he says. "There have been many magazines targeting mothers and they predominantly have pictures of mothers and kids and the readers are mostly women. This magazine is new in appealing to both mothers and fathers and letting them know what raising kids is all about and that raising kids can be done by both."

It seems to make sense that a parenting magazine aimed at both men and women would come from the former editor of *Nikkei Trendy*. Kazuo says that while he was there, he discovered that despite the oft-quoted statistic—that the average Japanese father spends seventeen minutes a day with his kid—Japanese fathers would like to spend more time with their children. He points to the fact that more and more Japanese men are buying toys for their children, when gift shopping was once the sole province of mothers. Amusement parks are also reporting an increase in attendance by fathers and their children, when as recent as a decade ago, it was just mothers and their kids. "There was an image of Japanese fathers as workaholics,"

Kazuo says. "On the weekend, they just go home and rest, not spending time with the family. But now this is changing. This is not entirely true of every family, but there is this shift in which fathers want to return to their families and spend more time with them. This tendency is on the rise and it's going to be a big hit and that's why this company decided to publish this magazine."

Kazuo himself grew up in the typical Japanese family. "My father dedicated himself to work—he even worked over the weekend and he's not retired yet," he says. "My mother was the so-called housewife." Yet at the same time that he calls himself "average," he urges me to look deeper beyond that definition. "My father was always trying to enjoy time with me, by playing catch," he says. "He took our family on trips. He knew how to enjoy family time."

The changing roles of Japanese fathers hits particularly close to home for Kazuo because he himself is navigating those waters. He's married with two kids: a nine-year-old boy and a four-year-old girl. "I'm the perfect target audience for this magazine," he says. "I always make sure to go home as early as possible in the evening. Over the weekend, I make sure to have time with my kids. I'm always thinking about what's going to be fun or how to create new fun with my kids."

Fatherhood, he says, has changed him. "Before I had my own children, I was a very different person," he says. "I worked hard, and after work I would go out drinking with my coworkers. I was the typical Japanese husband. Once I had a baby, I suddenly changed so much. Now I enjoy life with my family."

His wife works for a publishing company. "She used to work in the office but now she is doing freelance editing," he says. "She is quite busy working as a writer and editor." Kazuo points out that if women want careers, because they didn't have them before, it's only natural that men will want a family life, because it's the piece that was missing for *them* before. "Men want families now because work does not have to be the primary focus, unlike the older generations," Kazuo says. "It's happening to women as well but especially to men because men are supposed to be the main workforce in the family. Now the men are getting tired of society as a whole. They need something much more pure that they can grow and care for. Something that they can love and that has their own blood. When I interact with men in conversations and interviews, they always talk about their lives as children and how it was so beautiful, unlike the life they are having right now. By looking at their own child, they fall into the nostalgia of thinking about their own childhoods. Men want to go back to those pure and innocent days, and children can be one of the best tools for them to feel like they are back in their own beautiful childhood."

The bubble bursting meant that men have, albeit slowly, begun to loosen their ties with corporate Japan. "I can say that less men than before are saying that work is their priority," Kazuo says. "One of the reasons why they are coming to think like that is that companies are not providing everything in the recent days. Before—only about twenty years ago—if you were employed you don't really have to worry about your future life because the company provides everything, even after you're retired there's a pension. But now the economy does not allow the company to provide all kinds of benefits that they took for granted only less than twenty years ago. The men have to think about being responsible for themselves, so they don't feel like dedicating themselves to only work cause it doesn't really mean anything these days." Interestingly, he says, "Men choose their children for their top priority but not many men choose their wives as their top priority."

When I ask him why, he gives me one of the most thoughtful answers I've received in the years of researching this book.

"The modern man has been impressed with the women's achievements in Japan—both what they have done and will be able to do in the future," Kazuo says. "Looking at those women, the men get overwhelmed. It's not like the men don't like the recent women or anything like that, they're just overwhelmed—like looking at an object they have never seen before—like 'Wow!' There is no hatred in it, but there is no special affection in it either—they are just overwhelmed." I'm struck by what he says: the "Wow!" with no hatred, but no special affection either.

It's easy to forget that in the land of Hello Kitty, Puffy Ami Yumi, and Pokémon, that until very recently, family had been quite a strident, regulated, serious thing. Behind closed doors, a generation of Japanese grew up with fathers they never saw and mothers who were long-suffering housewives. *Nikkei Kids* is powerful because while the government is wringing its hands about the dropping birthrate and the media is going on and on about the latest fad, be it parasite singles or *make inu*, people are still getting married, people are still having children. This new generation of Japanese parents would like to create a different home life than the one they experienced, but they don't really know how.

10

REVOLUTION AT
BULLET TRAIN SPEED

*How Women Are Forging Change
and Tradition in Japan*

She is only thirty years old. But already Kanako Otsuji has made Japanese history—twice. In 2003, at the age of twenty-eight, she became the youngest person ever elected to the Osaka prefectural assembly (the equivalent of a state congress). The fact that she is a woman made her youth and success even more incredible. At that time there were only seven women in the 110-member assembly. Then last year, a year after her election, she came out of the closet, becoming the first openly gay politician to hold a major office. She had never hidden her sexuality, but both her fellow colleagues and the journalists politely ignored it—a fact that made her uncomfortable. After her election, she wrote a memoir, simply titled *Coming Out,* which was accepted by Kodansha, one of the most important publishers in Japan.

Sitting in her Sakai City office, she seems both anxious to

talk about her experience and wary of being misquoted and misrepresented. Her office is small and there are two assistants on her staff; one of them is her girlfriend. She has short brown hair that is cut in a pixieish style. She's wearing a light blue turtleneck underneath a dark brown suit. This has been a hard meeting to schedule. The assembly meets only four times a year. But Kanako works hard at researching the issues she raises on the floor and preparing responses to items that are being discussed. "To prepare for the questions you have to go around and interview people and study different topics," she says. "Another important job is to let the voters know what kind of activities you've been working on. Generally after the assembly ends, I write up an assembly activity summary report. So I send those off to voters. I have summary meetings." She also keeps up an active lecture schedule: speaking at universities, welfare centers, women's groups.

Kanako Otsuji was born in Nara and grew up in Osaka. When she was in middle school, her family moved to Kobe. Her father was a typical salaryman. Her mother teaches mentally disabled students. Always athletic, she was an Asian Junior karate champion in high school. She enrolled in college, dropped out, and eventually reenrolled at Seoul University, with the hopes of studying taekwondo and qualifying for the Sydney Olympics in 2000. When she didn't win a place on the national team, she returned to Japan, enrolling at Doshisha University in Kyoto. It was there that her interest in politics started to grow. "When I was a junior in college, right before going on to my senior year, I did an internship for an assembly member," she says. "It was for a member of the Ibaraki City assembly in Osaka. That's when I had my point of contact with politics.

"I was just starting to look for jobs and when I was finding out about different types of occupation, I wanted to know what kind of work an assembly member does. In Japan, most politicians are covered in the media when they are involved in scandals, and you don't really know what these people do exactly. So I wanted to know and I applied for the internship. Another reason was that I interviewed with a female member of the assembly and when she asked me why I wanted to intern, I told her that I was a lesbian and that I wanted to see what politics can do to change certain things. And that's how I got the position."

Five years after graduating from university, Kanako won her assembly seat, wrote her memoir, and came out of the closet. "After I published the book, there was a part of me that felt a sort of relief and a part of me that was stressed out because of it," Kanako says. "But overall, nothing's changed about me just because I published a book. The only difference is whether the world found out about it or not. In terms of my political stance, I don't think anything has changed. I think it's been hard on my family. Of course they felt puzzled at first."

Kanako's coming out was especially hard on her mother. "She didn't have accurate information about homosexuality," Kanako says. "And then she hears her daughter is coming out of the closet, and she has to deal with relationships with the neighbors as well as relatives and I think there was some anxiety there."

The role-model question is a tough one for her. I try to rephrase it and ask her whose opinion she trusts. "That's a difficult question," Kanako says. "I think there are two roles for the member of the assembly. One is to hear what the voters have to say. But if you listen to voter's voice, sometimes your point of view can lean toward the public opinion. That can be a demerit. I also have to voice my opinion and create the public opinion. The balance between these two are difficult. With me, most people that supported me in my election worried because I announced that I was gay. Never in the history of Japan has a member of the assembly come out and said that they were gay, so we didn't know how people would react. I believe that I have to be in the front and be the opinion leader. I listen to many different opinions, but in the end I do think I am the one to make the decision. It is a job for the member of assembly to make decisions. We've been entrusted by the people to do so."

She is confident about her work, but getting other people to take her seriously is a full-time job—hence the extensive research she undertakes before the quarterly assembly meetings. "In my assembly there are 112 seats and only seven are women," she says. "Which is about six point some percent. So when you go to an assembly of that sort, a young woman's opinion is not taken seriously. I've experienced that. Those men work only with same type of men, so to them, I am like their daughter. The average age in the assembly is in the late fifties. Those are the people that make decisions in our world. Those are the people that decide how to use people's tax money. Politics can be conservative in any country but in Japan, when you think about women's advancement, it's really behind. So I do think it's still difficult for women to work in a collective environment. It doesn't mean that there's no hope. The Osaka governor is a woman. The first woman governor in Japan. The head of the biggest labor union in Osaka is a woman. This also is the first in Japan. It's true that anything that's a 'first' becomes news, but I do think slowly changes are happening."

The Osaka governor is now famous for what is referred to as the "sumo incident." Every spring, the grand sumo tournament takes place in Osaka. Traditionally, when the winner receives the Governor's award, they receive it directly from the Governor, but because the Governor is a woman, she can't get up on the sumo ring. Rather than argue with the old myths about females defiling the sumo ring, the female governor simply doesn't award the prize rather than challenge the rules of the national sport. In Japan, even a female governor cannot escape the gender discrimination.

"The Governor's award comes out of the citizens' tax money, about three million yen," says Kanako. "So I think that there's a problem here if the organization that we are investing our tax money into is discriminating against women. It wouldn't be a problem if it didn't have anything to do with public funds. If it were a private company, then it wouldn't matter. Sumo takes place at the Osaka prefectural gymnasium, which is built by the people's tax money, and the Governor's award is also using the public tax money. So there is something to think about. But it seems that the Governor's also sick of being noticed just through this incident. It becomes news every year in March."

As a young politican, Kanako must circle her own version of the venerated men's-only sumo ring. "Being a young woman, you really stand out in assembly. People wonder who I am," she says. "People don't think I am a member of the assembly, they think I am a secretary or an official staffer. Or sometimes even a tour conductor. There is still a stereotype of assembly members being old men. That's why I get a lot of attention." She adds, however, that at least during the meetings, the men behave themselves. "None of them pick on me. It looks bad for an older man to tease a young woman their daughter's age."

Still there's a way of withholding information that can be just as effective as putting you down. "My colleagues are all around my father's age," Kanako says. "All of them give the younger men in assembly more chances and not the women. They tell them what would be helpful for them to succeed in the future, what to study, what they should know. With women, it doesn't feel like they want to educate us or give us any chances. So I have to go out there and get my own chances. I have to be very clear when I feel that it should be my turn to work on an issue."

Sometimes Kanako feels that her arms are too short to box with the powers that be. One of the things that she finds so tiring is the feeling that she must always, always be on her guard. "I am in a very conservative environment even within Japan," she says. "Even when I tell people that work in the corporate world, they are surprised by what I have to go through. One thing that troubles me is that I can't make any jokes. I am a young woman so they already look down on me. So I think if I say a stupid joke, they won't take me seriously. If an older assemblyman says the same joke they wouldn't consider him dumb but it's different for a young woman. So I have to always show that I am studying hard and that I am together."

Kanako is also trying to address Japan's race issues. "Japanese people generally think that they are homogeneous," she says, "even though that's not true. In Osaka there's about one hundred and fifty thousand ethnic Koreans. There are the Ainus as well as the Okinawans and they have their own language and culture. We are not taught about diversity in our education. And as a member of the assembly, what I do is look at the problems. For example, foreign residents in Japan do not have voting rights. Even if they are permanent residents, they don't have voting rights in local elections. Japan is clearly behind in these terms. At immigration, there are incidents where human rights are being abused. The biggest problem is that Japanese people are unaware of these things. They lack interest. I am trying my best so that they will be more aware of their surroundings."

She worries that economic stagnation is being addressed by an us-against-them mentality. "People in politics are trying to strengthen solidarity by saying that we are of one ethnicity and one culture and one value," she says. "Even when you look at issues about textbooks in Japan. When they say things like 'Japanese culture is beautiful,' does that include the Ikuno district in Osaka city where one third of the population is composed by ethnic Koreans? Does it include the war-displaced Japanese in China? Does it include sexual minorities? Does it include the mentally, psychologically, and physically handicapped? Does it include homeless people? Osaka has the largest homeless population in Japan."

Kanako knows that if she lived abroad, her sexuality and her gender wouldn't be such a big deal. However, she's not interested in leaving Japan. "When I speak to people that live in foreign countries, I notice that there are no perfect places," she says. "I know a Japanese-American lesbian who lives in San Francisco, and I also know a Japanese-Canadian that lives in Canada and what they both say is that the biggest issue is race, more so than being a sexual minority. In America, depending on where you live, being gay is extremely dangerous. So there are merits and demerits anywhere you live. I think it's important to first work in the town you live in. To try to make changes there first."

It's hard to believe that there are still some people who say that Kanako has had it easy, winning her first election at such a young age. "There is some jealousy, I think," she says. "Before I came out as a lesbian, I spoke about sexual minorities human rights in assembly and I was shut down. They said, 'How could you know about minorities and human rights? You graduated from college and were elected at your first try. You are on the winning team.'

"But I'm a lesbian so I'm not on the winning team. Members of the assembly are not on the winning team, we have to deal with being unemployed every four years. I am risking a lot by announcing that I am a lesbian. There might be harassments. I am the one that has to deal with pressure from my family. So I am the one that's taking the risk. But I guess if people complain about me, it also means that they are noticing me. That's a plus for me." Still, I'm struck by the language she uses. There are winning teams—people who achieve success at an early age—and there are nonwinning teams—sexual minorities, racial minorities. There are losing dogs—single, over thirty—and there are winners—married before thirty. In every society, women must measure up against the expectations of her family, society, her peers, herself. However, it seems like in Japan the decisions about your value are made in a startlingly abrupt fashion—just like in sumo, you can be thrown out of the ring in two seconds flat.

Kimie Oshida is kneeling on a stage, holding a fan and a hand towel, dressed in a traditional kimono. She looks not entirely different from any photograph you might have seen of other traditional Japanese women. But as it soon becomes apparent, when she launches into her act, Kimie is a comedian. As she tells her story, the fan becomes a pair of chopsticks, a cigarette, scissors, a pen, and then a pipe. The hand towel becomes a book, then a stack of bills. She's engaging in *rakugo,* a three-hundred-year-old Japanese art form. Kimie, who runs her own *rakugo* troupe, calls it sit-down comedy as opposed to the stand-up comedy of the West.

Rakugo was traditionally performed by men. A lot of the humor was based on the fact that you saw male performers using a female voice and making exaggerated feminine gestures as they portrayed a geisha, or a little girl, or a nagging wife. Kimie says, "I don't get the same laughs when I play female characters, so I reverse the sexes." You know something is changing in Japan when a woman can wear the pants in a comedy troupe—and get all of the laughs.

Kimie, thirty-four, and a lecturer at Meikai University, first got the idea to perform *rakugo* when she attended a conference in New Zealand about humor. What she heard again and again was that the Japanese aren't funny. Or at least, the context seemed to be, Japanese people aren't funny intentionally. Even within Japan, the Japanese are so often the butt of the joke (just check out www.engrish.com)—whether it's the way they mix their l's and their r's, the red-faced drunk salaryman, the *Star Wars* theme-oriented "love hotels," or the vending machines that sell "used schoolgirls panties"—there's never any shortage of stories to tell about "those wild and crazy Japanese."

What interests me about *rakugo* is that here's a young Japanese woman, building on a comic tradition, translating it into English, and with her comedy troupe finding an audience both among the Japanese and the foreigners. Anyone who has spent any time with a professional comedian knows that the power is in being the one telling the joke, not being the butt of the joke. In this way, I think Kimie Oshida is mighty powerful. She says, "Western comedy tends to feature punchy one-liners and jokes about body parts and functions. In Japan, we find most of our humor in conversation, rather than short jokes. In *rakugo,* there's a fifteen-minute story and then the punchline at the end."

Kimie is the only woman in her *rakugo* company, but she has never had any problem asserting her authority. "In my troupe, I'm the big boss!" she says, laughing. "The men have a lot of respect for me. They feel I have done something they could never even think of on their own—translate *rakugo* into English. They thank me all the time. I translate and write *rakugo* scripts for them, train them, arrange the performance tour, raise money, produce shows, and take them to perform in front of the audience."

It's easy to forget in the land of *American Idol* and reality TV, the stage is actually a platform. For a Japanese woman to step front and center as a performer takes more than just talent and courage, it takes a willingness to be the nail that might get hammered down. While Oshida's troupe performs internationally and throughout Japan, she knows that it means a lot for young women to see a smart, intelligent woman on the stage. "The students respect my work outside of campus. Many of them come to see my performance, especially girls. I think students admire the kind of work I do, the kind of social status I have, which was not something women could have before. I'm independent, both professionally and financially."

To be a woman performer in Japan has always been a political act. The arts have not been the refuge for women in Japan as they have been for women in the West. In the seventeenth century, long before geishas ever strolled along the river Kamo in Kyoto, women performed on stages in the dry portions of the riverbed. One woman, above all, stood out: Izumo no Okuni was Josephine Baker, Marlene Dietrich, and Madonna all rolled into one. She scandalized her audiences by dressing like the randiest of dandies in brocade trousers and animal-skin jackets. Her dances were erotic, and her sketches were risqué. She was even known to dress up as a priest when performing her dirtiest routines. Her performances were deemed *kabuku*—the Japanese term for "wild and outrageous"—and so the kabuki theater was born.

The kabuki soon became a predecessor to the modern sex show as troupes of sexy young women sought to follow Izumo no Okuni's erotic lead. At that time, the line between courtesan and actor was very thin. The shows were meant to turn the audiences on, an advertisement for the services that might be provided afterward. Although the shogunate, the ruling government at the time, banned women from kabuki in 1647 on charges of immorality, it is widely believed that it was only when samurais began to fight over the most popular kabuki actors that the shogunate stepped in.

Young men then took over the kabuki roles, but the problem remained the same, as beautiful young men proved to be equally tantalizing. Eventually, they too, were banned from the stage. Finally, only adult men were allowed to perform on stage and we get the kabuki of today where all of the parts, including the female roles, are performed by men. I like to think, however, that the spirit of Izumo no Okuni is embodied by all the hundreds of thousands of Japanese women who refuse to play by the rules.

Today in Tokyo, a more staid, but no less dynamic performance is taking place. It is Sunday afternoon at the New National Theater in Tokyo. The lights dim, the curtains raise, and the audience sits mesmerized as the Tokyo City Ballet begins a rollicking, erotically charged performance of *Carmen*. What gives this particular rendition so much power is that Carmen, the seductive Spanish gypsy most famously portrayed in Bizet's 1875 opera, has been transported to twenty-first-century Japan. Reinterpretations of the classic are nothing new. In the 1950s, Otto Preminger recast the title role as a fiery African-American woman in *Carmen Jones,* giving Dorothy Dandridge the defining role of her career. A black Carmen, fighting in the quintessential Carmen way to hold onto her freedom at any cost, made a powerful statement about Jim Crow and segregation at the time. In the 1980s, French New Wave director Jean-Luc Godard portrayed Carmen as a nineteenth-century bank-robbing moll in the vein of Bonnie and Clyde. In 2005, director Mark Dornford-May moved the gypsy heroine from Seville to a shantytown in South Africa in *U-Carmen eKhayelitsha* and translated the lyrics from French to Xhosa. Carmen, always sensuous, always independent, is the perfect lens with which to view a woman's role in any given community. It makes perfect sense that, in Japan, Carmen becomes a career woman.

In the first act, Carmen is portrayed by prima ballerina Etsuko Adachi Uchikawa. The first scene takes place in that quintessential Japanese setting: the commuter train. Dancers hang from straps and make their way in and out of the moving car. Our Japanese Carmen is working for corporate Japan. We see the dancers move in and out of cubes that are meant to symbolize computers, desks, and of course, cubicles. Office sounds, such as the stacatto of typing, modulate the dancer rhythms. We get a sense of the monotony of office life. After hours, Carmen seduces the company's security guard, Jose. He is hopelessy naive and, of course, hopelessly in love. We soon realize after that our Carmen is stealing company secrets. When she is in danger of getting caught, she sets up Jose to take the fall. Fighting for his innocence, he brutalizes his boss. Carmen gets away scot-free.

Nobuyoshi Nakajima, who conceived this interpretation of *Carmen,* says that he definitely had the changing roles of Japanese women in mind. "Carmen has always been a very mysterious woman for men because she never seems to be satisfied with anything," Nakajima told reporters. "I have the same feeling about modern women, who seem to be continuously seeking new things from jobs to clothes to hobbies in the expectation that this will make them happier. So through this ballet, I want to examine what women are looking for, in general, in modern society and what they will ultimately get as a result."

After the performance, I met with Etsuko Adachi, who portrays Carmen. She is dressed in a black turtleneck, blazer, and slacks. A far more conservative presentation than the character who was writhing above her lover, onstage, just a few hours before. Etsuko, who is forty-five, tells me that she does not dance full-time. In Japan, dancers—even prima ballerinas with big-city dance troupes—don't earn enough through performances. "In Japan, we don't have companies like in New York or America or Europe," she says. "They pay you for the performance, but not a salary. Fortunately, I could get a job in music instructing, so I teach music, acting, and ballet classes. Of course, I teach ballet classes here at the Tokyo City Ballet."

Etsuko's father was a government officer. Her mother was a housewife. She has one younger sister. She says, "My father has very Japanese ideas. Everything was decided by my father, so my mother had to ask permission for everything. He didn't want me to do ballet. He wanted me to go to university. I had already decided to be a ballerina so to hide it from my father I went to university."

Etsuko began studying ballet at the age of three. Because her father was in the government, they moved a lot. She remembers, "I wanted to be a ballerina, but I had no confidence." Even so, dance became a through line, a constant she could count on. "Everywhere I went, I always did ballet," she says. During her second year of university, she entered a national competition and won a government scholarship. Finally, her father started to come around.

Like Carmen, Etsuko's life as a dancer has allowed her the kind of freedom few women in Japan can enjoy. "I will speak about my sister," she says. "In ballet, men cannot dance women's parts so we are equal on the stage. But my sister is a scientist. In this field, men and women are competitive and because this is Japan, we have a lot of discrimination. She married a Japanese man and moved to America. She realized it was so different. We begged her to come back and find a job.

But she says, 'Oh I cannot work in Japan because I can't take care of the Japanese men around me in my job, I can't be concerned with what they want.'"

What is it that Japanese men want? "They want women to not be more clever than they are," Etsuko says. "They want the women to not show she has more knowledge. In Japan, if a woman knows the answer, they try to stop her from saying it. My sister's been in America a long time now and she talks, that causes conflict." Her sister's growing independence actually led to her divorce. Her Japanese husband couldn't handle it. "She's so much more direct!" Etsuko says. "When I was with her in New York even the way she spoke to the taxi driver was so forceful, I was shocked. She just speaks her mind. I think if she still lived in Japan, she would still be married." Etsuko sees the difference between what she and her sister have been able to achieve and her mother's life in stark terms. She says simply, "Me, I have ballet. Even if I stopped dancing, I could teach. My sister has her career as a scientist. My mother had nothing."

When she was younger, Etsuko dreamed of dancing with a company outside of Japan. But now, she says, "I feel that this is my place in life and I'm happy to be here." She has friends all over the world, former classmates who have joined different companies. Last year, she went to visit her former professor who lives in Monte Carlo. Going abroad then coming back home helps her to see the changes in Japan more clearly. "Maybe we Japanese women are very conservative, but it's changing compared to twenty years ago, or even ten years ago," Etsuko says. "I think Japan is always following the U.S., following your system and maybe your way of thinking. I want to think though that we shouldn't abandon our traditional feelings. We want to get rid of discrimination or unfair things but good things like modesty, that kind of feeling, I want to stay in Japan. Otherwise, we are not Japanese. Like in ballet, too, when we are dancing *Swan Lake*. All the over the world they are dancing *Swan Lake*—American *Swan Lake*, French *Swan Lake*, Russian *Swan Lake*—but not all the methods are the same. In Japan, when we dance *Swan Lake*, we are putting some Japanese poses and feelings in it, that feeling is very important."

Etsuko points out in much the same way that teen trend researcher Yasuka Nakamara did that among Japanese women in particular, there's always a strong predisposition to being in a group. "Traditionally, women don't want to be individuals," she says. "Now many people are thinking as individualists." Choosing a career in dance forced Etsuko to step apart from the group, to "talk" in the way that her sister had to when she moved to the States. "On the stage we need to have personality, individuality, originality, but in Japan that kind of thinking is very new," she says. "And the educational system in Japan doesn't prepare you for it. When I was in elementary school, the teachers asked us to do things all together. At the time, I was doing ballet, that was very expressive so somehow I was trying to hide."

It can be hard to imagine how much being overly expressive can be a liability in a culture that values a conservative sameness. There's a funny scene in the movie *Shall We Dance?* in which the lead character runs into a coworker in the men's room and he realizes that unless he is very, very careful, even his walk will reveal his secret—that he is studying ballroom dancing in the evening. Along the same lines, I can imagine that as a young girl, Etsuko feared that her ballet dancing lessons would somehow burst out at the wrong moment, making it clear that she was somehow different from, and less than, her classmates. In the U.S., a girl who is good at ballet—good enough to one day become a prima ballerina with the Tokyo City Ballet—would be proud of her achievements. In Japan, you share neither your successes nor your failures.

In the Japanese ballet, Carmen is a sexually liberated woman; some of her movements are almost graphic. I ask Etsuko if she thinks that women are more sexually liberated in Japan these days. I'm thinking, in particular, about the girls in the host club. She demurs, "Mr. Nakajima is the creator of the ballet. He believes it and I think that's why he put this kind of sexuality into Carmen. But I don't think so."

Etsuko, who has been married for ten years, does not have children. For her, it was a tough choice to make. "I wanted children," she says. "But I am very interested in dance so I had no time to stop. And at that time, I didn't want to stop. It is difficult to have children and remain a dancer. Especially in Japan." Her marriage, however, has been a great source of fulfillment—and fun. It helps that her husband is a rock musician. "We respect what each other does and we also understand what we are doing," she says. "If I need to concentrate on my dancing, he will help me. He doesn't say, 'You have to make food or you have to clean up.' I am sure my father would have told my mother to stop. At the same time, my father has been so generous and helpful, to both me and my sister. I think my father understands somehow that if a lady has talent, they have to use that talent. But it's different when he thinks of his wife. For my father's generation, when he was a child, he was taught that the man should not enter the kitchen. Even if he wanted to, it would've been considered shameful. I learned that my father loved to sing and dance when he was little. But that wasn't the thing for men when he was a child. When he was quite older, he tried ballroom dancing and he loved it."

Etsuko's comments about her father remind me of the "Men in the Kitchen." Her father's finding ballroom dancing after abandoning his youthful impulses for so many years highlights how poignantly both men and women in Japan are learning new steps. As for Etsuko, she is planning her next act.

"I am so lucky to still be dancing," she says, reminding me that few prima ballerinas continue to get starring roles in their forties. "I want to try to continue to dance, but I'm also teaching younger people. I am also thinking that I would like to direct a company. My husband is helping me think it out. He is also changing his focus. He's continuing his career, but he's beginning to compose for other people." Directing would be a huge step forward, but Etsuko feels that she's ready. After all, she's been practicing her grand jetés since she was three years old. In a society where women are making great leaps, a female dance director has more than a fighting chance.

In the film *About Love* three different couples in three different cities, Shanghai, Taipei, and Tokyo, fall in and out of love. Thirty-five-year-old Haruko Nagatsu, a rising star on the Japanese film scene, wrote the Japanese portion. The day we meet, she's dressed in a sleek cream turtleneck and jeans. I'd heard a lot about Haruko and was anxious to meet her. Films are our dream factories and they do a great job of portraying iconic women. But from living in Los Angeles, I know that no matter how many women command power on the screen, behind the scenes, women are still struggling to make their mark.

Haruko's father worked in real estate. Her mother was a housewife. Her father loved classical music and from the time she was six years old she played piano. Unlike Etsuko's father who was initially against the idea of her pursuing a career in ballet, Haruko says, "My parents let me do anything that I wanted to. So I played piano. One reason why I chose to be a screenwriter is because my father loves films very much. He would often listen to music and try to create a story from that music. I think that's how I write and make stories, because of my father."

Initially, Haruko wanted to be a director. She still wants to direct, but "I haven't had the chance and honestly I don't have any idea how to direct." She studied film at Syracuse University and stayed in the U.S. for five years. There she met a Taiwanese director who asked her if she knew how to use the Avid, a digital editing system. Thanks to film school, Haruko did. The director invited her to come to Taiwan to work on his film. But soon after she got there, his production company went bankrupt. Haruko was at a crossroads. "I didn't want to go back to Japan, so I started teaching Japanese and English at a Japanese school in Taipei," she says. She was enjoying her life abroad. "I was speaking Chinese and seeing so many different kinds of people and cultures," she explains.

It was while teaching in Taipei that she started writing screenplays. "There are many competitions in Japan for TV and movie scripts," she explains. "So I wanted to send in my works. I wrote five or six screenplays in one year. I sent them all to competitions and they all won." In a classic show of Japanese modesty, Haruko immediately starts to downplay her accomplishments. "I misunderstood and thought I was talented," she says, lightly. "I thought I was a gifted writer. So I moved back to Japan."

Interestingly, for Haruko, there wasn't a huge difference between the U.S. and Japan. Taiwan, she says, was very different. "In Taiwan, there's an environment where there are many women presidents in business," she says. "Women stand up and speak out, so the film industry is much easier for women. I think in Taipei women and men are equal. I didn't see much equality in the U.S. film industry. Men are always on a higher level than women. My friend in the U.S. always told me that if you want to get a good job, you have to use anything you can. I said, what? But she does. In Taiwan, they are not so beautiful like in the U.S. They are like the men. They don't wear makeup, they wear ties and boots. When I ask them why they dress like men, they say, 'Because it's comfortable, why not?'"

Coming back to Japan from Taipei was a culture shock for Haruko. "It's tough," she says. "The screenwriters are underpaid and the producers regard people like me as objects. They don't give me the right to be important in the film. The value of the writing itself is low. Here the producers only care about copyright and they always ask me, 'Can I just put my name under your credit?' But you didn't write anything." I hate to be the one to break it to Haruko, but that's how screenwriters all over the world feel. Women, Haruko argues, are treated especially poorly. "Females are no longer devoted to their family as a wife as a mother so the producers want to use them as screenwriters," she says.

"There are many screenwriters who are housewives because being a housewife is very comfortable. Most of films not showing in theaters cannot guarantee pay to the writer. A housewife, however, they can easily pay because she has a husband who earns money. One of the producers told me so. 'She's a housewife so it's very useful.' Some of them are talented, very talented, and they wanted to be a screenwriter from the beginning but they had children. It's different for me. I don't have a husband who supports me but I get the same little pay." At the same time, she says she will always write scripts. "I want to continue screenwriting until I die. For life. Forever," she says. "Come interview me when I'm seventy or eighty." Then Haruko pretends to stoop over and makes a shaky, old person voice, "Ok, how long will you continue writing? Until the day I die."

Haruko has a boyfriend that she's been seeing for four years. They've discussed marriage, but it's Haruko who put the brakes on moving the relationship forward. "I'm a writer so I work twenty-four hours a day," she says. "So if I want to marry the guy he has to understand my job, my lifestyle." Like the producers who hire housewives, Haruko's parents support her screenwriting because they think it's a job she can continue when she has children. She wants to have children, "many children," she says. But right now there's just too much she wants to do with her career. Her sister, however, is pregnant, "She is going to have a baby this March." Haruko, quite the dramatist, acts out a traditional scene of gratitude, reminiscent of a scene from *Memoirs of a Geisha*. Feigning a soft, but emotional voice, Haruko says, 'My sister is pregnant. I say good. Thank you, my sister—now I can be free.'"

It is eerily reminiscent of the scene that is being played out in the Imperial Palace. While Crown Princess Masako suffers from depression and the puppetry of the all-powerful Imperial Household Agency, who is furious with her for not having a son, her younger sister-in-law has broken free from the palace walls entirely. Princess Sayako, now thirty-six, was married in November 2005 to a man who works for the Tokyo Metropolitan government. Following the Imperial Law, any princess who weds a commoner must give up her royal status. Sayako has lost her title, her palace allowance, the royal status of her future children—but she is free. And by all accounts, thrilled at the prospect. Had she wed a person of royal status, a distant cousin for example, there would have been pressure for her to have a son—as that son could have become Emperor. Instead, she married a childhood friend, a man she became reacquainted with at a tennis party that her brother, Prince Akishino, threw two years ago. While the wedding of the Crown Princess was an affair of the state, Sayako got married in a simple, white tea dress and pearls. She will live in a rented apartment until the condominium she and her new husband have purchased is ready. She has taken driving lessons and her very first trips to a public supermarket. What she lacks in Masako's diplomatic and educational background, she has made up for in the dramatic act of throwing off her title. She is the first princess, in forty-five years, to give up her title. In Japan, as Lady Diana once was, she is the princess of the people's hearts. "It's like someone above the clouds is coming closer to ordinary people like us," one young woman told the Associated Press.

Back beneath the clouds, Haruko Nagatsu is writing a novel. "I am trying to show life in your thirties for the Japanese woman." She's also planning to direct. "Five years is the cycle of my life," she says. "I spent five years in the U.S. Five years in Taipei. In the next five years I want to direct my original story. I am going to shoot a short film with my friends—I have a few friends in the industry. So I'm going to make it and show to them, take it around to producers and say: 'This is my work, what do you think?' And if they like it, they will ask me for more work. I don't want to ask producers for money for my short, I just want to shoot it."

Haruko's plan to direct her own film is a powerful indicator of how much things have changed in Japan. In the early nineties, when Nike launched its globally successful "Just Do It" campaign, Japan was the only country where it didn't work. Everything in Japanese society sent the opposite message and it was hard for young people to understand the spirit of what seemed, all around the world, to be a simple inspirational phrase. These days, things are different and I can't help but think that women like Haruko, Etsuko, the ballerina, and Kimie, the *rakugo* comedienne—are the reasons why.

In the early nineties, they were called *"onnanoko shashinka,"* the wildly popular group of young Japanese "girl photographers" who captured the beauty of the everyday with their Polaroid-like prints. Young women in Japan saw their own lives writ large on gallery walls, men were intrigued into what many saw as the secret life of teenage girls. Mika Ninagawa is part of the second wave of *onnanoko shashinka*, but she's also defining a turf that's much greater than the term "girl photographer" might imply. She's won all of the important prizes, including Canon's New Cosmos Award. She exhibits at the high-end galleries, but also in the more trendy ones in Harajuku. She's published a half-dozen books and manages her business with the discipline and organization of a much older master photographer. While her photographs often focus on young Japanese girls, in bright clothing and intriguing poses, she has begun to branch out, producing technically impeccable still lifes as well as travel photography that shows a world much bigger than Tokyo, much bigger than the teen life that the first generation of women photographers seemed, eventually, to be obsessed with.

When we meet in her Tokyo office, Mika Ninagawa, is dressed like a quintessential artist—all in black, with a frilly blouse and lots of necklaces and rings. Gold glitter eyeshadow make her eyes pop. Unlike the classic salaryman father, housewife mother story, Mika's father is a director and producer. Her mother and her cousin are actresses. "I grew up in an environment where I saw so many creators," she says. "I always wanted to be a creator, if not necessarily a photographer. But when I think about my life now, I think photography is the only job I could ever want."

In Japan, the path to becoming a professional photographer is very similar to the path you might take in the U.S. Usually, you attend art school or college. And then, after graduation you usually work for a studio as an assistant or an assistant photographer. You work your way up to becoming an assistant to a prominent photographer, and then you strike out on your own.

In Mika's case, she was awarded a prize in a photography contest when she was twenty-two years old and still a university student. "When I won this prize I suddenly became a professional photographer," she says. "I didn't do any kind of general course before I actually became a photographer. I also didn't have any experience as an assistant. I was lucky and that meant I was quite a target of jealousy from everyone who wanted to be a photographer."

Eleven years later, Mika has a solid career built on strong reviews of her gallery work as well as her amazing publishing career. Her books sell briskly to young women through her Web site and are also sold at every major museum and bookstore in Tokyo. "Still there are some negative opinions about me that come mainly from men," she says. "My work isn't based on study and training. My work is based on my artistic sense, on my hunches and my feeling about what is beautiful. It's not based on skill itself. So I am attacked by other photographers. Some photographers who have the skills are not necessarily as successful as I am. Men, in particular, are always finding fault with my work."

Like many of the *onnanoko shashinka,* Mika used herself as a model in the beginning. Some of her early self-portraits were nudes. "Most people think because I showed my own nudity to the public that meant I like sex and anything goes," she says. "So when I met with this one gallery director he asked me to go to bed. I said, 'No thanks, I'm not that kind of woman,' and I walked away from working with him." One wonders if her more overtly sexual pictures don't end up arousing the same kind of men who favor pornography that features cute young girls. Mika says, "I always shoot whatever I think is pretty or cute or beautiful. My purpose is not to be sexy even if that's what the picture shows. When I have exhibitions with pictures with a lot of sexual images, those exhibitions are quite appealing to women and girls, not so much to men. So the customers are usually women."

The challenge for Mika is to use being a woman to her benefit without actually feeling exploited. She jokes that when she's carrying around her heavy camera equipment, being a man would be more beneficial. But she also says, "When I go abroad to photograph children and when I ask to take pictures, most people say yes because I look like the harmless Japanese woman. So I prefer to take advantage of it. I've had a lot of [criticism] in my career [because I'm a successful woman], but I don't give it too much thought. I just try to let it go."

Like jewelry designer Yoko Shimizu, Mika finds that working with young women in her studio can present challenges. She wants to give young women opportunities, but at the same time she questions their commitment. "My assistants are younger than me, they are in their early to late twenties," she says. "I just find that they always have some way to escape from hard work. Usually marriage is a road out for them. If a woman wants to marry and be a housewife, they don't have to work that hard in this society. That's why female workers can be braver than men can be. Women take risks because marriage is a safety net for them."

Mika herself is married and says she would never consider quitting her job. Again, her unusual family is her inspiration. Before her father found success as a film and theater director, he didn't make much money. During this period, her father took care of the children. Until she was five, her father was her primary caregiver. "My mother was the one making money," she says. "So from the beginning there was no thought in my mind that women have to do a particular thing and men have to do a particular thing. My thought about the family is that people should do what they can."

Then, before it has even started, my interview with Mika Ninagawa is over. She's a busy woman. She's getting ready to shoot her first feature film and says, "This is the biggest project so far. I am going to direct and this is my first attempt at that." Going forward, she has even greater ambitions. "I have five axes for my activities: films, fashion, making branded goods, gallery exhibitions, and book publishing," she says. "I hope that I can achieve top ranking for each of the five." Five is a number that is significant for her. "I also want to have a baby in about five years," she says. "But I want to make it clear. Even if I have a baby, I will never quit my job." She points to the floor: "Come back and see me, and you'll see my baby playing right here in this office."

The first time I saw snowboarder Junko Asazuma, I was sitting in a no-frills sushi restaurant in Los Angeles, waiting for the screening of my friend Joe Doughrity's short film, *Seven Days in Japan*. There was a TV over the bar and someone had put on the Winter X Games. I saw a snowboarder fly up off the half-pipe, then spin in mid-air. For what seemed like forever, I held my breath while she pirouetted in the air. Then after she'd come down, I watched her take off her hat and sunglasses. She was a Japanese girl! I spent the next year and a half reading about her—how she'd come out of nowhere, joining Burton's Team Asia after only two years of professional boarding. She was flawless on the half-pipe and was impressing judges with an impressive "McTwist," an inverted aerial in which she rode forward on the half-pipe wall, became airborne and rotated 540 degrees in a backward motion, and then performed a front flip and landed, riding forward. Only five feet two inches, she was becoming a crowd favorite—both young men and women cheered her "amplitude."

Finally, finally, after a year of faxed requests and the rigors of her competition and training schedules, I'm able to meet her. I take the long train ride out to Chiba prefecture and we meet up at the OB Café. It's the kind of restaurant you expect to find in a ski town—a log cabin structure, with a huge wood-burning stove. I won't bore you by telling you that Junko Asazuma is smaller in person than she appears on television. She comes into the restaurant, dressed simply, a silver cross around her neck, a burgundy camisole underneath a camoflauge puffy jacket. She looks like the cool, older sister of the half-Japanese model, Devon Aoki. After we order hot drinks, she tells me that she started snowboarding when she was twenty-one. It was just a hobby for four years, though people kept telling her that she could go pro. Finally, at twenty-five, she decided to go for it. She needed to be certificated to go pro, meaning she had to compete—and place—in an exhibit game. She finished in the top three.

First, she joined the Japanese pro circuit. Every year, she ranked number two or three in the country. She kept feeling that she was in danger of becoming the perpetual big fish in a small pond. In order to really elevate her game, she needed to compete internationally. She went to Canada, finished in the top three, and earned a place on Burton's Team Asia.

Junko grew up in Chiba, not far from the OB Café. Her father was a maintenance engineer for Japan Airlines. Her mother is a housewife, although she started out as a licensed home healthcare worker. She has one older sister, who is an office lady.

As a child, Junko was always athletic. She ran track and

played basketball and volleyball. "The training was quite rigid," she says. "The coach was quite tyrannical." Tired of being bossed around, she abandoned sports in junior high school—with the exception of the occasional pick-up game of basketball with her friends. In high school, she went even further in the other direction—joining the home economics club. Chiba, however, is a city that lends itself quite naturally to the sporting life. The city offers easy access to beaches and the mountains. Sometimes, when she was still a student, Junko joined her friends for surfing or snowboarding.

From eighteen to twenty-one, she says she did "nothing in particular," working various part-time jobs and hanging out with her friends. "I didn't have any dreams when I was younger," says Junko, now thirty-one. "I didn't ever imagine that I could be a professional snowboarder." What she thought is that she'd hang out with her friends, meet a nice guy, and become a housewife. Her family, she says, are just as surprised as she is that she's now an internationally recognized athlete. "They say, 'Your life is so exciting now.'"

During the snowboarding season, from January through July, she travels a lot to the U.S. On a typical day, she's up at 7 A.M. and gets to practice by 9 A.M. She practices at least four hours a day. After practice, which is murder on the joints, she goes to the jacuzzi, sees her masseuse, and exercises in the pool. In the evenings, she says, "I go to drinking parties and *onsens* (hot springs) with my teammates." Welcome to the life of the extreme athlete—work hard, play hard.

In the off season, August to December, she says, "I don't want to do anything too hard. I just want to stay relaxed." Sometimes she competes on an indoor track and there's a fairly full publicity schedule for Burton, but for the most part, her time is her own. One thing she is committed to, however, is her teaching. "I'm an instructor for young kids," she says.

"I'm quite motivated to get the younger generation excited about the sport."

Even on the half-pipe, however, there's the equivalent of pouring tea. In Japan, there are lots of exhibits and games just for men. "The prize money is also different for the sexes," Junko explains. "Women always get exactly half of what the prize money is for men. The standard prize at an event is 2 million yen (roughly $19,000) for men, 1 million yen for women." In the U.S., she says, things are a little better—most games are for men and women. "There are many more opportunities for men and women to come together," Junko says.

She plans to compete for an additional two years. She's quite involved in the designing of boards and gear for Burton. "I'd also like to manage a café like this one," she says. "That's why I like to meet here. I'm always checking out what cups they are using, what they are offering on the menu."

She dates a lot, but doesn't have a serious boyfriend. "Men tend to be intimidated by me," she says. "Especially if they've seen me compete before they meet me. They always say, 'You look softer and nicer than I thought you would be.'" She would like to have a child, mostly so she can return to someone the love and support that was given to her. "I have parents who have always taken care of me," she says. "They always supported me in my extracurricular activities, from piano to boarding. I'd like to give that kind of thing to my own child. I want to give someone that kind of support." She thinks about it and then adds, "I'm not going to force them to snowboard, even though I was a professional boarder."

I think about what a different world we live in, a world where a kid could go to school and say, "Yeah, my Mom used to compete in the Winter X Games. She was nice on the half-pipe."

I ask her what it's like—when she's executing her signature McTwist and there's nothing beneath her board but air. "It's a mixed feeling," Junko says. "I'm so scared and I'm so happy." And I think that, at the best of times, her words capture what every independent woman in Japan is feeling these days.

Although I doubt she could execute a McTwist, Yoko Tajima knows a thing or two about the extreme sport of being an outspoken, public figure in Japan. She is referred to, by many, as the most important feminist thinker in Japan and is as well known as Gloria Steinem is in the U.S. When I arrive at her home office in a residential neighborhood of Tokyo, it is not even nine o'clock in the morning, and a small army of young women are already busy at work: researching her speeches, copyediting her many publications, coordinating her media appearances. Her inner office, a large well-appointed room on the first floor, is filled with a library of books along one wall and a collection of images of Tajima on the other wall. There is a large framed poster of her advertising Virgin Atlantic airways. A bus stop–size ad shows the sixtysomething Tajima in a sign that says: Stop AIDS. Nearly two dozen cartoon illustrations of her frame the wall behind her desk, like the back wall at Sardi's.

The interesting thing about the illustrations, all done by different artists, is they all focus on Tajima's lips, a telling detail for a woman who makes her living by speaking her mind. In one cartoon, she looks like the Edna Mode character in *The Incredibles*. She's parachuting down to the ground and shouting through a bullhorn at a group of Taliban women. The caption, in Japanese, reads: "Now you have to be independent and show your faces." In another image, she looks like a rock star— Yoko Ono with Mick Jagger's lips. In yet another, her strong profile is carved into the side of a mountain. In one cartoon, her likeness has been emblazoned on the body of a rocket and in the one next to it, her face has been transposed onto the body of a duck. It's a lot to take in, all before you meet the woman herself. An assistant brings up cups of buckwheat tea, and I wonder, is it different pouring tea when your boss is the nation's leading feminist? Then Yoko Tajima herself walks in. She is wearing a hot pink turtleneck and a camel wool suit. The black bob is the same as it is in the photos and she's wearing gold frame glasses. As for her iconoclastic lips, they are engaged in a broad, welcoming smile. We sit down to talk.

Yoko Tajima never meant to become a media figure. "For thirty years, I was teaching women's studies and literature at a college," she says. "People think of me as a sociologist, but I'm not. My research specialty is nineteenth- and twentieth-century British literature." Still, there was always a feminist slant to her work as she wrote about such topics as the missing figures of mothers in literature. It's only been in the last ten years, that Tajima has become known as a talking head on television. In particular, she became known as the sparring partner of Beat Takeshi, a comedian who has gone on to become a respected, provocative, filmmaker and director—Woody Allen meets Quentin Tarantino. "When I first appeared on TV, the feminists didn't like it," she says. "They didn't think TV was an appropriate medium for me to appear on."

Tajima felt differently. "If you publish books and magazines, maybe a thousand people might really read what you have to say," she says. "When I'm on television, I can reach twenty million people. I think TV is the best medium for me to express my ideas." Her party line is simple, perhaps maddeningly so: "Japan must elevate the status of women." Yet in the U.S., where we are used to a diversity of voices on women's issues from Naomi Wolf and Hillary Clinton to Ann Coulter, it's easy to forget what a lone wolf Tajima really is. If she covers a lot of ground, it's partly because she has to. There simply aren't a dozen media-friendly, outspoken feminists who have a national platform in Japan.

"They call me Mad Tajima," she says, with a laugh that suggests she doesn't actually find it funny. "I'm always angry about something." One of the things that makes her angry is the Equal Opportunity Act of 1985. That one didn't quite take, so the government passed an additional Equal Rights Act in 1999. Still, they are widely regarded as being meaningless pieces of legislature. "The Japanese government is not ready to be severe," she says. "They are not really putting pressure on the companies to act." So Tajima does: she gets on TV, on the radio, in a hot air balloon—at least in the imagination of one cartoonist—and she says things have to be different.

In a country where women still, sometimes, speak in a softer tone of voice around men than they would around their girl-friends and cover their mouth when they laugh, it isn't easy to be Mad Tajima. There's a Japanese ghost story about a woman who dares to be the bearer of bad news. One day at Himeji Castle, I heard this version. Okiku was a servant of the great samurai, Tessan Aoyama, who was planning to overthrow the reigning feudal lord. Okiku learned of the plot and reported it to her lover, a loyal warrior. When the plot failed and Aoyama learned that it was Okiku who had foiled him, he decided to kill her. He accused her of breaking a priceless plate from the royal castle. She was tortured to death and her body thrown in the well. At the well, outside of Himeji Castle, it is said that you can hear Okiku counting the pieces of the plate, "*Ichi, ni, san . . .* seven, eight, nine . . ." The story is that when she gets to the number ten, she lets out a blood curdling scream and starts at number one all over again. The message is clear: a woman who goes up against a powerful samurai will be punished.

Yoko Tajima has faced down her own samurai, but her story ends much better than Okiku's. When she was a regular guest on Beat Takeshi's talk show he was known as a very macho fig-ure. Like a guest from *Charlie Rose* wandering into the studios of *The Tonight Show,* Tajima often found herself as the lone academic on a dais of entertainers. Over time, she and Takeshi developed a platonic version of what Japanese couples call a *sogo rikai,* or mutual understanding. "He was very masculine," she says. "And he was always sitting right next to me. Over the years, he was very changed by our conversations. He started to understand me completely. He developed a great respect for me and the audience could feel it. That started to change minds."

Still Tajima, who is a tall and handsome woman, felt the sting of those who felt she was the wrong woman to be paired, even intellectually, with a heartthrob like Takeshi. "The first time I appeared on TV, people called me names," she says. "They said I was not pretty, I was ugly, a dog, nasty." The fact that she has never been married only made her more vulnerable to public attack. Think about the prime minister who says that women who had not borne society any children did not deserve a pension. It's really important to remember that in Japan, it's okay for powerful men to say the most childish, awful, chauvinistic things. "The men I argue with think that because I wasn't loved by a man, that's why I became a feminist," Tajima says. As in the U.S., the very word "feminist," is going by the wayside. "They don't use the term so much anymore," Tajima says. "When you fight for social problems, you find that there are both men and women who don't like you." She pauses, then adds, "It's okay if they don't use the term, as long as the ideas are spreading."

How are the ideas spreading in Japan? Tajima points to all kinds of signs: in fashion, in the workplace, in the media. She thinks the style of young women who wear pants underneath their skirts points to a rejection of earlier fashions that projected delicacy and helplessness. She says the number of women who are working after marriage is growing—and this is a victory. But most of all, she loves seeing commercials she never thought she'd see: commercials for detergent where the *men* are doing the laundry, another commercial where the woman puts the rice on the table and tells her husband, "Now, you have to deal with supper"—and he does. Tajima actually grins when she describes these commercials, as if she were a feminist fortune-teller and her television were a crystal ball, looking into the homes of Japanese families everywhere.

After we meet, I continue to wonder about this. Am I just so cynical that I'm not wowed by a television commercial with a man who does laundry? (Full disclosure—in our house, my husband does the laundry.) But I think Tajima is actually very smart. I also think it takes a lot to keep putting yourself out there—as an easy target to an indifferent government and an unrestrained media. It must be very hard to continually be called unattractive, to have your loneliness thrown back in your face. I think of the words Tajima used to describe her marital status. Of course, there are things that get lost in translation but she didn't say, "I've never been married," the way most women do. What she said, describing her debating partner's cruel words, is: "He says it was because I've never been loved by a man." I think *love* is a very interesting, very vulnerable, word for an activist to use. If Tajima gets excited over progress in a television commercial, it's because images are powerful—and because you have to mark your progress when you put yourself out the way she does, otherwise you begin to feel that all your sacrifice is for nothing.

I ask her what it feels like to be a role model, as many women have told me that she means a lot to them. Married women sneak their books into their houses, young women who would like the world to think they are happy-go-lucky parasite singles are transfixed when she appears on TV. She rejects all pedestals completely. "Each woman has to find her own way. I don't believe in role models," she says. "I don't like this idea. I can give you the perfect 'model'—working women taking care of their children, taking care of their parents. It's so much pressure it's killing them. Women have the kind of pressure to think they have to have it all. If you want to have it *all*, you have to be very rich so someone can do *most* of it for you. If women want it all, the government has to support them and have a system for them. Maybe the idea of a role model serves men, not women. Maybe if there were such a person for a man, it's easier for him to follow. The role model is useful for men because it's really about a successful career. Women want a successful home *and* career."

I ask Tajima about the wall of images that depict her in so many different ways. She tells me that the weekly news-magazines actually run contests to see who can draw the most outrageous cartoons of her. After they publish them, they send her the winners. She is saddened, she tells me, that no one depicts her in a flattering way. "It's always the giant teeth and the mouth," she says, with a sigh. I wonder what she thinks of Freud and his theory of the vagina dentata, but I'm not sure it's an appropriate context in which to bring it up or if my making the connection might not seem even more unflattering. She tells me that she's quite busy with commercial work these days. In addition to Virgin Atlantic, she also hawks such big companies as Microsoft. In this, as in everything else, she makes her own rules. "I never appear in pharmaceutical commercials," she says. "I don't drink so I don't do alcohol ads—though they ask me. I also don't do ramen commercials." I think of her delight in the commercial where the man is forced to cook the rice. No man is ever going to see Yoko Tajima showing how easy it is to make ramen on TV. If he's hungry, he'll have to figure it out himself.

* * *

The truth is that in many ways, it was my own loneliness that drove me to write this book. Before I went to Japan, I heard a million stories about how every night my Japanese colleagues would take me out drinking, how I would be forced to drink whisky after whisky, and how they would try to test my mettle by having me eat blowfish (a fatally poisonous dish, if not prepared correctly). It never occurred to me that these stories were told to me by men. A sign, I guess, to how equal I feel in my American workplace. But when I got to Japan, I discovered that the Japanese men I met during the course of my workday did not invite me drinking, to hostess clubs, out for blowfish. I spent each night alone. I did meet some women in the course of my meetings, but they were efficient, professional, distant. I had no idea, back then, the kind of struggles they were up against. I think now of the nights I spent in Tokyo restaurants like T.Y. Harbor, talking to Japanese women friends and friends of friends about work. I can close my eyes and see them, beautiful, stylish women, each with a wicked sense of humor. I see us sharing plates of pasta (family style is the preferred method of ordering in Tokyo, especially for a night out with the girls), pouring one another wine. In Tokyo, my female friends do the same dance that we do in the U.S. We peruse the dessert menu, all agree that we couldn't possibly eat another bite, then decide to get one or two desserts "to share" and then tear into them with gleeful abandon. It has taken years to get to know these women, to make these connections. But during my first trip to Japan, I did not have years. I had three months and the few attempts I made at reaching out to other women socially were swiftly rebutted.

One afternoon, I was walking back to I-House and I found myself thinking of a song I used to hear on television when I was a kid. "Who are the people in your neighborhood?" the song asked. "They are the people that you meet each day." I walked up to the doors of I-House and there was Jun Takahashi, the bellboy who had checked me in on my very first day.

"Would you like to have a drink with me?" I asked Jun.

He looked surprised and I did not know what to expect: a bill estimating the time spent, a very polite "We'll see," which really meant no, or some unseen, unheard of repercussions that would only be felt later on.

He said, "I'm sorry. My English is not very good. Can you say it again?"

His English was great and I was beginning to be embarrassed. But I repeated the question anyway.

He said, "Let me see if I understand you. You go to a bar. I go to a bar. If you see me there, you will act as if you know me?"

Now I was confused.

"We could go to the bar together," I suggested.

He paused. Then he said, "May I ask why?"

I wanted to say: "Because I am so lonely. And I'm so far away from home and I can't afford another $100 phone call to my mother. Save me from myself, please!"

What I said was: "I was thinking maybe we could have a language exchange. You could help me with my Japanese and I could help you with your English."

He smiled. "I like this idea."

We made a date for that Friday night.

The following day, I ran into Jun again. He said, "Would you mind if I invited some of my friends who are also wanting to practice their English?"

I agreed, happily.

Finally, Friday arrived. Jun called up to my room and I came downstairs to find four young men waiting for me. They were all dressed up as if they were going to a job interview. Jun intro-

duced them as Haruki, Kazu, and Hiro. He said that there was
a local restaurant they wanted to take me to. I was beyond
excited to see that it was a place I'd tried to visit before. Most
people have seen the Japanese restaurants with their plastic
reproductions of food in the windows. But what I found was
that many restaurants that did not have English language
menus did not want foreigners in their dining room. "If you
don't like what you order then they lose face," Mama-san had
explained. "What if you refuse to pay? There could be problems." I explained that I was adventurous and happy to just pick
and try anything on the menu. Mama-san just looked at me and
said, "That is not how one eats at a restaurant." I began to
understand that the casualness with which I had approached
my time in Japan could be seen as callous or insulting.

Escorted by Jun and his friends, I was welcomed into the
restaurant I'd been turned away from before. We were led to
a small tatami room, where we removed our shoes and sat
cross-legged around the table. Jun ordered and each dish was
more delicious than the next. There was no pretense with
these guys—all in their senior year of Keio University—and
soon the idea of a "language exchange" was dropped. I ate and
listened happily as they insulted one another, frat-boy style, in
both English and Japanese. I felt like Elaine starring in my own
Japanese version of *Seinfeld* and something in me shifted. I
wasn't merely a foreigner, bowing and saying good morning to
strangers, *sumimasen*-ing my way from one end of Tokyo to
another. I'd had a glimpse into a more intimate way of life and
although the meal satisfied, it left me hungry for more.

The boys, as I quickly began to call them, walked me back
to I-House. Hiro asked me if I had ever heard of haiku.

"Of course," I said.

"Oh, really?"

He was surprised as so many people I encountered were

that news of Japan—culture, history, heritage—had made its way to the West. I didn't have the heart to tell him that I'd learned about it in the fifth grade, and that the only haiku poems I remembered involved my classmates' three-lined odes to ponies and Smurfs.

Hiro asked me if I had ever heard of Basho, the great haiku master. I admitted I had not.

"I have memorized many of his poems," he said. "If you like, I will share one with you."

"I would like that very much."

He put his hand on my shoulder and pointed up at the night sky:

> *Clouds appear*
> *and bring to men a chance to rest*
> *from looking at the moon.*

Just then, Jun, Haruki, and Kazu came running up to us, making wolf sounds at the moon. They were laughing so hard at Hiro's rendition that they were doubled over, clutching at the wall as if it could hold them up. I looked over at Hiro, but he wasn't embarrassed at all.

"Don't listen to him," Jun said. "He's full of himself."

"This guy has another name," Kazu said.

"What's that?" I asked.

"Bansho."

"Like the poet?"

"No, no, no." Kazu said. "The haiku master is Basho. You can call this guy, Bansho."

Haruki explained that they called Hiro "Bansho" because he was bossy.

"*So desu ne,*" I said, using one of the few Japanese phrases that I had at the ready. Technically, it means, "I understand."

But like *sumimasen,* it has many meanings, from "I see what you mean" to "That's it, exactly" to "Keep talking, I'm listening."

"Your Japanese is very, very good." Haruki said, commending me on my apt use of exactly three words.

The next morning, I went to the I-House front desk to receive a fax. The gentleman at the counter, Mr. Kuriyama, whom I had seen every day for weeks on end, leaned over to me conspiratorially.

"Chambers-san, I would like to ask you a personal question. It is within your rights not to answer."

I was worried. What had I done wrong? What past repercussion was coming back to haunt me?

"Go ahead, ask."

"Chambers-san, is it true that you had dinner with the bell-boy?"

I laughed. "Yes, we had a language exchange dinner," trying to keep it official lest Jun get in trouble at his job.

Kuriyama-san coughed and then leaned forward once again. "Would you be interested in having dinner with the front desk staff? Also to practice a language exchange?"

I said: "I'll have dinner with just about anyone."

He smiled: "I will arrange everything."

So it was that I ended up having dinner with the front desk staff, the back office staff, and the librarians. But it was Jun and his friends that ended up being my truest and dearest friends. I heard a lot of trash talking about Japanese men in the course of reporting this book, but if it weren't for my guy friends, I would've never returned to Japan at all.

During my last visit to Japan, I went to the Metropolitan Museum of Photography. There, I visited one of my favorite prints, "Unknown Woman Arranging Plum Blossoms." It is credited to the "early Meiji era," believed to have been taken in the mid-1800s. A woman in a kimono, sits kneeling down, placing a graceful stalk of blossoms into an ebony vase. Although they are plum blossoms, I think of them as cherry blossoms. In Japan, during cherry blossom season, there is a kind of national frenzy similar to the crowds gathered on New Year's Eve in Times Square to watch the ball drop. Companies hold parties, friends gather for picnics, stores offer special desserts. News organizations dedicate themselves to "Cherry Blossom Watch" with the same ferocity and pride of purpose that weather announcers in the U.S. track hurricanes. If you are a true cherry blossom fan, you can follow the bloom from the southernmost tip of the country through the north to Hokkaido: every year, thousands of people do. The beauty of a cherry blossom is fading; it reminds us of the preciousness of life itself. One of the many things I love about Japan is that even in all of its super-high-tech speed, the entire country hits the pause button to appreciate the beauty of something that will not endure. A cherry blossom's peak is short. Once they are at full bloom, they will fall off the trees within a week. Even quicker, if there is rain or snow.

My own season of charting the changes of women in Japan runs longer, but is to me as precious. *Giri ninjo*, my Japanese friends taught me when I first came to Japan, is a term meaning loyalty and humility. They made gestures of cutting off their own pinkies and told elaborate tales about the Japanese mafia, samurai legend, Buddhism, and haiku master Basho. Somewhere in the midst of this convoluted story, I was made to understand that bowing is all about putting your neck out there. To bow before a person is to say that I trust that if I expose my neck, you will not lop my head off. And I can't help but think this contains not just the essential element of my experience in Japan—my putting myself out there—but the very nature of life. To live is to put your neck out there and to trust that when you return to standing, your head will be attached to the rest of you. Certainly, writing this particular book, was a process of a thousand bows—literal and figurative—and all the modesty and vulnerability therein.

The story of how Japanese women are evolving at bullet train speed, continues to change and grow. The women in this book are the kickboxing geishas, the ones who both respect the traditions, while simultaneously trying to knock parts of it out. I have not only been writing about Japanese women, but like a musician sitting in with a large and legendary orchestra, I have been taking up the melody. Sometimes, I am doing something different altogether and I hear the words, like a few bars of music, of a woman that I have interviewed. Hip-hop DJ Naomi Chida talking about delivering papers to buy records and saying, "Girls don't do this, but I don't care. My curiosity wins." Mika Ninagawa saying, "So from the beginning there was no thought in my mind that women have to do a particular thing and men have to do a particular thing. *My thought about the family is that people should do what they can.*" Or Miss Monday, when she says, "I am seriously studying and will not do thoughtless things."

I, too, am seriously studying Japanese culture and I am so grateful to these women for letting me sit in while they take up the melody of the women who came before them and continue the all-important business of composing their own lives.

ACKNOWLEDGMENTS

I am grateful for many people, but primarily to the Japan Society who awarded me the Media Fellowship that enabled me to first explore Japan. I thank especially Ruri Kawashima and Betty Borden of the Japan Society. My former *Newsweek* colleague, Jonathan Alter, offered early encouragement in my explorations in Japan as did Kay Itoi and Greg Beals. The friends who visited me in Japan, helped me see old things with fresh eyes: Michelle Burford, Ruth Tenenbaum (way back in the day), and Jerry and Mary Clampet.

I am inspired by the writing of Peggy Orenstein and Banana Yoshimoto. I return to their books again and again.

In Tokyo, this book would not have been possible without the help of Kazuko Koizumi of the Foreign Press Center. She is a godsend. Manami Tominaga and Mie Anton provided invaluable translation assistance. I had the privilege of interviewing many amazing women, but I owe a particular debt of gratitude to: Erina Noda, Naomi Chida, Mina Takahashi, Ritsuka, and Kaori. The Anton family in Shizuoka provided a haven of music, good food, and great conversation. Karen Hill

Acknowledgments

Anton is intelligent, generous, and honest. Bill Anton is quite the DJ. Lila Anton provided valuable insight, as did Marsha Krakower. I am grateful, always, for the thougtful and diligent research of Judy Ganeles.

I learned so much from my editor, Emily Loose. Writers dream about being challenged and encouraged with as much skill and grace. I have admired Martha Levin for years and am so happy to finally be publishing this book with her. Thank you to Maris Kreizman for her editorial input, as well.

My agent, Christy Fletcher, is not only Harajuku *sugoi,* but whip smart.

Last, but certainly not least, I must thank Jason Clampet who in the midst of writing his own book (*The Rough Guide to Baja California, in stores now!*) agreed to make Tokyo one of the many places we've called home.

ABOUT THE AUTHOR

VERONICA CHAMBERS was formerly an editor for *The New York Times Magazine,* a culture writer for *Newsweek,* and a senior associate editor at *Premiere* magazine. Her articles have appeared in many publications, including Japanese *Vogue, Glamour,* and *O, The Oprah Magazine.* She is the recipient of many fellowships, including most recently, a Bellagio from the Rockefeller Foundation. She lives in Samsonite and Tumi with her husband, Jason Clampet, a travel writer.